DON'T GO THERE

A Tour of the World's Most Sinister Spots

J. W. Ocker

QUIRK BOOKS
PHILADELPHIA

Library of Congress Cataloging-in-Publication Data
Names: Ocker, J. W. author
Title: Don't go there : a tour of the world's most sinister spots / J.W. Ocker.
Description: Philadelphia : Quirk Books, 2026. | Summary: "A compendium of mysteriously dangerous places around the world and their histories" —Provided by publisher.
Identifiers: LCCN 2025042940 (print) | LCCN 2025042941 (ebook) | ISBN 9781683695028 hardcover | ISBN 9781683695035 ebook
Subjects: LCSH: Dark tourism
Classification: LCC G156.5.D37 O25 2026 (print) | LCC G156.5.D37 (ebook)
LC record available at https://lccn.loc.gov/2025042940
LC ebook record available at https://lccn.loc.gov/2025042941

ISBN: 978-1-68369-502-8

Printed in Malaysia

Typeset in Novel Pro, Duskey Stamp, and Overpass

Designed by Elissa Flanigan
Production management by Chadd Keim

Quirk Books
an imprint of Andrews McMeel Publishing
a division of Andrews McMeel Universal
1130 Walnut Street, Kansas City, Missouri 64106
quirkbooks.com

The authorized representative in the EEA is Simon and Schuster Netherlands BV, Herculesplein 96 3584 AA Utrecht, Netherlands.
(info@simonandschuster.nl)

10 9 8 7 6 5 4 3 2 1

MIX
Paper | Supporting responsible forestry
FSC® C016973
FSC www.fsc.org

To Zach Sanzone, for the safe harbor

And to Becky Shott, for standing by me

CONTENTS

INTRODUCTION

SERIOUSLY, DON'T

Every travel book ever published focuses solely on recommending the places that we should visit on this planet. Not enough warn us about avoiding the places that we shouldn't. After all, this planet isn't all exciting cuisines and world wonders and cultural touchstones and exotic experiences. The world is also terrifying, horrible, and dangerous, so much so that sometimes you have to wonder what we're all doing here in the first place.

We are so blissful within the fragile bubbles of our artificial cities, suburbs, and towns, viewing the world from the distorted vantages of our beach vacations and national park excursions, that we make the mistake of thinking that Earth was made for us; that it is hospitable to us; that it protects us. It isn't. It doesn't. It's hospitable only in the comparative sense when held up against the choking, unending void of a cold universe. But don't be fooled: This hurtling rock does not care for you or me. The sites in this book are proof.

In this book, I'm going to call out those places where you shouldn't go, not because of their crime rates nor any ongoing wars or travel embargoes; nothing so pedestrian. This isn't a guide to protect your person: It's one to secure your soul. These places need to be avoided because they are laced, latitude and longitude, with weird forces that seem to cause strange deaths, mysterious disappearances, and inexplicable, reality-shaking phenomena. And we're not talking mere haunted castles or abandoned asylums—sites of odd occurrences bounded comfortably inside four walls that are easy to avoid. We're talking entire landscapes, full-on towns, massive stretches of water: what some call *vile vortices*, where the environment itself seems to be cursed, where around every bend in the road, beneath every wave, is not just something out to get you but an entire roulette wheel of existential and physical misfortunes.

Here are the sites where lurk an ecosystem of competing and unsolved horrors: extraterrestrial encounters, scary monsters, dimensional rifts, bizarre mysteries, and even worse things. These are the scariest places known to humankind. For the love of your own sanity and existence, don't go to any of them.

And, sure, some places in this book are technically tourist attractions. Some are heavily advertised and heavily monetized and heavily visited. But don't fall for it—that's only because these sites need to feed, and a steady diet of ignorant travelers is an ideal repast.

Here be worse than dragons. Here be the terrifyingly unknown.

Don't say I didn't warn you.

FEARSOME FORESTS

The woods are a scary place all on their own. They don't need ghost tales, serial killers hiding bodies in their substrate, UFO landing spots, occult ritual meeting places, or lumberjack tales of weird monsters. They are, in and of themselves, scary: The labyrinth of unending trees. The feeling of inescapable enclosure. The mysterious sounds. The lack of glowing red exit signs. Maybe that's why we set so many stories of caution and terror there, from old fables like "Hansel and Gretel" and "Little Red Riding Hood" to modern horror films like *The Evil Dead* and *The Blair Witch Project*. The woods don't need additional weird and inexplicable reasons to be scary. But when you add new and strange reasons to be scared into their undergrowth and overstory, it can become hard to see the forest for the screams.

PINE BARRENS

LAND OF MONSTERS AND MOBSTERS

LOCATION: Southern New Jersey, USA	**INFAMOUS FOR:**
SIZE: 1.1 million acres	The Jersey Devil, mob burials, deadly fires, ghosts, ghost towns
MAIN FEATURES: Pitch pines and acidic, low-nutrient soil	

The 1.1 million acres of New Jersey forest known as the Pine Barrens have been the site of strange beastie sightings, abandoned towns, mob crimes, disappearances, deaths, and paranormal legends that range from witches to ghosts to the infamous Jersey Devil. This massive green oasis that covers 22 percent of the state in the middle of an extremely developed part of the eastern seaboard is just... creepy.

The Pine Barrens gets the first half of its name from its prevailing species of tree, although it also has some oak and cedar amidst all the pine. It's also known for its swamps and bogs, as well as its sandy, low-nutrient soil. That's where it gets the latter half of its name, via European settlers who found the land bad for farming—and bad in general. Polish writer Julian Niemcewicz described his relief in exiting the Pine Barrens in his 1799 book *Podróże po Ameryce* 1797–1807, writing: "There are no longer bogs, sand, gloomy cedar and pine forests, but an open and fertile country. My eyes wearied for a long time by the sunken emptiness were cheered by this sight."

Before the European invasion, it was the home of the Lenni Lenape, who would be displaced by those settlers and decimated by the Old World contagions they brought with them. The settlers included the Swedish, Dutch, and English. During the Revolutionary War, the Pine Barrens became a hiding place for Tories—those loyal to the British crown—and various industries thrived in its depths, including timber, pitch, shipbuilding, bog ore, and glassworks. Those who lived in the Barrens, especially over multiple generations, were often called Pineys—at first derogatorily, although today the term has been reclaimed to express local pride. In 1979, the state partnered with the federal government to officially designate the Pine Barrens as a preserve.

And now that we've got through the basic background, it's time to give the devil its due. The Jersey Devil is the most famous denizen of the Pine Barrens. Its story is part folklore, part cryptid sighting, and part boogeyman tale. The legend goes like this: On a stormy night in the Barrens in 1735, a woman named Mother Leeds was pregnant with her thirteenth child. She didn't want it, so she cursed it. As a result, she birthed a monster—horse-faced and horned, with bat wings, a forked tail, and hooves. It attacked everybody in the room and then shot up the chimney like a cannonball to haunt the Pine Barrens as the Jersey Devil.

In January 1909, the Jersey Devil emerged from whispered lore into the lives of locals. For a week, sightings of a strange flying beast that left cloven tracks in the snow were reported all over the Pine Barrens and further north in the state, as well as across the border into Pennsylvania. According to the New Jersey Historical Society, a city councilman named E. P. Weeden awoke in the night in his Trenton home to something beating at his door. He looked out an upper-story window and saw a line of bipedal hoofprints in the snow on his roof. Other people in Trenton heard strange screeches in the night, saw more hoofprints, and even witnessed the thing itself flapping in the sky.

Meanwhile, various sources state that the winged creature was seen across the Delaware River in Bristol, Pennsylvania, as well. For instance, police officer James Sackville got close enough to shoot at it. Postmaster E. W. Minister described the monster as crane-like, with long wings and the horned head of a ram. He even claimed that it glowed with an unnatural light. Liquor store owner John McOwen saw something eagle-like hopping on the ground outside his window. He described its cry as like a phonograph record scratch combined with a factory whistle.

It didn't take long for people to connect the unusual sightings to the old folktale of the Pine Barrens and start screaming Devil. Schools and businesses across the region shut down. People armed themselves. Hunting parties were formed. A local dime museum even exhibited a painted kangaroo with cardboard wings, claiming it was the captured Jersey Devil.

But the Devil isn't the only strange resident of the Pine Barrens. Bigfoots are regularly sighted loping through its trunks—although to be fair, bigfoots have been sighted all over New Jersey (almost sixty reported sightings since 1966, according to a 2018 article in the *Asbury Park Press*, with at least a third of those in the Barrens). But bigfoots aren't unique to the Barrens. If you believe the stories, they lurk in forests all across America and are about as common as squirrels.

But the Jersey Devil and the occasional bigfoot are perhaps the least frightening parts of the forest's story, because the Pine Barrens is not merely the domain of monsters. It's also a big graveyard full of murder victims. "Victims Dumped in

Ocean Woods," blared a headline from the front page of the *Asbury Park Press* on March 25, 1987. The article about the Pine Barrens went on to claim: "Since 1962, one body a year has been found deep in the woods in sparsely settled areas." But who are these victims? According to the *New York Times*, not all of these bodies are mere unfortunate campers or suicides. A headline in its February 5, 1973, issue proclaims "Mobs Favor Pineland Burial." The article goes on to claim that "of the almost 50 murder cases Ocean County has reported since 1966, about half involve the pinelands." And many of those murder victims had found themselves on the wrong side of the Italian-American Mafia.

To name just a few victims, an armed robbery suspect turned informant named Anthony Scanella Jr. was found freshly killed in the middle of the forest in 1964. That same 1973 article says of his discovery, "The killer, apparently not a hunter, disposed of the body on the first day of hunting season." In 1967, the body of Angelo Sonnessa, who was a member of the Mafia in New York, was found buried under a chicken coop, hands and feet bound and a plastic bag over his head. Nearby, an unidentified victim's corpse had dissolved in an oil drum filled with hydrochloric acid. Another member of the mob, unnamed in the article, was found dumped on the side of the road in the Pine Barrens in 1969. The body of gangster Frank Franco was uncovered in 1970 after being buried in the woods near Manchester Township. Even when bodies are found outside the Pine Barrens, some of them were probably meant for the Pine Barrens. The article states that when the body of Emanuel Gambino, nephew of mob boss Carlo Gambino, was found (a week previous to the article's publication) a few miles north of the Pine Barrens, one of the responding officers commented, "They must have gotten lost. They stopped too soon."

The connection between gangsters and the Pine Barrens has become so culturally pervasive that an entire episode of the turn-of-the-century HBO series *The Sopranos* was dedicated to it. Entitled "The Pine Barrens," this third season entry explored the plight of two henchman, Paulie "Walnuts" Gualtieri and Christopher Moltisanti, as they wandered the Barrens lost and cold after the corpse they went there to bury disappeared. The Pine Barrens were Paulie Walnuts's idea—he said:

> *It's perfect: It's fuckin' deserted down there. We take him in the woods, dig a hole, end of story . . . the best part is, we'd be like twenty minutes away from AC. We'll get a room, freshen up, play a little blackjack . . . we'll go to Morton's, get a steak. This way the day won't be a total loss.*

But it wasn't just the mob hiding victims in the voracious swamps and sandy soil. During the trial of Manhattan real estate scion Robert Durst for the murder of Susan Berman in 2000, the prosecuting attorney John Lewin included in his opening arguments a brief tutorial on murder in the Pine Barrens. He said he could prove that Durst had also killed his wife back in January 1982 and hid her in the mafia's favorite disposal grounds, stating: "The soil at the Pine Barrens is sand. It doesn't freeze, so if you kill somebody in the middle of winter, you need to have sand you can dig into."

Murder isn't the only cause of death in the Pine Barrens, either. On July 12, 1928, a young aviator named Captain Emilio Carranza Rodríguez met his fiery end in the woods. The media called him the Mexican Lindbergh because of all the flying records he had set before the age of twenty-two—although, tragically, there wasn't to be an *after* twenty-two for Rodríguez.

On that summer day, the intrepid aviator was flying from New York to Mexico City when he hit a storm above the Pine Barrens, crashed, and died. A twelve-foot-tall stone marker dedicated to him now looms on the site of the crash.

The Pine Barrens are strewn with ghost towns of past settlements and industries: the village and ironworks of Atsion, the Hampton Furnace, Fries Mill, the Weymouth Furnace, Harrisville, the Hermann glass factory, and the dried-up cranberry bog town of Friendship. Perhaps the most notorious set of ruins is off Pasadena Woodmanse Road. The Brooksbrae Brick Factory includes remnants of walls and tunnels and pits, all of which are so thick with graffiti that it's practically an art installation. The brick factory had barely started spitting bricks when it became a pile of bricks itself. In 1915, the building was sitting idle because the death of its owner had left it in limbo. A pair of caretakers, Julian and Katherin Tomaszewski, lived in a building on the property. One night they lit a fire. Apparently, the chimney was faulty. The building burned to the ground, and both Tomaszewskis perished. But they weren't the final victims of the brick factory: The rest of the complex was burned down a couple years later in another fire. In 1917, watchman Gildo Plazziano was found dead in bed among the flames that were engulfing the plant, along with the body of a twelve-year-old neighbor girl named Harriet Chattin. It was believed to be a murder-suicide—with all the nefariousness that implies.

Not all fires in the Pine Barrens are set by humans—wildfire has been a crucial component of the region's ecology for thousands of years. But that doesn't stop some from speculating about supernatural causes behind these frequent wildfires. There's a local legend about the Pine Witch and the Pine Wizard. In life, they were said to be an ordinary married couple from the nineteenth century named Peggy and Bill Clevenger. When Bill died, he sent a message to Peggy from the afterlife by boiling the water in their well. Peggy eventually joined him when she was killed during a combined burglary/arson. The Pine Witch and the Pine Wizard have been setting fires ever since.

Bill and Peggy are far from the only ghosts in the woods. Another notable specter is notorious pirate Captain Kidd (it wouldn't be an East Coast state if there weren't a Captain Kidd legend within its borders). Kidd supposedly hid treasure in Barnegat Bay, and now his ghost has been sighted wandering the coastal forest (even though he died in England), sometimes alongside the Jersey Devil itself, and often headless (even though he died by hanging). The Jersey Devil has a full dance card, in fact. He's also been seen cavorting with the Golden-Haired Girl, a woman in white ghost who died pining for her lost sailor lover (although some versions of the story say it was the son of the Jersey Devil itself whom she pined for). If you see the Black Dog, it's harmless—just a ghostly hound that was killed during a pirate attack along with his young master. And if you see the White Stag, it's a good omen—it has stopped travelers from inadvertently driving their carriages over washed-out bridges. The Ghost Boy in the town of Atco can be called up at will. He was supposedly killed when he was hit by a truck on Burnt Mill Road after chasing his basketball into the street. To conjure him, there are two methods: You can either park your car on the road and kill the engine, or honk your horn and flash your lights three times each.

Once you get past all the monsters and Mafia activity, the Pine Barrens are a pretty nice place. People hike there and camp there. Entire towns are located within its borders. The times I've visited have been disappointingly pleasant and terror-free. Still, the Pine Barrens of New Jersey are over a million acres, and those million acres contain a million stories, a million mysteries, a million horrors, and every day more are added. The local papers are regularly filled with disappearances, deaths, and strange sightings, with most of the articles taking an "It's the Pine Barrens, after all" angle. Say what you will of the Pine Barrens, they'll never be barren of dark history and disturbing lore.

BRIDGEWATER TRIANGLE

BAY STATE BIZARRE

LOCATION: Southeast Massachusetts, USA **SIZE:** 200 square miles **TRIANGLE POINTS:** Abington, Freetown, Rehoboth	**INFAMOUS FOR:** Strange creatures, murders, disappearances, Satanic cults, UFOs, ghosts

The Bridgewater Triangle has it all when it comes to the strange and macabre: UFOs, monsters, Satanic cults, murders, cattle mutilations, cryptic stone carvings, ghosts, disappearances, and more. But the Bridgewater Triangle is not some obscure, dark corner of this round planet: It's in Massachusetts, the land of shiny sports dynasties and comfy bowls of clam chowder.

The Bridgewater Triangle was officially dubbed as such in April 1980, conjured into reality by an article in *Boston* magazine written by Peter Rodman and Loren Coleman, the latter of whom coined the term and who at the time was well on his way to becoming the world's foremost cryptozoologist. Coleman, a transplant to the state from Illinois, was working as a social worker for rural families during the day and investigating Fortean phenomena by night. As he researched, he kept coming across a trio of adjoining towns known locally for strange phenomena: Bridgewater, East Bridgewater, and West Bridgewater, which are in the southeast part of Massachusetts

before it curls into Cape Cod. However, Coleman observed that the range of strange wasn't confined to those three municipalities but seemed to extend into a much larger triangle. This triangle measures two hundred square miles from the towns of Abington to the north, Freetown to the east, and Rehoboth to the west, and its angles include all or parts of the towns of Easton, Taunton, Berkley, Dighton, Brockton, and Raynham. In the article, he and his coauthor conclude:

> "These areas are the focus of much unexplained, strange, sometimes violent activity of the ancient and recent past. Will they be the site of astonishing events of the future? Keep an eye on the Bridgewater Triangle."

Three years later, Coleman would publish his book *Mysterious America*, in which he dedicated almost an entire chapter to the Bridgewater Triangle, bringing the Massachusetts oddity to a national audience.

I don't even know how to tell the story of the Bridgewater Triangle. There's not a single throughline that unites the disparate weirdness and dark violence of this part of the Bay State. I barely knew how to explore it, driving from forest to graveyard to quarry to town to swamp, searching out all the sites of all the strange stories within its boundaries. The only commonality that the area seems to share besides tax rates is that it was one of the many bloody chessboard squares in King Philip's War.

That war took place from 1675 to 1676, mainly between the Wampanoag tribes and the English colonists in southern New England, with the Wampanoag being led by Metacom

(English name: King Philip). The war was short but vicious. Three thousand native people and six hundred colonists were killed—both civilians and fighters—in addition to widespread destruction of homes and food supplies. It took decades for the colonists to recover. The native people never did. A 2020 article for Connecticut Public Radio called it "America's most devastating conflict."

The war ended with a musket ball to King Philip's heart in Rhode Island. His head was removed and displayed on a pole in Plymouth, Massachusetts. Cotton Mather, famed colonial minister and infamous witch chaser, had such animosity for the Native American leader that he wrenched the jaw off King Philip's skull and took off with it.

According to tradition, one of the places King Philip often camped during the war is a cave in Norton, Massachusetts, near the center of the Bridgewater Triangle. That cave still exists today and is named after him (although it's more of a tunnel through an outcropping of large boulders). By day King Philip's Cave is a hunk of rock marked by an historical placard in a residential neighborhood. By night it's a ghost hunter's paradise, with stories of Native American specters, phantom campfires, spook lights, and the invisible striking of drums.

These same paranormal phenomena are also recounted ten miles to the southwest in Rehoboth at Anawan Rock. This site was named for one of King Philip's leaders, who was captured there soon after the Wampanoag chief's death. Anawan was also sent to Plymouth, where he was executed, and his decapitated head likewise put on a pole for display.

Then there's Dighton Rock. This forty-ton boulder was found in the Taunton River in Dighton, near the bottom edge of the Triangle. One of its large faces was covered in obscure petroglyphs. Over the years, the engravings have been attributed to everyone from the Phoenicians to the Portuguese to the Norse, but it's most more likely of Native American origin (although that doesn't help decode the symbols on the rock). Today the boulder and its mysterious message have been moved to a small museum dedicated to it on the shore near where it was found.

So, sure, there is a lot of violent and mysterious aboriginal history in the Bridgewater Triangle, but welcome to America; every square foot of the continental US is haunted by the history of brutality against the indigenous peoples. This history doesn't explain the cryptids, the modern ghosts, the UFOs, and the strange crimes the Triangle also contains.

As to cryptids, the Bridgewater Triangle is a scary zoo full of weird beasts, including phantom big cats, giant snakes, thunderbirds, and devil dogs. But the two dominant species here are bigfoots and puckwudgies.

The Bridgewater Bigfoot makes its home in Hockomock Swamp, one of the most notorious parts of the Triangle. Its name means "place where spirits dwell" in Algonquin, although English colonizers were less poetic when they dubbed it Devil's Swamp. Hockomock takes up 17,000 mucky, murky acres in the heart of the Triangle. Witnesses have been reporting something tall, hairy, and smelly in it for decades. One of them is Joe DeAndrade, a Bridgewater resident whose sighting of a bigfoot on the edge of a pond in 1978 received mainstream press for decades. He described the encounter to the *Boston Herald* in 1998: "I saw what I will never forget for the rest of my life. It was 200 feet away and it was walking slowly, like Frankenstein, into the brush." A few years after that sighting, John Park, from West Bridgewater, had a similar encounter. He was setting muskrat traps from his canoe in the swamp one night when he was stalked by a large, hairy presence on the shore. He told the *Boston Herald* in that same article, "I knew it wasn't a human because when it passed by me, I could smell it. It smelled like skunk—musty and dirty. Like it lived in the dirt."

The Triangle is also supposed to be prickly with puckwudgies. However, these creatures are less from cryptozoology and more from Algonquin lore. Puckwudgies are diminutive, gremlin-like creatures with porcupine quills extending from their backs and heads. They bear poison-tipped spears and arrows and have magical abilities, including shapeshifting, invisibility, and the power to confuse people's minds. It's said they like to lure victims to their deaths over a nineteenth century quarry wall called Assonet Ledge in Freetown Forest, which is in the southeast corner of the Triangle. The lore is so prevalent in the region that in 2017 the local police capitalized on it and temporarily placed *Puckwudgie Crossing* signs around the entrance to the five-thousand-acre forest to surprise drivers into slowing down.

Not only is the Bridgewater Triangle full of weird wildlife, it also seems to be one of the levels of the afterlife. Ghostly suicides disappear after jumping from Assonet Ledge. Phantom trucks tailgate drivers on Copicut Road in Freetown. Hitchhiking spooks beg for rides on Route 44 in Seekonk. And the area has plenty of haunted historic buildings as well, from Taunton Hospital and its mysterious man in white and screams in the night to the one-room Horbine School in Rehoboth, with its ghostly students and phantom bell tolling.

And then there are the UFOs, as if the boundaries of the Bridgewater Triangle extend upward into space. Flying lights and strange craft are regularly sighted in the skies. The most famous encounter occurred in the spring of 1979. Two local radio reporters, Jerry Lopes and Steve Sbraccia, were heading to the Raynham Dog Track. When they hit Route 106, a strange bright light appeared above the treetops, extraordinary enough that the two men pulled over. The lights adorned a dark object that Lopes described in the 2013 documentary *The Bridgewater Triangle* as shaped like a "baseball home plate" and Sbraccia described as "an arrow." The object measured more than a thousand feet in width, with a "cord" dangling off it that emitted sparks. The object hovered for a bit and then flew overhead, seemingly close enough the observers could have hit it with a thrown rock, and passed out of sight. Lopes, also an Air Force veteran, said that one of his immediate thoughts was, "That's not one of ours." Over the next week, reports of more strange aerial sightings poured into the local papers and the police stations. But the extraterrestrial visitors to the Triangle were harmless—unlike some of its human visitors.

I would need a ten-season true-crime podcast to examine all the murders, attacks, and disappearances in this region. Almost every article about the Bridgewater Triangle lists a different series of crimes and accidents, depending on when it was written and what the freshest wounds are. For instance, on Halloween in 1998, the *Standard-Times* of New Bedford, Massachusetts, ran an article listing the most heinous crimes committed in the Freetown Forest from 1978 to 1991. They included:

- The murder of a teenager named Mary Lou Arruda, found tied to a tree (1978)
- The ritualistic murder of three sex workers by a trio of Satanic cult members (1979)
- The abandonment and death of a newborn male infant (1983)

- ▷ A "drifter" who was beaten, shot, and burned to death (1987)
- ▷ Two men discovered naked and dead from shotgun wounds (1988)
- ▷ The theft of the body of Elizabeth Gregory, who died in 1868 at age eighty-six and was buried in a forest cemetery (1988)
- ▷ A teenager stabbed, beaten, and buried under leaves for three days, who would suffer brain damage and lose both legs to frostbite (1991)

The list ends with a chilling "etc." At the time of the article's publication, many other violent cases in that area were actively being investigated by police, including "physical and sexual assaults, attempted murders, suicides, car burnings, animal mutilations, and ritualistic activity."

As for crimes and tragedies from this century, it doesn't take much googling to see they have continued—but neither did they start in 1978. One of the more interesting historical artifacts in the Triangle was found because of a missing persons case from the early 1900s. In 1916, a journalist was trying to locate Evelyn Packard, who was believed to have fallen victim to the Hockomock Swamp while on a solo canoe trip. What he found instead was a large stone with a poem engraved on it, dated to 1862. Turns out, it had been engraved by a local minister and eventually forgotten by the twentieth century. Packard's body was found three days later, not far from the stone. The thirty-two-word poem about the beauty of nature and seclusion gave the stone its current name, the Solitude Stone—replacing a previous nickname, the Suicide Stone, after a man named John Crane shot himself at the site in 1880.

Some locals have a more practical view of the horrible

events within the Triangle. The same *Standard-Times* article referenced earlier quotes a police detective, Lieutenant Alvin Alves, as saying, "You've got probably 300,000 people in New Bedford, Fall River, Taunton and the surrounding towns who are within 20 minutes of one of the most secluded places in the state. It's used as a dumping ground."

Of course, there are plenty of sites in the Bridgewater Triangle that aren't weird or dark. It has its strip malls and neighborhoods, its fast-food restaurants and golf courses, bowling alleys and grocery stores. Hockomock Swamp and Freetown Forest themselves are full of beautiful scenery, pleasant hiking trails, and idyllic camping spots. It's just that, for some reason, interspersed among all those bits of life and beauty are lots of death and tragedy, like moth holes in fabric.

And maybe you could trace a triangle around any section of the country and find it similarly riddled with weird lore, strange tragedies, and heinous crimes. Certainly, the bizarre events of the Bridgewater Triangle bleed over its borders. The infamous Lizzie Borden house misses being in the Triangle by a couple miles, as does the site of the mill in Easton that was supposedly built in the eighteenth century by a wizard named Nathan Selee, with the help of what a sign on the site calls "satanic imps"—my guess: puckwudgies. Or it could well be that this stretch of southeastern Massachusetts is much more moth-ridden than most. We can only, in the words of Rodman and Coleman way back in 1980, keep an eye on it.

HOIA-BACIU

THE WORLD'S MOST HAUNTED FOREST

LOCATION: Cluj-Napoca, Romania	**INFAMOUS FOR:** Disappearances, UFOs, bioplasma
SIZE: 1 square mile	
MAIN FEATURE: Poiana Rotundă	

Hoia-Baciu is an old-growth forest in northwestern Romania in that famous region known as Transylvania. That's right: Dracula country. However, the forest has nothing to do with vampires—unfortunately. It is, though, if you believe the tales, the locus of a series of strange phenomena that range from the paranormal to the ufological. It's like related content for Romania: "If you like Vlad the Impaler, you may be interested in Hoia-Baciu."

Hoia-Baciu (sometimes written without a hyphen) is a surprisingly small bit of woodland for one vaunted as "the world's most haunted forest" in the echo chambers of the internet. It covers only a square mile and is far from isolated—sitting only a few miles west of Cluj-Napoca, Romania's second largest city. The forest is full of vampire-stake-worthy hardwoods like maple, beech, and elm and is inhabited by all the usual sylvan creatures—bears, foxes, deer . . . bats. On any given pleasant day, it will also be populated by hikers, bicyclists, campers, and sports enthusiasts participating in archery and paintball. School groups often go on nature walks here.

However, despite its recreational usage, there's something eerie about the forest. Swathes of trees throughout the woods are misshapen—twisted into spirals, bent into zigzags, arched into gateways. Branches grow in the wrong direction, toward the ground instead of toward the sky. It also features an oblong bald spot of a meadow measuring approximately ninety-three by seventy-seven yards. The meadow is called, among other names, the Poiana Rotundă, and it is said that no trees can grow there—either because of the radioactive soil from all the UFO landings or the residual magic from all the occult and esoteric ceremonies conducted there. A tour guide named Alex Dan told ABC News in October 2021 that he once witnessed people practicing rituals in the spot. He said, "I came across a group celebrating spirits that are well-known in Romania folklore. They told me they were trying to harvest energy from other dimensions."

Hoia-Baciu also has a reputation for swallowing people whole (and sometimes returning them years later) via interdimensional portals or injuring them with mysterious rashes and burns. It makes visitors feel anxious, nauseous, uneasy. Like they're being watched. It causes electronic devices to fail under its overstory. Lurking among its trunks are shadowy figures. Strangely shaped objects hover in its sky. Hoia-Baciu, some believe, is a place where matter and beings normally invisible to the naked eye can become visible, upending our myopic understanding of reality. Adrian Pătruţ, a professor of chemistry at Babes-Bolyai University in Cluj-Napoca and the authority on Hoia-Baciu, says in his 1995 book *The Phenomena of the Hoia-Baciu Forest* that:

> "No one, or almost no one, knows what is really going on there, but everyone or almost everyone has heard of extraordinary phenomena."

But how did these rumors get started? And when? Certainly, Hoia-Baciu is an ancient place, with a history of settlements dating back thousands of years. The remains of the oldest Neolithic settlement in Romania, Gura Bacului, lie close to its northern edge. The dirt is riddled with old bullet casings and buttons that date back to World War I, the remnants of minor skirmishes of a major war.

The oldest stories about the forest are vague, always shared without names or dates. One that is circulated online time and time again concerns a shepherd who supposedly entered the forest with his flock of sheep hundreds of years ago. Neither shepherd nor sheep returned. That's one of many theories on how the forest got its name, as Baciu could be a Romanian translation of a Hungarian word for shepherd (although Baciu is also a common name for villages in Romania, one of which is just two miles north of the forest). Other unsourced and vague tales include that of a five-year-old girl who disappeared for five years in the forest, only to return the same age and in the same clothes she had disappeared in. She had no memory of where she had been. Then there's the spirit of a woman who wanders the woods in a wedding gown for unknown reasons. Again, no names, no dates, no context. Always credited to local folklore.

But on August 18, 1968, that all changed, and something new and more specific emerged from the tangled trunks of Hoia-Baciu, something that Pătruţ called in his book a "modern form of folklore." An engineer named Emil Barnea, who worked at the University of Art and Design in Cluj-Napoca, was hiking in the Hoia-Baicu with three companions when they spotted a UFO above the Poiana Rotundă. It hovered and rotated there for a leisurely two minutes, and Barnea was able to get a series of five carefully composed photos before it sped off. They show a silvery object above the treetops. It was about one hundred feet in diameter and shaped much like the top hat token in a game of Monopoly, as if thrown into the air in anger by a player after being bankrupted by a Boardwalk hotel.

The photos caught the attention of the international press, and for the first time Hoia-Baciu was on the map. Almost literally, as even the name hadn't quite been pinned down yet, and to that point the forest had mostly been known as Hoia. Barnea had called it Baciu Forest during interviews about his photos, and so the hyphenate was formed. According to Pătruţ, "This entrance onto the world stage is fully deserved because the images of Emil Barnea from Hoia-Baciu represent one of the best, if not the best, series of UFO photos ever obtained." Now Dracula had some competition.

After Barnea's UFO photos turned this thin tract of Eastern European woodland into an internationally known extraterrestrial hotspot, it brought global attention to the work of Alexandru Sift, a botanist at a research institute in Cluj-Napoca who had been obsessively documenting bizarre occurrences in Hoia-Baciu for decades. Sift's work helped bolster the reputation of Hoia-Baciu as "the world's most haunted forest." He should have a bronze statue in his likeness in the middle of the Poiana Rotundă for his efforts. Except what he was documenting was no mere ghost or alien spacecraft. Enter bioplasma.

According to Sift, his first experience with the odd

phenomena of Hoia-Baciu was in 1948, when he was eleven. Sift was in the forest with his father when he saw a V-shaped formation in the sky that seemed to be made of translucent gray smoke. It flew slowly across the sky. When he got home, a similarly shaped red mark appeared on his arm, where it would stay for the next two years.

His next encounter was as a teenager in the summer of 1953, when he witnessed another of these V's disappear inside a hawthorn bush. When he poked his hiking stick into the bush, both it and his arm turned invisible. He felt a sudden heat and pressure and fled for home, where he grew nauseous and vomited. He continued to experience these ill effects for days. But the biggest side effect was that it kickstarted his obsession with the forest.

For the next four decades, Sift regularly visited the forest, taking almost constant photos. And everywhere he pointed his camera, something strange appeared on the film. More V-shaped fogs, glowing spheroids, misty lumps flying in formation, columns of light, clusters of cruciforms. But they weren't always invisible to the naked eye: Sometimes they would materialize to the point that he didn't need his camera to view them. Sift claims to have witnessed black pyramidal objects scorching grass and tree branches as they landed. He saw shadowy figures dematerialize in front of him. At one point, he observed a group of four-foot-tall humanoids with dark, reddish-brown skin, large heads, and canine faces alongside a pear-shaped object. They went invisible soon after the sighting.

Over time, he started to theorize that he was seeing manifestations of what Pătruţ would later call *bioplasma*, or organized systems of particles or energies that are invisible to the human eye but which we can interact with psychically.

According to Pătruţ, who would befriend Sift after reading a 1974 interview with him in a magazine called *Flacăra*, Sift believed that he was witnessing "structures, forms, or plasma appearances, which are not objects or bodies and, in no case, terrestrial or extraterrestrial vehicles."

At this point Pătruţ would join Sift on investigations and launch a few of his own, pulling in friends and colleagues to create entire teams of investigators combing Hoia-Baciu. They would find shocking manifestations of bioplasma that revealed themselves after the photos were developed. One of the photos Pătruţ's team took showed a disembodied head in the grass—which looked exactly like one of the investigators. Another time, a large dragon-shaped "plasmoid" appeared in the photos. Another photo showed a man with no shadow, despite everything around him having one.

Sift died in 1993. Tragically, the estimated 60,000 photos that Sift took over the course of forty years and all his accompanying notes were allegedly stolen a few months after his death (Pătruţ blamed "gypsies") and sold to a recycling center for "the price of two bottles of beer." Pătruţ tracked the center down but could only rescue a handful of them that had escaped pulping.

With Sift's death and then Barnea's in 1994, that left Pătruţ as the last-standing academic to be the spokesperson and PR agent for the forest. Pătruţ would continue to further theorize and systematize his and Sift's findings, as well. In his book, he stated that "in most cases, the free state bioplasma, in a white, black, gray or even colored variety, unstructured or structured in different shapes, is invisible to the naked eye. However, it interacts with the photographic film and generates focused images. Respectively, it produces physical, chemical, and biological effects.... In a few cases, the structures are sufficiently condensed to be observed visually."

Pătruţ believes that these "bioplasmic formations" are present throughout the world and explain everything from UFO sightings to ghost encounters to religious visions. But it's only in Hoia-Baciu where that layer of reality can be readily observed and documented. There's just something about the place.

These days, Pătruţ is still the go-to interviewer when paranormal shows descend on the forest every Halloween (the busy season in Transylvania). When the forest hits the news during any other time of year, it's usually because development has started to encroach on the forest and various organizations are fighting to preserve the valuable land for public use. Part of those efforts is continuing to broadcast its status as "the world's most haunted forest" to bring in the tourists, even if "most haunted" doesn't begin to approach the strangeness that Sift and Pătruţ believed to be the truth of the woodland.

According to Pătruţ in his 1995 book, "We consider that the research of bioplasmatic manifestations, as well as of other macro-paranormal phenomena, represents a necessary path for the progress of psi research and for the development of a new worldview. Having come so far, we ask ourselves, 'Are we prepared and are we ready to open Pandora's Box?'"

Maybe just check out Dracula's castle while visiting Transylvania.

NAHANNI NATIONAL PARK

VALLEY OF THE HEADLESS MEN

LOCATION: Northwest Territories, Canada **SIZE:** 12,000 square miles **CENTRAL FEATURE:** South Nahanni River	**INFAMOUS FOR:** Disappearances, decapitations, giant wolves, cannibal bigfoots, lost treasure

It is an extremely isolated land, untouched by the last ice age, guarded by mountains, largely untapped by modern humans, and rumored to be full of prehistoric and mythical creatures. Its waterfalls and rapids are among the most spectacular on the continent and its canyons could swallow skyscrapers. It is a land warmed by volcanic activity and chilled by arctic blasts, a land coated in mists that coax forth unique flora. Its valleys are full of mysterious sounds and its mountains rumored to be stuffed with bounties of gold. It has been called a lost world. Oh, and a bunch of people have been found headless there over the years and an entire aboriginal people reportedly disappeared within it.

In the southwest corner of Canada's Northwest Territories, right along the continental divide, is Nahanni National Park. When it was established in 1976, it spanned more than 1,800 square miles. In 1978, it became one of UNESCO's inaugural Natural World Heritage Sites, along with Yellowstone National Park, Simien National Park, and the Galapagos Islands.

However, despite that status of planetary jewel, very few people visit—only about one thousand per year. That's in part because it's extremely hard to get to. The least inhospitable window for entry into the park is short, from June to August. The rest of the year, it is a virtually impenetrable mountainous icescape. There are no roads into Nahanni National Park. Visitors must either arrive by floatplane or by helicopter or take long, arduous hikes that the cheerful Parks Canada website calls "ambitious and demanding." Those who make it into the park find no end to the daunting dangers of the harsh landscape and unforgiving weather, and many have succumbed to it over the past two centuries. And then there are the rumors of giants, monster wolves, decapitations, mysterious disappearances, evil spirits, and other strange terrors with which visitors may need to contend.

The central feature of the park is the South Nahanni River, which, when it's not armored and fanged by ice, rages for more than 330 miles, building its fury into Class IV and V rapids (on a scale of I to VI). The river cuts through a series of canyons, the deepest of which descend more than three thousand feet. According to the 2017 *National Geographic Guide to the National Parks of Canada*, when American outdoorsman Fenley Hunter attempted to paddle up the river in 1928, he called it "an impossible stream" and remarked that "a stiff rapid is met on average every mile, and they seem countless." At one point, the river hits an almost 400-foot-tall limestone spire, jutting up like the tusk of some monster, before diving 315 feet down Virginia Falls, which is beflowered at its banks and base by rare orchids that thrive in the billowing mist.

To the northwest are the Ragged Range of mountains, the tallest in the Northwest Territories and frosted with glaciers. The mountains include the Cirque of the Unclimbables, a series of towering peaks and cliffs with sheer granite walls. Throughout the park are hot springs, the most famous of which is Rabbitkettle, also in the northwest area of the park and which features—at one hundred feet high and two hundred feet wide—the largest tufa mound in Canada (tufa mounds are delicate rock formations created from dissolved minerals in the water). Visitors aren't allowed to enter that fragile ecosystem without a guide and must tread barefoot across the geothermally heated ground.

But it's the names of other features in the park that reveal the dark side of Nahanni. The Funeral Mountains are in the southeast, and Deadmen Valley is farther downriver. Inside of Deadmen Valley is Headless Creek, as well as Broken Skull River and Broken Skull Hot Springs. Then there is the nickname of the park itself: the Valley of the Headless Men. These names reflect the macabre human history of the park.

Today, Nahanni is unpopulated. But that wasn't always the case. The park is named for the original inhabitants, the Naha tribe. According to Parks Canada, our knowledge of these First Nations people comes from the oral history of a neighboring tribe, the Dene, who to this day use Nahanni as a hunting ground. The Naha were known by the Dene to be a particularly fierce mountain-dwelling people who delighted in raiding and ransacking the homes of other tribes. One day, the Dene decided to take a stand against their rivals. They traversed the inhospitable terrain, found the homebase of the Naha, surrounded the encampment, and ambushed it . . . only to find the entire camp empty. The embers of the fires still glowed, and the sleeping bags were laid out inside the tents ready for the weary returners who would never lay their heads down. The Naha had simply disappeared. Every one of them.

No one knows what happened to the Naha, but the

prevailing theory is that they headed south for unknown reasons (or for the same reason retirees do) and became the ancestors of the Navajo, an idea that is based on various linguistic similarities between the two peoples. But their abrupt disappearance is just one of the many strange mysteries of this land.

The first Europeans to see Nahanni were fur traders who arrived in the late 1700s or early 1800s. Toward the end of the nineteenth century, the Klondike Gold Rush brought hopeful prospectors laden with pickaxes and pans next door to the Yukon. Some of these men tried their luck in Nahanni, as well. The most famous were the McLeod brothers—Charlie, Willie, and Frank—who came to Nahanni in 1904 using various means of transportation but making the final push by dogsled. They set up in the area around Flat River, one of the tributaries of the South Nahanni, and spent a year or so panning and sluicing and searching for gold before leaving the valley. They apparently found enough gold to excite the two younger brothers, Willie and Frank, because they returned to look for more.

The two brothers recruited a Scotsman named Robert Weir to accompany them and made their way back to Nahanni in 1905. By 1908, the trio hadn't returned from their expedition, so older brother Charlie mounted a rescue party. And he found his brothers. Or at least their skeletons . . . both missing their skulls. Robert Weir's skull was also missing, but in his case, so was the rest of him. One of their dogsled runners had been carved with the phrase, "We've found a fine prospect." This led Charlie to speculate that the men might have been murdered by other prospectors for their gold. Or maybe even by the missing Weir, as a rumor circulated that he had been sighted in Vancouver, suspiciously wealthy.

As rumors of murders motivated by abundant gold spread,

other prospectors started searching for the Lost McLeod Mine, as it came to be known. At least twenty of them lost their lives in the pursuit. Nahanni has remained stingy, however. No gold of any appreciable quantity has ever been dragged from its mountains or dredged from its rivers, and the Lost McLeod Mine—if it ever even existed in the first place—has stayed lost.

And then it happened again—another decapitated body turned up in the valley. It wouldn't be the last time, either.

In 1917, a Swiss prospector named Martin Jorgenson was found dead next to his burned-down cabin. His skull was also missing. In 1945, a Canadian miner named Ernest Savard was found dead in his sleeping bag, his skull, too, missing. Were they all murdered by rival prospectors? Maybe. Did they starve or die by one of the 1,472 natural ways a person can die in Nahanni? Maybe. But the missing skulls fired imaginations.

Some theorized that the Naha were still in the valley, hiding and head hunting. Others thought that it was the work of a beast called the Waheela, a giant wolf similar to the dire wolf, that latter of which was supposed to have gone extinct 10,000 years ago. Amphicyonidae were also blamed—a family of creatures that look like a mix between a dog and a bear whose evolutionary line ended during the Pliocene period. There are similar rumors of living mastodons in the valley based on the many large bones found there, combined with some uncannily accurate Dene drawings of mastodon-like creatures that had been preserved on animal skin. And then there are the giant hairy cannibals that supposedly live in the hundreds of caves that perforate the mountains and who sometimes cook their food in the steamy depths of Rabbitkettle hot springs. Because, of course, somebody has to blame bigfoots—somebody always blames a bigfoot.

Among the more pedestrian theories, it's noted that lots of carnivorous animals make Nahanni their home. According to Parks Canada, Nahanni is home to 42 species of mammals, 180 species of birds, 16 species of fish, and a few brave species of amphibians. Animals that could kill a person (or at least abscond with their head after death) include grizzlies, black bears, wolves, wolverines, and lynxes. The bigger species in this list usually prey on caribou, moose, and Dall sheep, but a miner could be a good meal in a pinch.

To this day, nobody knows for certain what happened to these men or their missing heads. But their morbid fates fit the uncanny valley that is the Nahanni. According to Neil Hartling's 1993 book, *Nahanni: River of Gold, River of Dreams,* British explorer Raymond Patterson was advised before his expedition in 1927, "Men vanish in that country . . . and down the river they say it's a damned good country to keep clear of." This sentiment is echoed over and over by explorers of Nahanni. According to a 1946 issue of *Maclean's* magazine, Frank Henderson, a prospector who himself had a partner disappear in Nahanni, once said:

> "There is absolutely no denying the sinister atmosphere of that whole valley. The weird, continual wailing of the wind is something I won't soon forget."

Author Hammerson Peters in his book *Legends of the Nahanni Valley* quotes a story told by journalist Pierre Berton, who had visited the valley in the winter of 1947 on assignment for the *Vancouver Sun*:

> *We heard in the distance an eerie and spine-chilling sound. A low, howling whine swept out of the mountain down into the valley, died, and rose again in greater intensity. Was this the great evil spirit which the Indians claimed lurked in the mountains? . . . Standing there in Deadman's Valley, not far from the spot where the McLeod bodies were found, on that cold day in 1947, I felt it as strongly as anyone could. . . . The banshee wail made our hackles rise, for this was, without a doubt, the spirit sound so many men talked and whispered about.*

All myths, rumors, and speculations on how the headless prospectors died aside, it is a fact that scores of people have met their untimely ends in the Nahanni over the years. Some found death through the obvious means: drowning, freezing, starving. Many just disappeared, their deaths assumed and their causes, as a result, unknown. A woman named Annie Laferte, who was a member of a hunting party into Nahanni in 1926, was last seen by a Dene named Big Charley. According to a *Maclean's* account, he "saw her climbing a hill nearly naked. Concluding that a devil had got her, he refused to follow."

In 2009, Canada vastly increased the size of Nahanni National Park from its original 1,800 square miles to almost 12,000 square miles, dubbing this wider region the Nahanni National Park Reserve. According to the press release from the Canadian government, the expansion of the protected area "highlights our shared commitment as Northerners to protect and sustain the value and wonder of our region for the future." Sounds nice. However, this massive increase in the size of the preserve sounds suspiciously like the installation of a buffer, one that further isolates the mysteries and horrors of this Valley of Headless Men, keeping this lost world as lost as possible.

HAYNESVILLE WOODS

A TOMBSTONE EVERY MILE

LOCATION: Haynesville, Maine, USA	**INFAMOUS FOR:**
SIZE: 150 square miles	Vehicle accidents, ghosts, country music
MAIN FEATURE: US Route 2A	

You're driving down a dark, desolate road, the only light your headlamps. You're surrounded by dense forest of mostly conifers. Every so often a sign appears, reflecting your lights back at you and warning you of sharp curves or wildlife crossing (HIGH HIT AREA, the signs say under the silhouette of a leaping deer). As you gaze past your white knuckles on the steering wheel and into the blackness ahead, you might think, "I'm glad it's not raining or snowing." And, yes, you should be. Very much so. Because you're driving one of the most dangerous roads in the country. And inclement weather is the least of your worries.

Haynesville Woods is a one-hundred-thousand-acre patch of forestland in Aroostook County, Maine, in the northern part of the state that's surrounded by Canada on three sides. US Route 2A cuts through those woods, traveling directly through the tiny town of Haynesville (population: less than 100). And a forty-mile stretch of that road that cuts through Haynesville has garnered a reputation for both death and after-death.

In 1828, a military post was established in the town of Houlton, about twenty-five miles north of what would become Haynesville (William Wilson, the first settler in Haynesville, established his homestead that same year). The infrastructure was put in place because there was still contention about the border between the United States and the British-held parts of Canada. The Treaty of Paris, which ended the Revolutionary War and demarcated the new nation that had emerged as a result, just wasn't specific enough about that area of the continent. In 1832, a road was built from Houlton to transport military supplies to that border fort. It was known as Military Road. In 1839, the Aroostook War happened, which was not really a war but an escalation in tensions between Britain and the US. Militia on both sides were marshalled, but no actual combat occurred. Finally, in 1842, the Webster-Ashburton Treaty officially nailed down the border between Maine and what would eventually become Canada and everybody took their weapons and went home.

Military Road became US Route 2A (although portions of it are still called Military Road), and its main use by the middle of the twentieth century was trucks transporting lumber and potatoes from the forests and farms up north down to Bangor, Boston, and points beyond.

But it wasn't an easy haul. The road was notorious for its sharp turns and bad conditions, not to mention the region's already infamous inclement weather. At times, the route was practically lined with the carcasses of vehicles and the corpses of drivers. A 1980 article from the *Kennebec Journal* mentions seven truckers who died in the space of eleven weeks (although it doesn't mention the dates of these incidents). The same article interviews an eighty-year-old man named Lew Buddell, who "through the years . . . has used his team of horses to drag vehicles, some containing dead bodies, out of the ditches along the road."

In 1967, the *Bangor Daily News* interviewed a trucker named Clint Peary, a truck driver who had spent decades behind the wheel of a big rig. He described the conditions for a trucker up north back in the 1930s: "You could look through your floorboard and see your front axle. It was cold in the wintertime. We wore sheepskin coats. Some of the drivers wore felt boots as well. We'd stop at just about every town to get warm. Driving was just like working outdoors." Peary told stories of getting mired in mud up to the tailgate of his truck on that Haynesville road and traveling in caravans to cut through the snow. "One night in 1937 we went over the woods road and counted 58 trucks off the road due to the ice," he told the newspaper.

The deaths, injuries, and accidents weren't limited to those in the cabs. In August 1967, a tractor trailer traveling at a speed that the *Bangor Daily News* described as "not careful and prudent" hit and killed two ten-year-old girls walking along the side of the road. Their names were Janet Rouse and Melody Shorey.

That same year, a student named Sandra F. MacDonald wrote a paper on the local folklore for a University of Maine class. She based it on her own knowledge as a local. She mentioned many of the dangerous sections of the road—Santa Claus Hill, Beach Hill, Anderson Hill—that regularly jackknifed trucks. She called out Sawmill Turn, in particular, writing: "This curve has been improved a great deal over the past few years. I can remember when it was very sharp and they had a marker there stating how many people had been killed in car accidents on that turn. I don't remember the exact number but it was over fifty." In 2022, a *Bangor Daily News* reporter searched through the newspaper's archive to tally all the accidents on that stretch of road. They found reports of almost one hundred accidents going back to 1906. They also looked at reports from the Maine Department of Transportation, which had logged forty accidents since 2003. According to the article, almost all those latter accidents "involved deer or moose."

And that wildlife shouldn't be discounted. On my own visit to the road, I decided that since I was arriving late at night and had a car full of my kids, I wouldn't chance the Haynesville Woods right away. Instead I took the faster, straighter, better-lit Interstate 95 north. It parallels Route 2A, and my plan was that I would end up in Houlton, get a hotel, and then travel south through the woods on my return trip the next day. But even that stretch of interstate wasn't safe. It is, after all, only separated from Haynesville Woods by more woods. As soon as I got to the section of the interstate closest to 2A, I encountered, within the space of a few minutes: a bobcat on the shoulder, a coyote attempting to cross, and a steaming dead moose right in the middle of the highway, freshly hit by the car in front of me. By comparison, my trip back the next day via the dreaded Route 2A was peaceful and calm. Not a single creature attempted to face off with my car, despite the empty road and thick forest surrounding us as we drove. Something tells me skipping the night drive was a good call.

So the Haynesville Woods is home to a dangerous road, bad weather, and large wildlife, all of which can be deadly. And, of course, where there are frequent mortalities, there are ghosts.

One ghost in particular seems to haunt the road, a woman in a white dress known as the Haynesville Hitchhiker or the Haynesville Witch. She is, quite naturally, the victim of a vehicle accident, although the details of that accident vary. One story, repeated in multiple local newspapers and websites, involves the woman suddenly appearing on the side of the road in obvious distress. When drivers pull over to ask if they can help, she tells them that it's her wedding day, and she and her new husband have been in an accident. She enters the car or truck, but by the time it gets to the end of the road, she disappears. Another version of the story has the woman asking for a ride to a particular town where she lives, only to disappear when the trucker who picked her up stops for food. Curious, when he arrives in the town she claimed to live in, he asks about her—only to discover that she had died in an accident years ago. Other tales state that drivers see her walking on the side of the road but can never seem to catch up to her, until finally, she disappears into the dark.

In 2024, the *University Times*, a student newspaper of the University of Maine at Presque Isle, interviewed a resident of Aroostook County named Bob Chandler, whose dad was a trucker on the route in the 1970s and 1980s. He said, "I grew up hearing about the woman in white. Dad never saw her himself, but he would hear about her from the other drivers. . . . The truckers said that they would come upon a young woman walking along the road. They would, of course, pull over and offer her a ride. She would climb up in the passenger seat without making a sound, only to disappear into thin air when the poor driver tried to make small talk."

A major variation on the tale, or maybe even a second ghostly woman in white, seems to merge both the backstory and the ghost story. This version has her not as a bride, but a woman in a white party gown who suffers a flat tire en route to said party. While changing the tire, she is hit by a semi, although when the driver exits the cab to see what happened, all he finds is her bloody dress. Her body had vanished.

In 1993, the *Bangor Daily News* described a different kind of phantom hitchhiker. The newspaper reported an accident on the Haynesville Road where a pickup truck had rolled over. The driver was thrown from the truck and seriously injured . . . although he claimed not to be the driver. According to the article, the man said that he had picked up a hitchhiker, whom he had let drive the truck. After the accident, the hitchhiker immediately fled into the woods. According to the article, "Rescuers and passers-by conducted a search along both sides of the road but found no one. The exact cause of the accident is still under investigation." Seems like this ghostly hitchhiker might have been more scapegoat than spook.

Other stories involve phantom headlights that turn on and off without a car behind them, and a ghostly pair of hitchhiking young girls, potentially derived from the 1967 deaths of Rouse and Shorey.

The Haynesville Woods became so notorious that a country music song was recorded about them in 1965. The singer's name was Dick Curless, and he had written the song with his partner Dan Fulkerson. It was called "A Tombstone Every Mile." Curless drew from his own experience growing up and working in the area. He was from nearby Fort Fairfield and spent time on those potato fields during the Great Depression before eventually being employed as a truck driver himself, hauling loads down Route 2A. The lyrics of the chorus of the song went:

It's a stretch of road up north in Maine
That's never, ever, ever seen a smile
If they buried all them truckers lost in them woods
There'd be a tombstone every mile.

The song spent seventeen weeks on the charts, reaching as high as number five for two weeks.

Curless's tombstones were metaphors, but there are actual tombstones on the side of Route 2A as well. There are a couple of tiny, old cemeteries on the road, as well as a standalone tombstone. But the latter is not for any victim of the road: The gravestone marks the final resting place of Private Hiram T. Smith, who died in 1828 of pneumonia during the aforementioned and otherwise bloodless Aroostook War. As the road widened over time, its edge crept closer and closer to Smith's grave. Today, the asphalt is only about twenty feet from the grave—up a rise and into the forest. A Mrs. Donald Lowery, who used to tend the grave as part of the Daughters of the Revolution group—which erected the memorial stone—joked in the previously mentioned 1980 *Kennebec Journal*, "I can't believe Mr. Smith's toes haven't been run over."

But, for some reason, Private Smith isn't rumored to haunt the road or the woods. Maybe the area is already too crowded with spooks.

These days, Interstate 95 is the preferred throughfare for truckers on the East Coast. And Route 2A, despite its obsolescence, is a better maintained road. It's wider, smoother, and has decent cell service over most of it. As a testament to its gentling, those previously referenced forty accidents since 2003 in the *Bangor Daily News*? None of them were fatal.

Still, if you ever find yourself in that part of Maine, you should probably just take the interstate. But watch out for moose.

AOKIGAHARA

THE SUICIDE FOREST

LOCATION: Yamanashi Prefecture, Japan	**NAME TRANSLATION:** Blue Tree Meadow
SIZE: 13.5 square miles	**INFAMOUS FOR:** Suicides, angry ghosts, Logan Paul

Visitors to Aokigahara often describe how strange this Japanese forest feels. They say that the sound in the woodland seems deadened, that the wind doesn't blow, that rain doesn't fall. Wildlife seems scarce. Devices like phones and compasses malfunction regularly. The unease of these visitors, no doubt, is informed by one undisputable fact of the forest: At any moment, at any bend in the trail, over any rise in the ground, within any clearing, one might find a dead person dangling from a tree branch, curled among the mossy roots, or halfway outside the flap of a tent. Aokigahara is a place where many go to die by their own hand. So many, in fact, that people call it the Suicide Forest.

Aokigahara covers 13.5 square miles near the base of Mount Fuji, on the northwest side, in the Yamanashi Prefecture. The forest grew on hardened lava after an eruption during the ninth century. That porous bedrock is what makes the forest seem quieter than it should be, as the volcanic rock absorbs sound. It also has faint magnetic qualities, which is why it can play with a compass needle sometimes, and no forest needs a special reason for interrupted cell service. The bedrock is perforated by caves, including the Narusawa Ice Cave, the Fuji Fugaku Wind Cave, and the Saiko Bat Cave, which are known for their ice formations, echoless basalt chambers, and flying mammals. But it's to the green shadows of the trees that the desperate and the depressed go to end their stories.

The forest's name translates to "Blue Tree Meadow," and its less macabre nickname is Jukai—"Sea of Trees"—because the firs and cypresses and hemlocks that make up much of the forest grow close together, to the point that they seem to be blocking outsiders from intruding. The trees also give a creepy cast to the ground, as their roots must spread across the hardened lava horizontally and often twist above the dirt like surfacing serpents covered in bright moss. Despite the rumors, plenty of animals do call this dense, tangled forest home. Black bears are the biggest creatures, but it also provides habitat for minks, boars, flying squirrels, and around sixty species of birds. They're just skittish of the many visitors every year who go to the forest to hike and camp, search out stunning views of Mount Fuji and, yes, end their lives.

Aokigahara is one of the most popular suicide spots on the planet. A 2021 *Condé Nast Traveler* piece went so far as to rank it second behind San Francisco's Golden Gate Bridge. Ever since the 1960s, scores of people have ended their lives in the forest every year, peaking in 2004 at 108. More recent statistics are difficult to find as the authorities stopped releasing them in an effort to curb the high numbers. And the high numbers we do know don't tell the entire tale—first, they represent only the bodies that were found. The forest is so dense that the bodies of many who commit suicide are hidden forever. Second, some self-harmers don't even make the tally, as they end their lives in nearby forests, mistakenly thinking that they are in

Aokigahara. Finally, those tallies don't include the hundreds of attempts that were survived. The *Japanese Times* reported in 2011 that in in the previous year, 247 suicides were attempted in the forest. Of that number, only fifty-four were successful.

The same article featured an interview with a local named Hideo Watanabe. For three decades, he had run a café outside an entrance to the forest. He told the paper that in that time, he had saved some 160 people who were contemplating or had attempted suicide. He described one woman who walked past his eatery before attempting: "She had tried to hang herself and failed. She had part of the rope around her neck and her eyes were almost popping out of their sockets. I took her inside, made her some tea, and called an ambulance. A few kind words can go a long way."

The issue is so massive that every year since the early 1970s, hundreds of police and firefighters have combed the forest looking for human remains in what various newspaper accounts have macabrely described as a harvest. The responders follow the telltale strips of plastic ribbon that festoon the forest, bracing themselves for what they might find at the end of the trail. The strips are used by those who want to wander off the path and not get lost among the closely packed trees—maybe hikers. Maybe campers. Maybe those who haven't quite made up their minds whether to join so many others before them in the forest in death, or who want their bodies to be found. According to a 2000 article in the *Telegraph*, during that year's sweep of the forest, so many bodies were discovered that the local authorities ran out of space to store them.

But why do those looking for an end to the pain of life choose this forest in particular? There are practical reasons, of course. A psychiatrist named Dr. Yoshitomo Takahashi, who interviewed Aokigahara suicide survivors for a 1988 article in the journal *Suicide and Life-Threatening Behavior*, wrote that a main reason was "they believed that they would be able to die successfully without being noticed." However, Takahashi also opined that it was an act of solace: "Many people have committed suicide at Aokigahara; thus you won't die alone."

These days, the self-destructive seek this place out due to its reputation. But how it got that reputation is a mystery. Some say that the forest has always drawn tragedy. Early in Japan's history, Aokigahara was supposedly a site for the practice of ubasute ("abandoning an elderly woman"). During times of famine, family would leave the elderly and the very young to die in the forest so that the rest of the family could survive. However, no proof of the practice has ever been found, and most believe it to be a part of Japanese folklore.

Then there are all the angry ghosts that some believe flit among the thickly packed trees. In Japanese mythology, yūrei are vengeful spirits who died by an act of violence—including suicide. However, whether the tales of ghosts in Aokigahara pre-date the suicide phenomenon or are retroactive additions is unclear. Still, many subscribe to the idea. A Buddhist monk named Kyomyo Fukui, who was part of a group of fifty monks who traveled to Aokigahara in 2000 to set up an altar and pray for these spirits, told the *Independent*, "The spirits are calling people here to kill themselves, the spirits of the people who have committed suicide before. The spirits draw the unhappy people here. Prayers bring them peace and send them home rather than doing mischief."

The answer to why Aokigahara became the Suicide Forest lies in the past, but it's probably more cultural than supernatural. Japan has one of the highest suicide rates in the world among wealthy nations. The Japanese have no religious taboo against it. In fact, its acceptance dates back as far as the Feudal

Era and the practice of seppuku or hara-kiri, in which a warrior who felt the need to restore honor to himself or his family would disembowel himself with a short sword.

In modern Japan, the permissive attitude toward suicide prevails. In 2011, Yukio Saito, executive director of Inochi no Denwa ("Lifeline"), a suicide hotline, told the *Japan Times*, "Suicide is quite permissible in Japanese society, something honorable that is even glorified." Karen Nakamura, an anthropology professor at the University of California, explained to CNN in 2018 that many in Japan view suicide as a "rational decision." She explained, "One of the terms for suicide is jiketsu, which means to decide for yourself."

In 2009, CNN interviewed a man named Taro who had survived his suicide attempt in Aokigahara. The forty-six-year-old man had been fired from his job, was in debt, and had been evicted from his apartment. He explained, "My will to live disappeared. I'd lost my identity, so I didn't want to live on this earth. That's why I went there. You need money to survive." Taro's story is typical. Most suicides in those woods (and generally across the world) are middle-aged men, and the economic pressures on those men in Japan can be fierce. It's such a catalyst for suicide in Aokigahara that debt counseling numbers are posted at the entrance to convince would-be suicide victims to seek help instead of harm. Taro chose the latter, cutting his wrists inside the forest. Fortunately, he was found by a hiker days later almost dead from dehydration, starvation, and the frostbite that would take the toes of his right foot.

Popular media is also pointed to as an influence. In 1960, author Seichō Matsumoto published his romance novel *Nami no Tou* (*Tower of Waves*). In it, a woman kills herself in Aokigahara. The book has been so popular over the years that it's been adapted for Japanese television at least once a decade since its release. One real-life suicide victim was even found in the forest with the book as a pillow. Also found among the possessions of those who have ended their lives in Aokigahara is *The Complete Manual of Suicide*, a controversial book published in 1993 by Wataru Tsurumi that lives up to its title. He called Aokigahara "the perfect place to die." As recently as 2016, the American horror movie *The Forest* tells the story of a woman looking for a sister who disappeared in Aokigahara, and its story comes complete with yūrei.

In January 2018, the forest received intense international attention when twenty-two-year-old YouTube phenom Logan Paul (who had more than fifteen million subscribers at the time) posted a video of himself and his friends entering Aokigahara and finding a recently deceased body hanging from a tree. They blur out the face of the unfortunate, while making jokes, narrating to the camera, and generally projecting a nervous and excitable energy. In an introduction to the video filmed later, Paul talks about how the video "marks a moment in YouTube history," before segueing with, "Buckle the fuck up. Because you're never going to see a video like this again." Basically, they turned the tragedy into content.

The exploitative nature of the video was instantly criticized, and it was removed within twenty-four hours of upload while YouTube severed its business relationship with the young content creator. Logan would later release a statement apologizing for the video. But the damage had been done: A whole new generation had been introduced to the Suicide Forest.

Meanwhile, Japanese authorities and local residents are doing their best to stop the slew of suicides. They have installed cameras, regularly patrol the forest, and have raised the railings on bridges to discourage jumpers. They have also erected signs at the entrances to the forest with such messages as, "Your life is a precious gift from your parents" and "Don't agonize over problems yourself—please seek counseling."

Efforts to stop the suicides are ongoing, and locals hope that one day the Suicide Forest will be nothing more than a forest. A 2000 article in the *Independent* quotes a firefighter chief named Kiyotaka Oyamada, who was at the time leading one of the Aokigahara "harvests." It describes him as "looking round in despair at the three-camera crew and half a dozen reporters who have gathered to document his grisly mission." He said, "We'd love it if you media people would write about the walks and the trees and the beauty of it all, but the hikers stick to the other side of Fuji because they're worried that they'll be walking along with their kids, and suddenly there'll be a dead man hanging from a tree."

VYING WITH VILE VORTICES

Sometime in the late 1960s and early 1970s, Ivan T. Sanderson—the famed paranormal researcher, biologist, and inventor of the term *cryptozoology*—started playing with an idea, an idea born out of the widespread and raging fascination with a newly identified patch of the planet called the Bermuda Triangle. The Bermuda Triangle is strange by itself, but Sanderson went stranger. He postulated that the Triangle was just one of a series of twelve points on the planet where unexplained disappearances, time anomalies, and other unnatural phenomena occur. He called them "Vile Vortices." They included:

- Bermuda Triangle (see page 60)
- Mohenjo-daro in Pakistan
- Devil's Sea, near Japan
- Hamakulia Volcano in the Pacific Ocean, near Hawaii
- Algeria Megaliths
- South Atlantic Anomaly, near Brazil
- Zimbabwe Megaliths
- Wharton Basin in the Indian Ocean
- New Hebrides Trench, near Fiji
- Easter Island
- North Pole
- South Pole

Five of these vertices were found within the Tropic of Cancer and five within the Tropic of Capricorn, each of the vertices an exacting 72 degrees apart longitudinally and wrapping around the globe (72 degrees × 5 vertices = 360 degrees, a full circle), minus the two poles. Shape-wise, he most often described these planetary artifacts as *lozenges*—long ovals—but he also called them *blobs* throughout his writings.

The idea got some attention, and he was even invited onto the popular *Dick Cavett Show* on ABC to defend the idea. He arrived at the television studio with a globe tucked under his arm marked all over with vile vortices. Other guests on that episode included Lucille Ball and Carol Burnett.

However, Sanderson never quite arrived at any theories as to why these vortices existed, focusing his writings instead on the path to their discovery. In an article in the 1973 special UFO edition of *Saga* magazine called "The Twelve Devil's Graveyards Around the World," he merely concludes, "I really do think that it's about time we took this matter seriously."

And some do. Vile vortices seem to have a kinship with the paranormal concepts of Earth grids, ley lines, and energy vortexes. These ideas are sometimes tied to sacred geometry, a theory in which the universe has an underlying pattern that proves its deeper meaning and unity—the Force, basically. For instance, Sanderson's vile vortices form a regular grid around the Earth that can be extrapolated into a twenty-sided geometric figure called an icosahedron. Some claim the figure proves that the planet isn't just some random biology-riddled rock.

I don't know about that theory, but I do tend to agree with Sanderson's conclusion about taking these vortices seriously. To me, the implications of paranormal weak spots across the planet are clear and clearly terrifying. If the Bermuda Triangle is not an anomaly, but part of a pattern—in other words, not an exception to the known physics of the universe, but the rule—and the planet is pimply with these spots, it means the whole planet is scary. So don't go here, I guess.

WRETCHED WATERS

Every body of water on Earth is dangerous—oceans, seas, lakes, rivers, creeks, ponds, swimming pools, bathtubs. Humans, despite being the dominant species on this planet, are remarkably and ironically ill-adapted to a place that is predominantly water. We don't belong in the substance. Our bodies can only survive mere minutes if completely submerged. Creatures can attack us from all angles as we flail and splash with club-like limbs comically unable to maneuver us through a three-dimensional space made up of two atoms of hydrogen and one of oxygen. But some bodies of water are uniquely dangerous. They don't merely drown us. They don't merely chew us up with shark teeth or sting us with jellyfish tentacles. They present even more mysterious horrors not yet plumbed by science, story, or our most imaginative nightmares.

BERMUDA TRIANGLE

A SEA OF ACUTE MYSTERY

LOCATION: North Atlantic Ocean	**TRIANGLE POINTS:** Miami, San Juan, Bermuda
SIZE: 500,000 square miles	**INFAMOUS FOR:** Plane and ship disappearances

Here we go. The big one—the Bermuda Triangle. The Bermuda Triangle is, quite simply, the Bermuda Triangle of Bermuda Triangles: the grandaddy of mysterious places, a spot so influential that its mere shape has dictated the boundaries of other strange locales all over the world, from the Bridgewater Triangle to the Molyobka Triangle and beyond. It's a patch of ocean where ships and planes have been disappearing without a trace or any apparent cause for more than a century. And it's . . . off the coast of Miami?

That's right. This zone nicknamed "The Devil's Triangle" is not in some far-flung, isolated stretch of exotic ocean. The three points of the Triangle are roughly Miami, Florida; San Juan, Puerto Rico; and its namesake Bermuda, all three of which are destinations for millions of unsuspecting vacationers every year. The Bermuda Triangle encompasses some 500,000 square miles in the western area of the North Atlantic and about 500,000 bizarre stories. And those stories are . . . surprisingly repetitive. A lot of vehicles simply vanish at those GPS coordinates. The litany of mysterious disappearances covers both sea and air across time, from masted ships to modern cargo carriers to military planes to air liners.

But the story of how the Bermuda Triangle became the most infamous paranormal point on the planet is perhaps the most interesting thing about it.

The first mention in the media of the area being a place of no return seems to be an article in the *Miami Herald* on September 17, 1950. Titled "Sea's Puzzles Still Baffle Men in Pushbutton Age," it was written by a Florida-based Associated Press reporter named E. V. W. Jones. In it, he lists a series of mysterious disappearances off the coast of Miami from the previous five years.

In 1948, the British airliner *Star Tiger* vanished with its twenty-nine passengers upon nearing Bermuda. In 1949, another British airliner, the *Ariel*, disappeared heading in the opposite direction as it left Bermuda with twenty passengers. In 1950, the *Sandra*, a freighter crewed by a dozen men, departed Miami to deliver insecticide to Venezuela. It never arrived. All these disappearances were immediately followed by large search and rescue efforts. In the case of the *Ariel*, a fleet of US Navy boats that included aircraft carriers, cruisers, and destroyers were performing maneuvers nearby and immediately joined the search—to no avail. Not so much as a life preserver was ever found.

Jones also highlighted an unsolved event that would become the cornerstone of the Bermuda Triangle mystery—the disappearance of Flight 19. On December 5, 1945, five Navy TBM Avenger torpedo planes with a total crew of fourteen departed a station in Fort Lauderdale on a navigational training mission. Hours later, past the limits of their fuel, they had not returned. During the ensuing search and rescue (which Jones called "the greatest search in Florida's history"), a Martin PBM Mariner aircraft and its crew of thirteen also disappeared forever, following Flight 19 into what Jones termed a "limbo of the lost." According to a 2020 article in the *Telegraph*, without this multiplane, multitragedy event, there would be no Bermuda Triangle. Journalist Chris Leadbeater writes: "Flight 19 is the Bermuda Triangle legend—and the Bermuda Triangle is Flight 19. They are one and the same jumble of the unexplained."

The purpose of Jones's article wasn't to demarcate the boundaries of a new mystery, but to emphasize a broader point about how the dangers of exploration persist despite rapid technological advances. He writes:

> *We think [the world] is small because of speeding wheels and wings and the voice of radio which comes out of the void. A mile is only a minute's travel by wheel or a few seconds flight—but it is still a mile. The miles add up to a vast unknown into which a hundred and more persons have flown or sailed within brief memory, to be swallowed up just as ships were swallowed in the old sailing days.*

Jones went on to say that the 135 people he lists who disappeared "went forth confidently into a world they thought was small. But it is the same big world the ancients knew, into which men and their machines and ships can disappear without a trace."

As to why Jones used examples from that region of the North Atlantic, as a Florida-based reporter, it was basically his own backyard. An illustrated map accompanying the story marked the last known locations of each ship and plane disappearance. No boundary of any shape was drawn around the sites—the triangle would come later.

The story was circulated by the Associated Press, and eventually the idea of a "vast unknown" in the North Atlantic was promulgated by other publications in the 1960s and 1970s. *Fate* magazine published an article by George X. Sand in 1966 called "Sea Mystery at Our Back Door." In 1969, John Wallace Spencer wrote a book about the area called *Limbo of the Lost*. In 1971, a documentary directed by Richard Winer and narrated by Vincent Price debuted on the topic. It was called *The Devil's Triangle*.

But Winer wasn't the one to draw a triangle around all that weirdness. In 1964, fourteen years after the Jones piece, a writer named Vincent Gaddis gave the area a name and its dimensions in a story for *Argosy* called "Lost in the Bermuda Triangle." Four years later, *Argosy* promoted the topic to a cover story called "The Deadly Bermuda Triangle." The cover featured a human skull inside a red triangle along with the question: "Who will be its next victim?"

In a way, the answer to that question was all of us. Because the concept of the Bermuda Triangle hit the mainstream hard in 1974 when author Charles Berlitz wrote the (barely) nonfiction book *The Bermuda Triangle*. It sold more than eighteen million copies, was translated into thirty languages, and hit the *New York Times* best-seller list. According to a 2004 obituary of Berlitz published in *Skeptic* magazine, "Thanks largely to Berlitz, Trianglemania struck the world like a tsunami."

Over the course of these publications, more and more victims were added to the Bermuda Triangle's tally, both as new incidents occurred and as researchers discovered historical disappearances. In 1918, the USS *Cyclops* and the 306 people aboard disappeared en route to Baltimore after a brief berth in Barbados. The loss of life is the largest in the history of the US Navy outside of combat. The SS *Marine Sulphur Queen* vanished off the coast of Florida in 1963, taking 39 people and a hold full of molten sulfur with it. The HMS *Atalanta*, a British frigate, left Bermuda and known history in 1880 with 281 people aboard. Some even trace the first victims of the Bermuda Triangle all the way back to 1779, when South Carolina representative and signer of the Declaration of Independence Thomas Lynch Jr. and his wife Elizabeth went permanently missing while sailing to the West Indies.

In his article, Jones didn't attempt to hazard a reason for the disappearances other than it being the way of the world, but subsequent writers did, and their reasons raced at full speed up and down a spectrum of answers from the odd to the obvious.

Starting on the odd side of the spectrum (or maybe it's a seesaw), we've got abduction-happy extraterrestrials nabbing planes from the air and plucking ships from the sea as part of some kind of anthropological study of the planet. Steven Spielberg played with this theory in his 1979 movie *Close Encounters of the Third Kind*. In the film, ships and planes (including Flight 19) that had disappeared in the Triangle appear in the middle of deserts across the world as harbingers of the climatic landing of the extraterrestrial mothership on Devils Tower in Wyoming. Other theories place those aliens in the ocean at an underwater base, from which they sabotage trespassing craft. Another major theory is that the Triangle is home to an interdimensional vortex that pulls its victims into other times or other dimensions.

Then there's the theory that the waters of the Bermuda Triangle don't merely swallow people and machines, but entire continents. In this theory, Atlantis is said to be submerged off the coast of Miami, and the reason so many water- and aircraft disappear is because some remnant of the advanced technology of that vanished culture is disrupting the shipping lanes and fly zones. This theory was propounded by Berlitz, who, five years before his hit book on the Bermuda Triangle, published another barely nonfiction book: *The Mystery of Atlantis*. The evidence most often offered for this theory is the so-called Bimini Road, a long strip of flat, rectangular blocks resembling a man-made road fifteen feet beneath the surface of the water off the Bahamian island of Bimini. Turns out, despite their artificial appearance, the stones are completely natural and not all that uncommon of a rock formation.

Another interesting angle on the Bermuda Triangle mystery is that it is part of the Sargasso Sea. This area of the North Atlantic is a sea without shores, the only one of its kind, the shape of which isn't created by any coastline but by the four ocean currents that surround it and cut it off from the rest of the ocean. As a result of its watery isolation, the sea is often calm and dense with floating brown seaweed (sargassum). Christopher Columbus wrote about the Sargasso Sea in his journal because he thought the seaweed was evidence of shallow water and was worried his ship would run aground. Rumors have persisted that the sea traps ships with its lack of wind and entangling seaweed. In 1840, the French merchant ship *Rosalie* was found in the Sargasso Sea perfectly intact and complete with cargo, but, according to a contemporary report in the *London Times*, "not a human being was to be found on board."

More recently, in 1969, a thirty-six-year-old British businessman named Donald Crowhurst vanished in the Sargasso Sea while competing in a solo race around the world. Searchers found his yacht empty and his logbook full of delusions and strange speculations, including mentions of catching small ocean monsters and describing himself as a "second generation cosmic being" in a game among cosmic beings like God and the Devil. Those who have analyzed his life, the logbooks, and recordings he left behind believe that—having found his vessel not up to the task of an ocean voyage—Crowhurst started radioing in false positions to cover up his failure. The prevailing theory as to his disappearance is that he committed suicide by jumping into the Sargasso, his mind having collapsed under the intense burden of loneliness combined with his fears of failure, exposure, and financial ruin.

Moving to the middle of the spectrum, away from aliens and lost continents, are more scientific-sounding explanations for the vanishing crafts in the Triangle. Like magnetic anomalies and electric fogs that interfere with compasses. It is true that at one point in time the Triangle was crossed by the agonic line, where truth north and magnetic north align, confusing navigators who are used to compensating between the two readings. However, as the Earth's magnetic field has changed over time, so has the position of that line. These days, the northern segment of the line that once shot through the Bermuda Triangle has drifted westward, cutting through the North American continent. Then there's the methane gas hypothesis, theorizing that great belches of the gas rise to the surface, destabilizing the buoyancy of the water and pulling ships down or suffusing airplane engines and combusting them, although no firsthand evidence of the phenomenon has ever been found in the Triangle.

Eventually, though, you make it to the other end of the spectrum, where all the prosaic theories lie, but also possibly the truth: that the sea is a harsh mistress. The area is known for strong tropical storms and hurricanes. The powerful Gulf Stream current cuts right through the Triangle, continuously sweeping it clean of clues. The area goes from deep trenches of some 27,500 feet below sea level to the shallow shores of islands, making it tricky to navigate and burying its wrecks deeply underwater. And then there's human error, which is an easy thing to fall prey to on the open water—no matter how far technology has come, to Jones's point.

And speaking of human error, there's another prosaic explanation for the Bermuda Triangle—perhaps the most prosaic, in fact: that it simply doesn't exist. In 1975, during the heyday of Bermuda Triangle speculation, a single voice cried out in opposition. A research librarian at Arizona State University named Larry Kusche, who was also a pilot, published the book *The Bermuda Triangle Mystery—Solved*. By going back to original sources and doing a lot of follow-up work, he found issues with most of the supposedly "mysterious" disappearances in the Triangle. For instance, many happened outside the actual boundaries. Others not only didn't disappear without a trace, but the wreckage was found and unsurprising causes of destruction were determined. Many of the vanishings coincided with documented storms.

Most of the errors can be laid at the swim fins of Charles Berlitz. Kusche went so far as to say that Berlitz's research was so slipshod that "If Berlitz were to report that a boat were red, the chance of it being some other color is almost a certainty." And that includes the disappearances of Flight 19 and its rescue plane. Despite not being able to find any physical evidence, military investigators determined that it was a simple matter of human failure on the part of the latter (it was, after all, a training mission) and mechanical failure on the part of the former (the Martin PBM Mariner aircrafts were notoriously unreliable).

And today, the major organizations that know the seas best support Kusche's debunking. According to the website for the National Oceanic and Atmospheric Administration, "There is no evidence that mysterious disappearances occur with any greater frequency in the Bermuda Triangle than in any other large, well-traveled area of the ocean." In 2003, a historian with the US Naval Historical Foundation told *National Geographic*, "To say quite a few ships and airplanes have gone down there is like saying there are an awful lot of car accidents on the New Jersey Turnpike—surprise, surprise." The US Coast Guard had to create a FAQ about the Bermuda Triangle because of all the inquiries it was receiving. In it, they state, "The Coast Guard is not impressed with supernatural explanations of disasters at sea. It has been their experience that the combined forces of nature and unpredictability of mankind outdo even the most far-fetched science fiction many times each year."

On top of that, the Bermuda Triangle isn't even close to the most dangerous waterway on the planet. It didn't appear in the 2013 study *Accidents at Sea* by the World Wildlife Fund. According to that report, the places where you have the best chance of touring Davy Jones's locker are the South China Sea, the Mediterranean, and the North Sea.

Still, of all the waves on this mostly blue planet, it's the ones in the Bermuda Triangle that have fascinated us for decades, its three corners wedged deeply within our culture. Scooby Doo has visited there to investigate. As have Mulder and Scully and also Wonder Woman. Barry Manilow sang about it. So did Fleetwood Mac. Milton Bradley made a boardgame inspired by it.

The truth is, you've probably traveled through the Bermuda Triangle yourself, if you've ever been to southern

Florida, Puerto Rico, Bermuda, or the Caribbean. And even if this whole thing started because an AP reporter wanted to wax philosophical against a seeming onslaught of technology, it's still a special place as a result of everything that happened afterward. Its tale has inspired awe and wonder, sparked the imaginations of storytellers, and has generally made this planet a more interesting place to live. It's still the Bermuda Triangle.

LAKE LANIER

SWIM AT YOUR OWN RISK

LOCATION: Northwest Georgia, USA **SIZE:** 60 square miles	**YEAR CREATED:** 1956 **INFAMOUS FOR:** Drownings, sunken towns, ghosts

Lake Lanier is one of the most popular summer destinations in Georgia. More than ten million people a year visit this thirty-eight-thousand-acre reservoir in the northwestern part of the state to swim, boat, and do other watery activities. There's a resort hotel there, a water park, camping grounds, and restaurants. You can't get more fun-in-the-sun and what-I-did-on-my-summer-vacation than Lake Lanier. Yet, it has garnered a reputation as one of the most haunted and cursed sites in the country. And, the thing is, Lake Lanier might have the body count to back up the claim.

Lake Lanier is an artificial lake. It was created in 1956 by the US Army Corps of Engineers, who built Buford Dam to divert some of the Chattahoochee River. The sudden lake is named after nineteenth century poet and native Georgian Sydney Lanier, who wrote the poem *The Song of the Chattahoochee* (the full name of the body of water is Lake Sydney Lanier). It's shaped sort of like an ant lion, with a bulbous bottom and two thin jaws pointing north. Its seven hundred miles of shoreline touches five counties, zig-zagging along uncounted inlets and fingers that give the lake its ragged appearance when seen from above. The main purpose of the lake is to provide power, flood control, and, of course, drinking water to nearby Atlanta. That's right—Atlanta drinks haunted water. And, almost immediately after its creation, people started dying in Atlanta's reservoir.

According to the Georgia Department of Natural Resources, 216 people died in Lake Lanier between 1994 and 2022. In a 2021 article in the *Oxford American*, it was estimated that since the creation of the lake, 500 have met their end in its murky depths. Granted, this is a body of water where people party, so some fatalities are bound to occur, and if you do the math, that's less than ten out of the ten million visitors per year. (That means 0.0001 percent of the people who have visited Lake Lanier have died. Math makes things less scary . . . maybe.) That's still a far higher fatality percentage than those of comparable lakes. According to a 2024 article in the online edition of *Time* magazine, the Georgia lake with the next highest number of deaths is Lake Altoona, which is also an artificial lake created by the US Army Corps of Engineers. It receives around seven million visitors per year and counts less than a third of the fatalities of Lake Lanier. According to that same *Time* article, in 2023, thirteen people died at Lake Lanier, compared to only three at Altoona. For more context, Lanier's 2023 death total is more than the total deaths in 2023 for Lake Superior and Lake Huron combined, at six and four, respectively. Sometimes math makes things scarier.

How does Lake Lanier claim all those victims so disproportionately? Well, the more prosaic will cite boating accidents on the crowded lake and the general influence of alcohol in high-risk activities. And then, of course, there's the fact that people love to splash around in a chemical compound that can kill them in less than a minute if their heads are submerged.

Others, who cast a more suspicious eye on the water, tell tales of a ghostly Lady of the Lake who lures people to a watery grave. Of the curse borne out of multiple tragedies back when Lake Lanier was dry land. Of the crowd of ghostly hands that drag swimmers underwater to their doom. Surprisingly, each of these legends has at least some basis in history and reality.

The first two victims of Lake Lanier on record were Delia May Parker Young and Susie Roberts. In 1958, less than two years after the engineers high-fived each other over their impressive feat of terraforming, these two thirty-somethings were driving home from a dance in Dawsonville in a light blue Ford sedan. Except they never returned home—they just disappeared. A year later, the remains of a young woman in a blue dress were found floating on the surface of Lake Lanier, missing both of her hands and some of her toes. People speculated that the two girls had met their end in the newly created lake, but since the remains couldn't be conclusively identified and there was no second body, they buried the skeleton in an anonymous grave and kept hoping that maybe the two women were alive out there somewhere.

However, in 1990, during a bridge construction project on the lake, a light blue Ford sedan was dredged from the muck, ninety feet below the surface. Its license plate was dated 1958. A wristwatch inside had stopped at 11:30. And, most tellingly, the skeleton of Susie Roberts was found inside. She had sat in that coffin of a car under the lake for over thirty years. It didn't take long to connect this evidence with the remains recovered three decades earlier, which likely belonged to Delia. It appeared the two women had somehow skidded off the road or maybe a bridge and into Lake Lanier on that fateful night in 1958. And from that tragedy, Lake Lanier earned its first lore: the Lady of the Lake, who wanders its shores and roads, dressed in blue, her arms ending in nubs, drawing people into the lake to keep her poor, lonely corpse company in the cold depths.

But the land itself had claimed victims long before it was submerged. Forsyth County is one of the five counties that Lake Lanier extends across. It's also one of the origin points for the infamous Trail of Tears. Between 1830 and 1850, the US government forcibly removed five native nations from their homelands in the southeastern US so that colonial citizens could settle the areas. These nations were the Muscogee, Seminole, Chickasaw, Choctaw, and Cherokee, and they were required to move far away, to an area that would one day be the state of Oklahoma.

The territory of the Cherokee included the northwest corner of the state that is Forsyth County. According to the National Library of Medicine, of the sixty thousand native Americans evicted across the nations, about seventeen thousand were Cherokee, who were removed from their homelands in 1838. Of those seventeen thousand Cherokee, six thousand men, women, and children died on the grueling twelve-hundred-mile trek from Georgia to the new territory. Some say the land was cursed because of this original sin against these original inhabitants, and pouring water on it did nothing to wash away that stain. But it wasn't the only race-related tragedy to be drowned beneath 637 billion gallons of water.

Forsyth County was also home to the village of Oscarville, a mostly Black community that was founded in the latter half of the nineteenth century. On September 9, 1912, an eighteen-year-old white girl named Mae Crow was found on the banks of the Chattahoochee in Oscarville. She had been raped and her throat slashed. She would die fourteen days later without ever regaining consciousness.

Those two weeks were intense. Tensions were already high between whites and Blacks, with an attempted lynching days before. It was also a mere six years after the nearby Atlanta Race Massacre, in which mobs of whites destroyed Black neighborhoods and killed at least twenty-five Black Atlantans. In Oscarville, three young Black men were accused of Crow's murder and arrested on what appeared to be flimsy evidence: sixteen-year-old Ernest Knox, his eighteen-year-old cousin Oscar Daniel, and twenty-four-year-old Robert Edwards. Edwards was arrested first and jailed in the nearby town of Cumming, but a white mob pulled him from his cell the next day and lynched him on a telephone pole in front of the courthouse, before riddling his hanging body with bullets. Knox and Daniel were sent to Fulton County Prison to better protect them. But not for long.

Back in Oscarville, a white mob marched out into the streets brandishing torches and guns, burning down churches and businesses and looting houses. They drove off more than a thousand Black residents as sure as the government had driven off the Cherokee. In October, a jury convicted Knox and Daniel of Crow's murder in a deliberation that took about an hour. Five thousand people gathered and watched the two teenagers hang.

Today, the setting for all that violence and injustice is hidden under the shadows of jet skis and cannonball dives. When you take away people's homes and lives like that, you can't be surprised when ghost stories follow.

Oscarville wasn't the only area drowned under Lake Lanier. About fifty thousand acres of private land were as well, including buildings, farmland, and forests. The US Army Corps of Engineers dismantled most of the structures before flooding the land—at least anything wooden that could float and be a hazard in the water. They left much of the masonry behind, though—walls and foundations and such. A set of concrete grandstands from a racetrack surfaces every few years during droughts.

What was left behind makes for an eerie bottom-scape. It's murky and silty and strange shapes suddenly appear in the dimness. Sometimes it's a tree branch. Sometimes the corner of a brick wall. Other times what appears is more sinister. Lake Lanier's maximum depth is 160 feet (although it can get closer to 200 near the dam), but the danger starts somewhere around 35 to 40 feet down. Richard Pickering, the head of the Emergency Dive Response Team—a team of volunteers that searches for bodies in Lake Lanier—described the conditions in a 2024 Atlanta News First segment this way: "All light vanishes at 40 feet. Below that depth, it's pitch black. The bottom lake temperature is between 42 and 45 degrees year round." The trees are also a problem once the divers get below 35 feet. "When they flooded the lake, they did not chop down the trees," said Picker. In fact, they just chopped the tops off them to create that 35-foot space below the surface. "The trees are as thick now as the ones on the shoreline." It's no wonder that some thirty of Lake Lanier's victims have never been recovered, as they are probably tangled in a trap of tree limbs or hidden in the billowing silt of the bottom. In 2017, another local diver, Buck Buchanan, told Atlanta News First that he has felt body parts brush him while diving in the lake, saying:

"You reach out into the dark and you feel an arm or a leg and it doesn't move."

Speaking of recovered bodies, the many cemeteries embedded in the land, some twenty of them, were also denied the sky by the US Army Corps of Engineers. They removed as many of the remains as they could when originally constructing the lake, but it was impossible to find them all. Cesar Yabor, a spokesman for the US Army Corps of Engineers, told CNN in 2021, "While the Corps made every effort at the time to locate unmarked burials, the limited capabilities of the time make it probable that unanticipated finds of human remains are possible, whether from the antebellum and Civil War periods or of Native American origin from pre-colonial and ancient times."

It's easy to avoid the places that advertise their dangers: the deserts that want to desiccate you, the icefields that want to freeze you, the rough seas that want to drown you. But when that place is a sun-soaked vacationland with booze in every koozie and a sky full of volleyballs and Frisbees, that's where a person really needs to stay vigilant. Especially at Lake Lanier, which to this day is still adding to its body count. It really does seem that the lake never wants you to leave its watery embrace. You have to wonder—is it tree limbs and old fish netting pulling victims deeper into the depths, or the hands of the drowned dead and the ghosts of the poor souls twice buried under soil and water?

In the words of its namesake, writing about the source of Lake Lanier in *The Song of the Chattahoochee*:

The rushes cried "Abide, abide,"
The willful waterweeds held me thrall,
The laving laurel turned my tide,
The ferns and the fondling grass said "Stay."

ROOPKUND

LAKE OF SKELETONS

LOCATION: Utterakhand, India **SIZE:** 130 feet in diameter, 10 feet deep	**ELEVATION:** 16,500 feet above sea level **INFAMOUS FOR:** 800 mysterious skeletons

The place is like one of those thrift store paint-overs, where an artist buys a cheap landscape painting and adds something surprising to it: Slenderman looming in a flower-dotted valley. A T-Rex towering over a never-ending field of wheat. In this case, it's a lake scene, serene and surrounded by glaring glaciers and jagged mountains, with pristine water, the kind that bottled water companies pretend to sell you. Beautiful but generic enough to be default phone wallpaper or to adorn the vestibule of a hotel. Except that inside that pure mountain lake are hundreds of human skeletons.

Roopkund is a Himalayan lake in Uttarakhand, India. According to the 2019 book *Strange and Mysterious Places* by Muthanna Arthy Singh and Nainy Mamta, its name means "the appearance of a small reservoir" and is a reference to its origin myth, as a place created by the trident of the god Shiva so that the his wife Parvati could wash away the blood of demons she had killed. An alternate telling by anthropologist R. S. Negi in a 2013 lecture for the Indira Gandhi National Centre for the Arts says that Shiva created the pool because Parvati was

thirsty, and that while drinking from it, she witnessed her reflection in the perfect pool. The translation in that case would be closer to "an appearance or form in the small reservoir."

The lake is remote, a few days' trek from the nearest village, on the bottom of the slopes of Trisul mountain at about 16,500 feet above sea level. It's also small, roughly 130 feet in diameter and ten feet deep. This swimming pool of a lake is usually frozen and thickly frosted by snow. It is a spot that should have remained hidden and ignored, a small puddle amidst the grandeur surrounding it. Instead, for decades, it has made headlines around the world. That's because, during a brief window between August and September when it (sometimes) sheds its ice and snow, it's skeleton season at the lake. At its bottom and scattered around the surrounding rocky shore are the disarticulated bones and skulls of some 800 ancient human skeletons, some with mummified flesh still sticking to them. William Sax, an anthropologist who visited the lake in 1978, told *Business Insider* in 2019,

> "There are bones everywhere. It feels scary and disturbing . . . you can't take a single step without stepping on bones."

Some of the locals no doubt knew the lake's secret, and the skeletons had been mentioned obscurely by a few British explorers at the end of the nineteenth century and into the early twentieth, but the world at large didn't take notice of the skeleton soup until 1942. That's when Hari Kishan Madhwal, a member of the British Forest Service, and his team, who had been tasked with gathering alpine flowers, stumbled onto it at the right time of year to see the skeletons in all their gory, and he returned with his colleagues to check it out. A 1956 broadcast from All India Radio in Calcutta quoted Madhwal as he described the discovery:

> *We were face to face with a ghastly scene that made us catch our breath. The whole place was littered with scores of human bodies. Flesh like inflated rubber was sticking to most of the bodies. Their grinning faces made the scene still more hideous. Our porters were so much terrified at this gruesome site that they at once took to their heels, thinking that they had landed in a ghost land.*

Besides it being the right time of year to see the skeletons, it was also the right time of human history to get those bones into the headlines. In 1942, most of the planet was embroiled in the middle of World War II, so the British authorities to whom Madhwal reported paid attention to his find. They thought the skeletons might be the remains of a contemporary battalion of Japanese soldiers who had tried to sneak into India.

As news got out that Roopkund was a skeleton swimming hole, other theories were thrown around. Maybe the bones were the remains of Tibetan merchants, or plague victims, or religious pilgrims. Even victims of mass suicide. After all, the site was near the route for Nanda Devi Raj Jat, a festival that occurs every twelve years in honor of the goddess Nanda Devi. Maybe they were soldiers in the army of General Zorawar Singh, who had attempted to conquer western Tibet before his death in 1841. Some even hypothesized that the skeletons had something to do with the Pandavas, five legendary brothers from the Hindu epic *Mahabharata* who were born of deities, ruled as kings, and, when they were done with the world, trekked into the Himalayas to find the gates of heaven. Only the eldest, Yudhisthira, survived the journey to find the entrance. The only thing that was certain were Roopkund's new nicknames: "Mystery Lake" and "Skeleton Lake."

Then scientists got involved. In the 1950s, multiple expeditions were mounted to Roopkund to bring back samples, including one by the Anthropological Survey of India and another by the anthropology department of Lucknow University in Uttar Pradesh. The researchers verified Madhwal's observation that some of the bones still retained preserved flesh. However, not a single complete skeleton was to be found—only a thick carpet of dislocated bones and skulls that would have added up to some 800 full skeletons. More mystery for Mystery Lake. Besides human remains, the researchers found some clothing and artifacts as well, including leather chappals (sandals), bits of glass bracelets, and wooden utensils.

The scientists determined that the bodies belonged to two Indian ethnicities, some originating from western India who were taller than average, and others shorter and local. They hypothesized that the smaller locals might be porters and guides for the western Indians. The bodies included men, women, and children. Radiocarbon dating of the bones returned a date range of somewhere between the twelfth and fifteenth centuries, so these skeletons were at least half a millennium old; possibly closer to a full millennium.

As to the cause of death, nothing was conclusively determined, although different levels of mineralization in the bones seemed to suggest different ages for the remains. In other words, they hadn't all died at once in a terrible cataclysm: They had gradually accrued. It was hypothesized that many pilgrims had probably died over the centuries on the treacherous pilgrimage for Nanda Devi Raj Jat, although that wouldn't explain how they all ended up in the same spot—at the bottom of a lake. In addition, scientists discovered three sets of remains with compression fractures that suggested, among other scenarios, that the deaths could be a result of hail.

That last detail about the hail seemed to support a bit of local lore, one that was espoused as the solution to the mystery of Roopkund by Swami Pranavanand, a fellow of the Royal Geographical Society who had made a few expeditions to the lake around the same time as the Anthropological Survey of India and Lucknow University. According to R. S. Negi in his aforementioned lecture, Pranavanand published an article in 1959 called "The Rupkund Mystery-Solved," in which he stated his belief in the authority of a local folk song that seemed to explain all the skeletons. In that song, the Raja Jasdhawal of Kannauj, his pregnant wife Rani Balampa, and their entourage were traveling to celebrate Nanda Devi Raj Jat. However, they had dancing girls in the group, which made Nanda Devi angry. She turned those women into stones that, according to the lore, can still be seen on the pilgrimage route. Meanwhile, Rani birthed a baby girl, tainting the sacred land. This triggered more anger from the god. This time the divine punishment was a heavy hailstorm that killed the whole party.

For the next half a century, "pilgrims killed by hail the size of cricket balls" was the most widely accepted story of Roopkund. Still scary, but with enough of an explanation that it made the hundreds of skeletons a little less mysterious. Like when an astronaut dies in space—terrifying when you think about it, but you can at least lay your head on your pillow at night knowing pretty confidently that it'll never happen to you. In 2003, an expedition and analysis by National Geographic and Oxford University supported, popularized, and built on the theory. They determined that the remains dated back 850 years, and in opposition to previous findings, were all victims of the same catastrophe.

All that changed with further scientific findings, blowing that tidy explanation to skeleton bits. In 2019, researchers from Harvard and the Birbal Sahni Institute of Palaeosciences in Uttar Pradesh took advantage of advances in forensic technology to reexamine the Roopkund skeletons. What they found completely countermanded everything believed about Roopkund to date. In a study published in 2019 in *Nature Communications*, they announced two bombshells: First, the scientists found three distinct groups of people in their sample of 38 bodies. They found south Asians, which would be a local people; southeast Asians, which would be further afield; and eastern Mediterraneans—Greeks. Secondly, they discovered conclusively that the remains weren't the result of a single catastrophe, but multiple catastrophes over the course of a thousand years, with the most recent being in the nineteenth century. In other words, either whatever killed these people continued its murderous rampage over the course of centuries, or there are just many, many ways to die in that frozen puddle in the Himalayas. Plague was also ruled out by the researchers' analysis of the bones, with the result being that now nobody knows what exactly is going on with Skeleton Lake.

Of course, there's a psychologically safe explanation to be found in those results, as well. In 2019, Kathleen Morrison, the chair of the anthropology department at the University of Pennsylvania, told the *Atlantic* when interviewed about the findings, "I suspect that they're aggregated there, that local people put them in the lake. When you see a lot of human skeletons, usually it's a graveyard." However, the area is so remote and hard to access, and the number of bodies so great, it seems like the easiest explanation is one of the most difficult to believe. Plus, no record exists of Roopkund being a funerary site. The findings do perhaps lend credence to the theory of deaths related to multiple religious pilgrimages over the centuries, except that doesn't exactly explain the multiple ethnicities represented in the bones or how they all ended up in Roopkund.

More disturbing to contemplate is that we will probably never know what happened to these people. And I don't say that in a cliché, end-of-essay kind of way. I mean the site is impossible to preserve intact. First, rockslides happen frequently in the mountains, and where Roopkund lies is no exception. In addition, ice is constantly resculpting the landscape. But the biggest danger to Roopkund is the hikers. As the Roopkund mystery grew in popularity, hikers came to visit, taking souvenirs and arranging bones in shrine-like piles, making the scene even more distressing—and useless as an archeological site. As tainted as if a woman gave birth there and angered a god. As early as 2007, government leaders were trying to find ways to preserve Roopkund. That year, Chamoli district magistrate D. S. Garbiyal told the Indian newspaper the *Deccan Herald*, "If steps are not taken soon all the skeletons may disappear."

In essence, none of the questions that flew through Madhwal's brain when he first saw the skeletons in 1942 have ever been answered. Who are all these people? How did they die? How did all their bodies end up in this tiny, frozen Himalayan lake? Most importantly, were there yetis involved?

Today, more than eighty years after the official discovery of the Roopkund skeletons, we don't know much more about them than we did in 1942. And that means we have no idea if more skeletons will join them in the future. Just to be safe, maybe cross this destination off your Himalayan bucket list.

SALTON SEA

OMINOUS OASIS

LOCATION: Southern California, USA **SIZE:** 350 square miles **YEAR CREATED:** 1905	**INFAMOUS FOR:** Wildlife die-offs, cyanobacteria outbreaks, toxic dust, ghost towns, broken dreams

I found myself standing among the graffitied ruins of what a sign called Bombay Beach. The gutted and rotted ruins of houses surrounded me. Couches and recliners had been pulled out of those houses and set up here and there in the dirt, like someone had set up front row seats to the apocalypse. A rank smell of decay tainted the air. All those chairs faced a large, still body of water that gleamed in the distance and was the source of the stench: the Salton Sea. This was a scary place, although this time not for any ghosts or monsters or mysteries. It was scary because this fetid morass was man-made.

The Salton Sea was a big mistake. Two big mistakes, actually. First, its existence itself is the result of a colossal error of judgement. Then, almost a century later, natural processes and myopic politics caused it to putrefy into one of the largest environmental disasters in California history. This accidental lake would become a smelly, disease-ridden pool filled with dead animals and toxic bacteria, surrounded by decaying ghost towns where lung-destroying, chemical-laden dust blows across an apocalyptic landscape in which only the hardiest and the foolhardy have hope.

At 350 square miles, the Salton Sea is the largest lake in California. It's up to 50 feet deep, features 110 miles of shoreline, and contains 7.5 million acre-feet of water (an acre-foot is the amount of water it takes to cover one acre of land under one foot of water, or 326,000 gallons). The sea is south of Palm Springs and north of the Mexican border. And it didn't exist before 1905.

Pre-1905, the acres of land that would be one day be flooded with water were the hardpacked dirt of an ancient lakebed. Over millions of years, lakes had come and gone again, depending on the vagaries of the Colorado River, which altered its course from time to time. First it would feed a body of water in the depression known as the Salton Sink, and then it would divert course, dehydrating it to death, only for the cycle to repeat.

All that movement by the Colorado River deposited valuable nutrients in the soil of what would one day be called Imperial Valley, the area surrounding the Salton Sea. That, along with the year-round warm climate, meant the land was favorable to farming. Of course, farming in the desert means fantastic feats of irrigation are needed, so engineers tapped the Colorado River in 1900 by digging a canal. However, within a couple of years, silt clogged the canal, choking the farms off from the water and panicking investors. So much pressure was put on the project that an engineer named Charles Rockwood made the desperate call to cut a hasty chunk from the banks of the Colorado River to bypass the blocked canal. It was a decision that engineer H. T. Cory would call, in a 1912 edition of the proceedings of the American Society of Civil Engineers, "a blunder so serious as to be 'practically criminal.'"

Of course, Cory was speaking from hindsight, because in

1905, rains flooded the Colorado River and that ill-conceived breach was overwhelmed. Water broke through the weak spot and drained into the Salton Sink, eventually swallowing the town of Salton, a long stretch of Southern Pacific Railroad track, and the Torres Martinez Desert Cahuilla Indian Reservation. It took two years to repair the breach, but not before it created a veritable sea in all that desert—the Salton Sea.

Still, the lack of inlet and the intense summer heat (the area can reach temperatures greater than 120 degrees Fahrenheit) meant that water would, like its prehistoric forebears, eventually evaporate. But unlike previous appearances of lakes in the Salton Sink, the hundreds of thousands of acres of farmland in Imperial Valley were flourishing, and their irrigation runoff was finding its way into the Salton Sea—enough of it to keep the body of water on what a 2018 *National Geographic* article would call "long-term life support." At first, the people of Southern California loved their new watery wonderland.

By the 1950s, the Salton Sea was a vacationer's paradise, rivaling its neighbor to the north, Palm Springs. People flocked to the lake to fish its newly stocked depths, splash around its shallow beaches, and ride boats (the lake's high salinity from the runoff combined with it being 230 feet below sea level made boats especially buoyant; many speed records were broken on its surface). Luxury hotels were erected. Marinas and yacht clubs were built. Real estate investors capitalized on Lake Mistake and parceled off plots of this sudden oasis to sell. Celebrity entertainers even hung out there, including Bing Crosby, the Beach Boys, the Marx Brothers, Frank Sinatra, Desi Arnaz, and Jerry Lewis. During its peak as a resort destination, the Salton Sea lured 1.5 million visitors a year, beating the visitor tallies for Yosemite National Park at the time.

Meanwhile, the lake grew in ecological importance. It was

stocked with a variety of fish—croaker, tilapia, corvina, and sargo—and became California's most productive fishery for a time. Those fish attracted more than fishermen. Some four hundred bird species have stopped at the Salton Sea as it became part of the Pacific Flyway, a major migration route that stretches from Alaska to Patagonia. It was a good thing, too, because elsewhere, the wetlands of California were disappearing due to development and drought.

In the 1970s, tropical storms hit the Salton Sea area, leveling and flooding much of the resort infrastructure and dealing a massive blow to the economy—at least as a vacation destination. The party was over for tourists, but residents hung on tenaciously to their lake lifestyles and investments. And then, over the course of the next two decades, the Salton Sea got yucky.

For years, scientists who couldn't be heard over the sound of boat motors and cocktail shakers had prophesied that the lake was not a sustainable resource. It was receiving almost all its water from farmland runoff, which was thick with salt and heavy metals such as mercury, arsenic, and copper, as well as herbicides and pesticides like the now-outlawed DDT. And being a mere man-made puddle, it had no outlet to drain away those impurities or natural inlet to dilute them. Worse, the intense heat evaporated the water over time, concentrating the contaminants. Eventually, the water was twice as salty as the Pacific Ocean.

The fish suffered first. The high salinity of the sea and extreme heat made oxygen less soluble in water and suffocated them. Every year, fish died off in the millions, lining miles of beaches in rotting flesh stretching 150 feet from the water's edge. On August 4, 1999, 7.6 million fish died in a single day. Today you'll find white beaches on the Salton, all made of bleached fish skeletons. On my visit, a step too far on those bones, I sank two feet deep into the disgusting muck, releasing a putrid stench and getting stuck. A friend had to pull me out, and I had to leave my boots behind, a permanent artifact in the mud of the Salton.

With the fish dying, so followed the birds who depended on them for food. By the 1990s, the lake was thick with bobbing avian corpses, which, in addition to starvation, were also victims of diseases such as cholera and botulism from the close quarters on the shrinking surface of the water. During one four-month period in 1996, fourteen thousand birds died, some ten thousand of which were pelicans (one-third of all white pelicans in North America visited the lake). Workers fired incinerators twenty-four hours a day for weeks to dispose of the giant carcasses.

The financial toll was massive. Gone were the days when the towns around the Salton Sea thrived—Bombay Beach, Salton City, Niland, Slab City. Many of the residents today are immigrant farm workers from Mexico, retirees who can't move anywhere else in expensive Southern California, welfare recipients, and artists who find the decaying landscape inspiring. One of the latter described it to *Palm Springs Life* in 2020 as "*Mad Max* meets *Bagdad Café* meets *Northern Exposure*." A 2014 documentary called *Plagues and Pleasures on the Salton Sea* portrayed those who lived near the lake as a quirky people scrabbling together a difficult existence while dreaming of better days and bemoaning promised futures.

But the physical conditions on the Salton Sea are even worse than the economic ones. The Salton suffers from regular cyanobacteria outbreaks—blue-green algal blooms that can quickly take over large swathes of the lake. According to the Environmental Protection Agency website, these blooms look like "floating mats of bad-smelling, decaying and gelatinous scum." They produce cyanotoxins that can harm the skin, liver, and nervous systems of people and animals, causing everything from rashes to flu-like ailments to death.

But the bad smell from the Salton Sea doesn't only come from the gelatinous scum. It also emanates from the dead organisms in this serial killer of a lake. The smell of the Salton Sea has been described as everything from rotten eggs to excrement, and can reach all the way to Los Angeles, 160 miles to the northwest. In September 2012, the stench from the sea was so strong and pervasive that Los Angeles gave the event its own name: "The Big Burp."

But perhaps worse than the flooded infrastructure, dead animals, fatal bacteria, and smell is the toxic dust. As the sea evaporates, it exposes land that dries out and is called playa. All those particulates from the farmland runoff—the pesticides and heavy metals—are no longer trapped in mud at the bottom of a lake. Now they blow freely across the landscape in brown clouds that cover cars and houses, obscure the horizon, and enter the lungs of residents. In a 2019 interview with NPR, Tim Krantz, a professor of environmental studies at the University of Redlands, explained,

> *These are super-fine silts, two millionths of a meter, two microns in size. I can get a hundred in the width of a human hair. . . . If you breathe these sediments into your lungs you can't cough them out, they're too small—they'll profuse directly through your lung tissue into your bloodstream, carrying with them . . . arsenic, selenium, cadmium, bad stuff.*

Bad stuff, indeed. According to a 2017 article in the *Desert Sun*, Imperial County has the highest rate of asthma-related

ER visits for children in the state of California. A 2019 study from the University of Southern California reported that 22 percent of children in the Salton Sea area have asthma—three times the incidence nationwide. Local schools use a flag system to denote air quality, with yellow meaning to act with caution, orange meaning stay indoors if you have asthma, and red meaning everyone should stay inside, regardless of respiratory health.

Meanwhile, politics and science, the two elements that should be working together to solve the crisis, are making it worse. First, farms have implemented advanced irrigation techniques to lower water usage. Michael Cohen, a researcher with the Pacific Institute, told the *Water Desk* (a University of Boulder publication), "We want to use water more efficiently . . . but the unintended consequence of that is that less water goes to the Salton Sea because it is entirely dependent on inefficiency."

Meanwhile, what water does run off from the farms is still valuable. It's a desert, after all. In 2003, a deal was reached among local governments and organizations for the runoff from Imperial Valley to be shunted to thirsty, wealthy San Diego County and Coachella Valley. After local protests, the deal was modified to allow some water to the Salton Sea through 2017, but after that, the Salton Sea was on its own. According to a 2017 article in *USA Today*, over the next three decades, the sea will shrink by about a third, exposing sixty thousand acres of toxin-ridden playa.

Local and federal governments have passed various legislation over the years to save the Salton Sea. In 2003, California launched the Salton Sea Restoration Act. In 2006, there was Proposition 84. Then came the Salton Sea Management Program in 2018. Everyone from California governor Arnold

Schwarzenegger to US President Barack Obama earmarked funds for the sea, but they always seem to dry up as fast as the playa. As recently as 2023, President Joe Biden dedicated $72 million to the cause. But no initiatives ever seem to progress, much less work. The task of saving the Salton Sea is too complex, too expensive, and takes too much long-term thinking to fit into a single political term. It might be too late for the Salton Sea.

And many think that "too late for the Salton Sea" means "too late for Southern California." First, like the canaries in the coal mine that are almost too literal to be a metaphor, the animals will disappear. Biologist Dan Cooper told the *Desert Sun* in 2017, "This is really the last big wetland we have in the interior part of Southern California, so once this goes, that's pretty much it."

Then the cities will go. Palm Springs and Los Angeles would suffer from rising levels of their already infamous air pollution. In addition, the Salton Sea Authority cautions that if the problems of the Salton Sea aren't addressed, it "will cause an air quality disaster of such enormous proportions that the valleys of Coachella and Imperial as well as southerly into Mexico may become uninhabitable." Since the Imperial Valley provides most of the country's winter vegetables, the supply chain of the entire country would be damaged. Basically, the Salton Sea can take down all of Southern California, and maybe a lot of other places while it's at it.

But there is hope. And that hope gleams, improbably, from the ornaments of Tesla hoods. In the early twenty-first century, a gigantic deposit of lithium was discovered under the Salton Sea. Lithium is a vital element in the production of batteries for everything from laptops to electric cars. The deposit is so big it could represent one-third of the global supply. A

Yahoo Finance headline called it a "$540 Billion Motherlode." The groundbreaking for the first extraction plant occurred in January 2024. With industry once again funneling money into the area, lithium mining could buoy the futures of those who live there and finance clean-up efforts for the deadly mess that is the Salton Sea.

Although, if the history of mining has taught us anything, it's that the pollution and politics of the process can outweigh the benefits. But the Salton Sea is used to that.

MANCHAC SWAMP

WITCHERY IN THE WATER

LOCATION:	**NOTABLE RESIDENT:**
St. John the Baptist Parish, Louisiana, USA	"Aunt Julia" Brown
SIZE:	**INFAMOUS FOR:**
200 square miles	Witch ghost, superfog, hurricanes, serial killers

Swamps are the worst of all worlds when it comes to dangerous environments: They're wet enough to drown you as dead as any ocean. Dense enough to disappear you without a trace as much as any forest. They can get hot enough to burn you crispy as any desert and cold enough to freeze you stiff as any tundra. They contain creatures deadly enough to kill you fast as any jungle. And they're as disease-ridden as the most crowded city. In fact, there is very little that could make these places more terrifying than they are already. You'd have to go supernatural, I think. Like maybe a swamp that's been cursed by a witch. Like maybe Manchac Swamp in Louisiana.

Manchac Swamp is a strip of marshland about thirty miles northwest of New Orleans in the parish of St. John the Baptist. It covers hundreds of thousands of acres between Lake Pontchartrain and Lake Maurepas and is similar to many of the swamps in the state. Tall cypress and tupelo trees hold up the sky and shade the shorter black willow and palmetto trees. Various species of swamp grass accent the scummy waters.

Hiding and hunting in that vegetable labyrinth are all manner of beasties—alligators and cottonmouths, nutria and muskrats, and an expansive variety of fish and birds and bugs. Much of its lore is typical for the area, too, including the rougarou (also known as the loup-garou), a werewolf-like creature imported from the spook tales of French settlers. The rougarou prowls the swamps and surrounding towns of the state, preying on unfaithful Catholics and misbehaved children.

But how Lake Manchac is unique, and how it ups its menace beyond alligator jaws, mosquito-borne diseases, and Cajun lycanthropes, is that the swamp is the home of a terrible curse, one that seems to have killed scores of people since the early twentieth century.

Back in those days, Manchac Swamp included a few small towns strung like pendants on the chain that was the railroad track connecting New Orleans to points north. The towns of Frenier and Wagram were established as farming communities by German colonists who produced cabbage and potatoes, lettuce and beets. The town of Rudduck was built around a sawmill, hungry for the cypress trees in the region. These towns were extremely isolated, without roads and only sparse patches of dry land interspersed among all the swampiness. Still, hundreds of people lived in these bayou communities, including a woman named Julia Brown—who may or may not have been a voodoo priestess.

Julia Brown was a native Louisianan, born Julia Bernard sometime around 1845. She married Celestin Brown in 1880. Two decades later, the federal government granted the Browns forty acres in the town of Frenier for them to farm. In 1914, Celestin died, leaving Julia alone. The people of Manchac Swamp called her Aunt Julia, and the stories call her a traiteuse, or healer. Some tales go further and declare her a voodoo priestess and claim that she could predict the future, or at least that she could predict people's deaths.

Helen Schlosser Burg, who grew up in Wagram in the early part of the twentieth century, told the local newspaper *L'Observateur* in 1988 that Aunt Julia "always sat on her porch and played a guitar and sang a song that she had made up. The words of the song said that when she died everyone would die with her."

By some accounts, locals steered clear of Julia because of her creepy powers and predictions. Other accounts say it was because she was Black in an area populated by white German descendants—and as such, perhaps she had good reason to dislike her neighbors and want to take everyone down with her. But whatever the reason, Julia's lyrical prediction came true.

Julia Brown died in late September of 1915. The exact date is unknown, perhaps because it was overshadowed by the date of her funeral: September 29. Because this funeral was suspiciously timed with the landfall of one of the most horrific hurricanes to ever hit the state of Louisiana.

The hurricane came up from the Caribbean, a Category 4, with winds as powerful as 125 miles per hour and storm surges as high as thirteen feet. The storm killed 300 people across Louisiana, some 60 of whom were in the towns of Manchac Swamp—or ex-towns. When rescuers were finally able to boat into the swamp two weeks later, they found that the storm had torn them down and engulfed them. Nothing was left of Frenier. Or Wampac. Or Rudduck. Well, almost nothing—corpses and rubble bobbed in the water and festooned tree limbs. According to Burg in that 1988 *L'Observateur* article, "The smell of decaying bodies and cattle was nauseating." Survivors told stories of 25-foot waves taking out buildings and everyone who was sheltering there; of children clinging to dog houses before finally succumbing to the waters or being drowned in the railroad box cars where they had sheltered. One survivor named Milton Brown climbed a cypress tree to escape the water. According to *L'Observateur*, as he clung to its limbs, "even with the wind blowing and the rain and noise you could hear friends screaming for help as they died."

But what about Julia Brown and her oddly timed death? According to a *Times-Picayune* article published a few days after the storm, her funeral didn't escape all that destruction:

> *Many pranks were played by wind and tide. Negroes had gathered for miles around to attend the funeral of 'Aunt' Julia Brown, an old negress who was well known in that section, and was a big property owner. The funeral was scheduled . . . and 'Aunt' Julia had been placed in her casket and the casket in turn had been placed in the customary wooden box and sealed. At 4 o'clock, however, the storm had become so violent that the negroes left the house in a stampede, abandoning the corpse. The corpse was found Thursday and so was the wooden box, but the casket never has been found.*

According to Schlosser Burg, in regards to the funeral, "Everyone that was there died in the storm."

Of course, some say this whole story that Julia Brown cursed the swamp is exploitative storytelling based merely on a snippet of remembered song and the coincidence of the timing of her death—that Julia Brown has been maligned and that the hurricane was a standalone event in an always unforgiving swamp often besieged by storms, even if this one was the worst the area had ever seen.

Maybe. But that wasn't the end of the troubles in Manchac Swamp, even with all the people and towns gone. In November of 1956, the swamp was the backdrop for a pair of unsolved murders. A man named Tom Hotard was found shot to death in his car near where the town of Frenier used to be. His companion, a woman named Audrey Moate, had disappeared. The case of the murder and disappearance went cold in that swamp until 1959, when a woman named Leonie Martinez—who was sitting in a car in the Frenier area while her husband Frank fished—was shot by a man who tried to pull her from the car. She was able to lean on the horn until her husband responded and chased the man away. The authorities were able to arrest the attacker, who ended up being forty-year-old Edmond Joseph Duhe. When police searched his house they found, according to a 2020 *L'Observateur* article, a "vast hoard of pornographic photographs in the house, along with five women's purses, 50 lipstick applicators, and over a dozen sex magazines." Moate's handbag was one of the five.

Duhe would go to prison for the Martinez attack but maintained his innocence for the Hotard shooting and Moate disappearance. Law enforcement couldn't prove his involvement because they couldn't find Moate's body or the murder weapon that killed Hotard, despite digging up the bog, using a powerful electromagnet on an eight-foot-long pole, and tearing down the abandoned sugar refinery where Duhe had once worked. Nor did they get any leads from the other four purses. Manchac Swamp just wouldn't give up its secrets. The case remains unsolved to this day.

A few decades later, death returned to the swamp, this time in the form of the Storyville Slayer. Between 1991 and 1996, police found the remains of twenty-four bodies, mostly Black women, in the highway ditches and canals on the edge of Manchac Swamp. They eventually pieced together the story of a murderer who was prowling an area of New Orleans that was once a red-light district called Storyville. Although theories abound, the case was never solved. More bodies in Manchac.

Meanwhile, along with hurricanes and serial killers, Manchac Swamp found a new way to accrue victims: the Manchac Swamp Bridge. Interstate 55 and US Route 51 cut directly through the swamp thanks in part to the twenty-three-mile-long Manchac Swamp Bridge—one of the longest bridges in the world.

On September 13, 1976, a barge hit one of the pilons of the bridge, causing several sections to crack and fall into the water, taking people and vehicles down with it. At least one person died (some bodies might never have been recovered), two were saved, and the damage to the bridge was in the billions of dollars. Although it could have been worse. Wayne Norwood, at the time a deputy with the Tangipahoa Parish Sheriff's Office, and one of the first rescue divers in the murky water, wrote in a 2021 piece for the local newspaper the *Daily Star*, "Because this was the only road over the pass, it was a miracle no one else was hurt or killed."

But the Manchac Swamp Bridge wasn't done racking up fatalities. On October 23, 2023, extremely foggy conditions and smoke from marsh fires combined to create what the National Weather Service called a *superfog*. The dense environmental phenomenon caused a 168-car pileup on the bridge. Eight people were killed and 63 were injured. Will Lee, one of the victims of the crash, described the scene to the local Fox television station: "I heard cars smash into each other for a solid 25 to 30 minutes. That's all you could hear—cars crashing, horns blowing. It was pandemonium."

Today, you can hire a tour company to take you into the swamp. They'll glide you by a fake graveyard representing the mass casualties from the hurricane in 1915. They'll tell you stories of sightings of a white-haired old woman wandering the swamp; of the creak of her rocking chair echoing across the water; of the special powers she had to foresee and cause people's deaths. And maybe those are just tales to fuel a tour business. Maybe Manchac Swamp is no more dangerous than any other swamp or bayou in soggy old Louisiana (in other words, extremely dangerous).

But even as entire towns and vehicles and victims have disappeared into the muck of that southern morass, the legend of Julia Brown keeps many of them alive in story. She at least has that power—and her song has lived on.

Here's hoping you never hear it.

TANGLING WITH DEVIL'S TRIANGLES

Traditionally, it's the pentagram that keeps strange entities contained. However, zooming out to the macro (and map) level, the paranormal always seems bounded by triangles. I've included three in this book, but there are so many others that the title could easily have become *Don't Go to These Triangles*. There are so many of these triangles out there that some have resorted to dubbing the entire category *devil's triangles*. Here are some examples of devil's triangles:

- Bermuda Triangle (see page 60)
- Alaska Triangle (USA)
- Bass Strait Triangle (Australia)
- Dragon's Triangle (Japan)
- Bridgewater Triangle (Massachusetts, USA—see page 19)
- Pag Triangle (Croatia)
- Bennington Triangle (Vermont, USA)
- Romblon Triangle (Philippines)
- Broad Haven Triangle (Wales)
- Nevada Triangle (USA—see page 160)
- Falkirk Triangle (Scotland)
- Lake Michigan Triangle (USA)
- Molyobka Triangle (Russia)

This list isn't exhaustive, but looking them up is exhausting. So why have people delineated so many spooky triangles across our planet? The answer, it turns out, may not be mystical. It may be practical.

An extremely cynical interpretation is that the triangle is an easy shape to draw on a map—it's just one more dot than the endpoints of a straight line. Another factor might be that the triangle is the least ridiculous-sounding shape in this context. For instance, the Bermuda Square? Sounds like it should be in the middle of a town. The Bermuda Circle? In a subdivision. The Bermuda Rectangle? Nobody takes rectangles seriously. That's why college campuses have quadrangles.

Maybe it's as simple as that. But maybe not. I think the real answer is something I've learned firsthand from writing this book: No word in the English language describes a slice of the earth, a section of the map, a stretch of the planet—an area bigger than a single building, bigger even than an entire town or city, but still smaller than a state or province. The word *place*, for instance, could refer to anything from a house to a whole country. The same with *site* and *locale* and *spot* and *zone* and all the other words Thesaurus.com is throwing at me.

We just don't have an adequate word for the concept—hence the vague title and subtitle of this book. That means that any time a new spooky place (or site or locale or spot or zone) is discovered, it's invariably called a triangle. Because without a good word to sum up the concept, it needs to piggyback off the branding work already done around the Bermuda Triangle. When you append that three-sided word to your subject, people know where you're going.

INSANE ISLANDS

Islands are the Jekyll and Hyde of geography. On one hand—the tanned and manicured one—they can be tropical paradises, each one rimmed like a bright margarita with white sand, all the stresses of the world pushed far away by vast stretches of crystal waters. On the other hand—this one clawed and warty—they are terrifying places where a castaway can be marooned without hope, separated from everything they love while starving to death, if they don't die by exposure or the teeth of local wildlife first. And those are just the normal islands that dot our oceans and seas and waterways. Some islands are even used to hide things: the treatment of plague victims, the burial of cursed treasure, acts of murder. Beware islands. Unless there's a resort with a bar in the swimming pool. Then you're probably safe.

CHARLES ISLAND

ONCE, TWICE, THRICE CURSED

LOCATION: Milford, Connecticut, USA **SIZE:** 14 acres **MAIN FEATURE:** Tombolo connecting the island to shore at low tide	**INFAMOUS FOR:** Native American curse, pirate curse, Aztec curse, buried treasure

As I stood on the shore, the path rose slowly from the cold ocean water as if raised at the command of some ancient underwater god. People had died traversing this thin strip of slippery rocks, falling into the waves and getting yanked by the strong rip currents until their lungs filled with water. Mine were currently filled with crisp late winter air that matched the chill up my spine. Was I really going to take this sudden and treacherous path? Especially since once I crossed that mile of curving wet rock, the challenge wasn't over—there was still the cursed island at the end of it to contend with.

On any given summer day, Silver Sands Beach in Milford, Connecticut, is like any other beach. The scantily clad slowly broil themselves on towels, splash in the water of the Long Island Sound, and pick through the shells strewn across the shore. The only difference seems to be a small island, dark with trees, looming so close it seems you could almost swim to it. Except that you don't have to—you can walk to this island.

Sometimes, anyway. Although you may not want to. The island is cursed. Triply so: by a Native American chief, an infamous pirate, and an Aztec ruler. Every business and residence ever built on the island has failed, and for more than a century, people have drowned or gone missing in the waters surrounding it. The island's proper name is Charles Island, but it's also known as Thrice Cursed Island.

The island covers fourteen acres and is about half a mile from shore. Twice a day, a path connecting it to the beach emerges from the drink. It's not technically a sandbar—although it's often referred to as such colloquially—but a tombolo: a strip of sand or rock that connects two bodies of land. However, taking that tombolo when it appears from the waters of the Sound means you risk slipping into that water, getting carried off by dangerous rip tides, or—if you make it across—marooning yourself on the island if you mistime the tides and the path disappears again. Warning signs on the beach state: *Danger! Sandbar floods twice daily with strong current and undertow* and *Walking on the sandbar can be extremely dangerous*. It might as well have a historical placard, as well, for all the stories of its past.

Before Europeans settlers colonized this part of the New World, the entire area that would one day be called Milford was the home of the Paugussett Nation. The land was called Wepawaug, and its chief was Ansantawae. He would use the island, called Poquehaug back then, as a summer residence. According to the website of the Milford Hall of Fame, a local volunteer organization, his wigwam was "richly furnished with furs, for whenever warriors or braves went hunting they brought their chief the prizes of their hunt."

The Europeans started showing up in the early seventeenth century, and in 1639, Ansantawae sold all the lands to the

English. According to *The History of a New England Hometown: Milford, Connecticut, 1639-1989*, the tribe received in exchange for all that beachfront property a paltry six coats, ten blankets, a kettle, twelve hatches, twelve hoes, twenty-four knives, and twelve small mirrors. But the arrangement was also strategic, as Ansantawae believed the English would be good allies against their enemies, the Mohawk. Today the bow-and-arrow signature Ansantawae used to sign the deed is part of the Milford Town Seal.

However, at some point, Ansantawae is said to have cursed the island where he once summered. There's not much to that story. According to a 2018 piece in the *Milford Mirror*, the legend goes that "he cursed the island, any structure that was erected on the island and anyone who tried to live there." The two potential motives usually assigned to the cursing are foggy. The first is that he regretted the sale of the land since the domination of European colonizers led to the dwindling of his people (in which case he would have really hated the Milford seal). Today, about a hundred members of the Paugussett Indian Nation live on two small reservations in the state. The second reason given is that Ansantawae's daughter was kidnapped, although no further details adorn that story. In fact, even the few details we have about the curse aren't validated by any actual record. In a 2024 interview for the *Record-Journal* of Connecticut, Michael Dooling, author of the book *An Historical Account of Charles Island: Milford, Connecticut*, said that the story of Ansantawae's curse just "appeared on the internet one day."

But that was only curse number one. Once the island was in English hands, it was renamed Milford Island, and over the next seventeen years it was sold three times, until finally, in 1657, it was bought by Charles Deal, who gave the island the name it bears to this day. He attempted to build a tobacco plantation there, which the people of Milford approved so long as he—according to the 1892 *History of New Haven County, Connecticut*—"would not trade with the Dutch or the Indians, or suffer disorderly seamen to make it a place of resort." It failed not too long after. Apparently welcoming disorderly seaman would have been a much better business model.

Speaking of disorderly seaman, the second person to curse the island was the infamous pirate Captain William Kidd. Captain Kidd was a Scottish privateer-turned-pirate. In 1699, he was looking to clear his name and perhaps to bribe his way back into law-abiding society. He set forth from the Caribbean up the coast of North America toward Boston to speak to his benefactor, the Earl of Bellomont, who had promised him a pardon. When he arrived, the earl, who feared being entangled as an accessory to Kidd's piracy, had him captured and sent to London. There, he was hanged (twice, since the rope broke the first time) on May 23, 1701. However, en route to the northeast, he stopped at Gardiner Island in the Long Island Sound and buried some of his treasure there, hoping to use it as a bargaining chip to circumvent punishment for his crimes at sea. This part of the story is all in the historical record.

However, it's hypothesized that Kidd was too cunning to put all his gold in one basket, so legend goes that he divvied it up between various islands in the Sound. Charles Island would have been a good candidate, as it was unpopulated at the time and only fifty miles from Gardiner Island. The legend even mentions the location of the treasure on Charles Island as near a boulder called Hog Rock. Then, like any pirate worth his skull and crossbones, Captain Kidd cursed the island to ward off nosy treasure hunters.

Slight evidence exists that Kidd did at least visit Milford in 1699. An undated letter published in an 1899 edition of *New*

England magazine describes Kidd's visit to the town. Written by a young woman named Patience Tuttle to her unnamed cousin, the letter was found in the attic of one of Milford's oldest homes. It states:

> *Aunt Prudence has told you of the visit from Capt. Kidd, from the craft wh. was seen to come in the harbour at 7 of the clock in the evening. He stayed in the house till in the early morning and sat all the night by the fire with Jacobeth and Thomas Welsh carrying himself in an uncivil and bold manner . . . when he came in the room he put his arms about my waiste, and kyssed me, wh. made Jacobeth laugh and Thomas Welsh cough. . . . I overheard Jacobeth say that Kidd was going on a long cruise, and that he had left some things with him. I am going to tell Aunt Prudence all about it, and find out what they are.*

"Left some things" indeed.

The ultimate proof, of course, would be if anybody found treasure on Charles Island. To date, nobody has, although there have been attempts. According to a 2016 article in the CT *Insider*, a treasure hunter claimed in 1992 to have detected multiple metal bars buried on the island. But that story ends with an annoying ellipsis because he claims he wasn't allowed to dig them up due to "environmental concerns and red tape." An older and more fanciful-seeming account was detailed in the 1838 *History of the Colony of New Haven*. In it, a group of youths braved the curses with shovels over their shoulders to find the treasure. The author writes:

> *After much preparatory ceremony such as drawing a circle around the rock and reciting some words of incantation, they began to dig, and so far succeeded as to hit the lid of an iron box.*

> *When looking up in the air, they saw coming down upon them "the figure of a man without a head." They dropped their spades and ran, as most others would have done, and escaped. Looking toward the spot, they saw it enveloped in smoke and flame. Returning to the island the next day, their spades had disappeared. They found the ground smooth and no traces left of its having been dug.*

According to this tale, not only is Thrice Cursed Island cursed, it's also haunted. Either way, that's only curse number two, because even after all these curses, buried treasures, and ghosts, the fourteen acres of Thrice Cursed Island have enough room for more lore.

The third curse is perhaps the strangest of all. In this story, a group of five sailors find a treasure in a cave in Mexico in 1721. Turns out, that treasure was the property of Cuauhtémoc, a real-life sixteenth century Aztec emperor who had been tortured by Spanish conquistadors who wanted the location of this treasure. He apparently never gave it up. Two hundred years after his death, the sailors nabbed his loot by happenstance. However, on the way home to New England, four of the five died, proving that this Aztec treasure was cursed.

The lone survivor of the plunderers hid the treasure in the basement of the Old Milford Inn, but someone stumbled across it while searching the cellar for booze. Panicked, the sailor grabbed the treasure and took a boat out to Charles Island to bury it, thus planting a cursed treasure in the soil of the already twice-cursed island. And that is curse number three.

And while no treasure—pirate or Aztec or otherwise—has ever been found on Charles Island, the place seems to have rejected all attempts to put it to practical use, to the point that in addition to the nickname Thrice Cursed Island, it's also been called Hard Luck Island. After Charles Deal's failed tobacco plantation, a New York merchant named John Harris erected a thirty-five-room mansion on that island that he eventually abandoned. The mansion was turned into a resort that failed, and then a fertilizer plant was built that also failed. A hotel put up on the island in the 1880s met the same fate as the other enterprises. Finally, a Catholic retreat in the early twentieth century didn't last beyond the 1930s (although some of its ruins are still there). And those are just the projects that were completed on the island. Over the years, plans for a yacht club, an amusement park, a military installation, and a nuclear power plant were all scrapped before a single shovel bit into cursed sand.

In 1976, Charles Island was purchased by the state of Connecticut. An article in the *Bridgeport Post* from that year noted the looming procurement, but also asked, "But what about the supernatural encumbrances that will undoubtedly accompany this tidy piece of real estate?" The article then described all three curses on the island before ending with, "So it comes as no surprise that State Representative Gerald F. Stevens has recommended no significant improvements on the state's proposed acquisition. Why tempt fate?"

The island was for the birds, so in the end, they made it for the birds. Today, the island is part of Silver Sands State Park and is an official Natural Area Preserve dedicated to nesting birds, which, according to the Audubon Society, have a natural immunity to curses (I jest). It is now the home of herons, egrets, terns, ibis, owls, and oystercatchers. The island is managed by the Department of Energy and Environmental Protection and is closed to the public from May 1 to August 31 so as not to disturb the nesting birds.

However, in the offseason, you're technically allowed to cross that tombolo. But it's still dangerous. According to a 2015 article in the CT *Post*, the owner of the nineteenth century hotel on the island had a heart attack while crossing the tombolo, and in 1929, a church group got caught in a storm on Good Friday while at Charles Island, all of them perishing. The latest death as of this writing was in 2017, when a twenty-eight-year-old man was swept off the tombolo and drowned, while his companion was narrowly rescued by boaters. Many more have died over the past hundred years, not to mention all the stranded people who survive via emergency rescues, which are carried out multiple times every summer.

So whether you believe in curses or not doesn't matter: Charles Island is plain dangerous. Although I did make it to the island and back alive, in case you were wondering. But as for the curses? Only time will tell if I escaped unscathed.

ISLA DE LAS MUÑECAS

ISLAND OF THE DOLLS

LOCATION: Mexico City, Mexico	**INFAMOUS FOR:** Creepy dolls, creepy dolls, even more creepy dolls
SIZE: 1 acre	
NOTABLE RESIDENT: Don Julián Santana Barrera	

Dolls are our go-to gift for bringing comfort and joy to children and our run-from object for instilling unease and horror in adults. These toy homunculi bother us for reasons that lie deep inside our brains. Dr. Thalia Wheatley, a cognitive neuroscientist at Dartmouth University who has performed research using doll faces, said this about dolls in a 2018 *Vice* interview: "There are these signals that are telling our brain this thing is alive, but we know it's not alive. And that juxtaposition is really creepy." Knowing the science behind the reaction does absolutely nothing to dispel the terror. But believe it or not, there is something scarier than a doll: a decaying doll—old and stained with missing limbs and cracked skin. A mini-corpse, shocking us with the simulacrum of a dead baby. But there is one thing even scarier than both a doll and a decaying doll: an island full of decaying dolls. And, unfortunately, the place really exists—in Mexico City.

This island that is also an uncanny valley is in the southernmost area of the city, in the canals of Xochimilco. These canals were built by the Aztecs, and in fact they once crisscrossed all of Tenochtitlan—the ancient center of the Aztec Empire which would one day become Mexico City, and which was originally established on an island in the middle of Lake Texcoco. The Aztecs built the canals by creating artificial islands called chinampas, on which they raised various crops. Eventually, most of those canals were destroyed by the conquering Spaniards and backfilled to support the foundations of Mexico City, except for this one neighborhood which preserves 110 miles of the original canals. Today, Xochimilco is a UNESCO World Heritage site, and, besides their important place in Mexico City's tourism industry, the chinampas are still used as gardens on which people grow everything from maize to the pungent orange marigolds used in the celebration of la Día de Los Muertos (the chinampas are also known as the "Floating Gardens"). But one of those historic chinampas has an odd and foreboding name: la Isla de las Muñecas, the Island of the Dolls.

And it's not just a name: This single acre of an artificial island is covered with more than two thousand decaying dolls, dangling from tree limbs in makeshift nooses, nailed to fences and walls and trunks, strung from clotheslines, and shoved into bushes and boughs. These dolls are aged by weather and neglect—some naked, most sans one or more limbs, and many with bleached eyes too bright in their moldy faces. They are cracked and crazed, begrimed and discolored; some mere decapitated heads shoved onto bamboo pikes. The whole island looks like the aftermath of an exploding nursery or the hideout of a notorious serial killer.

But the mystery of this island isn't the dolls which hang from the flora like some kind of unholy crop. The mystery is the man who festooned the island with these toys: Don Julián

Santana Barrera. Much has been speculated about Barrera and his eccentric island in the media, although little of him is really known. What seems definite is that he moved to the island in the early 1950s and then began decorating it with old, discarded dolls. Other than those two facts, everything else is speculation, even on the part of his relatives (whose accounts of his life often contradict one another).

Some accounts say Barrera moved to the island to become a hermit; others that he was banished there after being run out of his neighborhood for getting drunk on pulque and preaching the Bible too much. Some say he left his wife and child to move to the island out of some strange impulse; others that he lived on the island with a wife but didn't have any children (his great-nephew Rogelio Sanchez Santana went so far as to tell the *New York Post* in 2021 that the island itself made Barrera and his wife childless). But his backstory almost doesn't matter—at least not as much as his strange obsession.

Barrera's motivation for decorating his island with all those dolls is as vague as the rest of his legend. In one version of the tale, he discovered a young girl drowned in one of the canals, tangled in the water lilies. In another version, he saw the girl drowning but couldn't save her in time. Some of his relatives say that no girl ever drowned anywhere near that island and that the story is completely made up ... but not all of them.

His nephew, Anastasio Santana, told *La Nacion* in 2021 that after the death of the girl, Barrera was "terrified by the visit of evil spirits," and that his uncle told him that he could "hear the laments of a woman, voices, and footsteps" throughout the island. His great-nephew Rogelio Sanchez Santana added to the tale in the aforementioned *New York Post* article. According to him, Barrera "started seeing ghosts, and one day woke up and found all his crops had died. He tried many things to improve his crops but he couldn't because the spirit damaged it. He became more and more scared."

Some do think that the canals and chinampas of Xochimilco were haunted long before Barrera made them his home. Every tour guide will tell visitors to the canals the story of La Llorona, a vengeful ghost mother who haunts waterways because she drowned her own children after learning of her husband's infidelity. A 2017 article in the *Independent* tells of nahuales, sorcerers who transform into animals to cause harm to others. It quotes a Xochimilco tour guide named Tino, who says, "I have seen black jaguar-like forms pass under my boat, jump onto the banks, and disappear into the trees."

The area also has a less spectral history of death and terror. Many fled to these canals to escape Hernán Cortés and his conquistadors. Gerardo Ibarra, founder of a Mexican travel company called Ruta Origen, told the *New York Post* in 2021, "A lot of these people were women and children hiding from the conquistadores. And many women killed themselves rather than be caught and raped." Even today people drown in the canals. According to a 2019 AP News article, at least six people have drowned in the canals since 2005. It can be a dangerous place.

But back to Barrera and his island of creepy dolls. In one version of the story, he found the first sodden doll floating next to the dead body of the girl. In another, he found the doll the next day in that same spot. Yet another version tells that he found the doll in the canal after hearing the ghost of the girl screaming, "I want my doll!"

However it happened, the first doll was hung up by Barrera on the chinampa—whether to honor the drowned girl or ward off the evil spirits that were harming his crops or just because he thought dolls were neat, no one really knows. He then added to the collection throughout the rest of his life, fishing them out of the dank canals and the garbage cans of nearby neighborhoods, and bartering for them with the vegetables he grew on his island. He erected an altar in his tiny cabin and would wear the dolls around his neck. He even had a favorite doll, although accounts are muddled on whether it was the first doll he found or another. Some call that favorite doll La Muñeca and others Agustinita. Besides wearing it and displaying it in his cabin, Barrera would also play dress up with the doll, adorning her with necklaces and sunglasses.

I know what you're thinking: You're wondering why don't I quote from the doll collector himself and get the official version of the story. Well, apparently Barrera was never interviewed during his lifetime. But there is one more fact about his life that everyone seems to agree on: his death. He died in 2001 at the age of eighty . . . in a way that only added to the legend.

According to his nephew Anastasio, he and his uncle were on the island, fishing and singing at the edge of the canal in April of that year. Barrera told his nephew that he thought a mermaid was trying to drag him to his death, and that he had to sing to keep it at bay. Anastasio took a break to attend to some farming demands, but when he returned, he found Barrera face down in the canal, dead as a doll. The official cause of death was a heart attack, but according to the story that soon circulated, he died in the same spot in the canal where he had found the body of the drowned girl. According to his great-nephew Rogelio,

> "The spirit of the girl came to him and dragged him into the water."

After Barrera's death, Anastasio took over management of the island, hanging up even more dolls and welcoming tourists to visit and take pictures for a small fee. He died in 2019, and Barrera's great-nephew Rogelio took over. None of Barrera's descendants live on the island, though, choosing to keep their families safe on other chinampas.

Today, it's a popular tourist spot (except with those who suffer from pediophobia). Colorful gondolas known as trajineras take visitors around the canals that the Aztecs built and to Isla de las Muñecas to witness the strange ornaments and to see Barrera's original cabin with its trajinera-shaped altar and his favorite doll. People pay their respects by leaving trinkets and keepsakes and, yes, dolls. Also on the island is a small museum dedicated to the inadvertent outsider art project.

Many who have visited or stayed overnight on the island claim that they have seen the dolls animate—turning their heads, moving their arms and legs, whispering, trying to lure victims to the same watery fate as Barrera and the little girl. Tino, the aforementioned tour guide who was interviewed by the Independent, told the story of taking three girls to island. After Tino tied up the boat, the girls took off. Five minutes later, they came running back, one of them crying. He said, "Between her sobs, she screamed that the doll was laughing . . . so, I said I would go up to the island. I was going to check it out, to make them feel better, tell them they were wrong. But when I got onto the island, I could hear the sound of laughter, too. There was a doll, dressed as a rabbit and it was laughing, I promise you. I couldn't believe what I was seeing."

And it's not only tourists visiting Isla de las Muñecas. Paranormal shows love to film on the island, including *Ghost Adventures*, *Expedition X*, and *Buzzfeed Unsolved*. The hanging, broken dolls lend a creepy production value a hundred times beyond anything these shows' budgets could accomplish.

And there might be one more ghost haunting the canals and chinampas now: the ghost of Don Julián Santana Barrera himself. Toward the end of his life, Barrera used a cane to help him navigate the island. And since his death, it's said that you can sometimes still hear it striking the ground. Of course, what is true lore about the island and what is mere tourist lure is hard to detangle these days.

But what is absolutely inarguable about Isla de las Muñecas is that it's a terrifying place, haunted or not. Standing there, staring at the warped faces of the baby dolls and listening to the rattling of their plastic arms in the wind, you may find yourself thinking that an attack by ghosts would be a relief.

POVEGLIA ISLAND

SHORES OF HUMAN ASH

LOCATION: Venice, Italy **SIZE:** 17 acres **MAIN FEATURE:** San Vitale church bell tower	**INFAMOUS FOR:** Plague victims, mad doctor, ghosts, teenage shenanigans

Poveglia Island has seen some serious shit. The meager seventeen acres of this island in Venice have hosted battles, plague, human experimentation, executions, and hauntings. Today, it is abandoned and derelict, its buildings overcome by vegetation, its soil rumored to be half composed of human ash. The whole island is a ghost, haunting the waters of the Venetian Lagoon three miles from the center of one of the world's most visited cities. And rare is the publication that can avoid the temptation to call it the most haunted island (and sometimes location, period) on the planet. Including this one.

The island is located off Lido, home to the famous Venice Film Festival and one of Venice's two barrier islands that separate the Venetian Lagoon from the Adriatic Sea. Poveglia Island is triangular in shape, but divvied up into three portions so that, from above, it looks like a jigsaw puzzle. A canal snips the base off that triangle, which is connected to the central island by a pedestrian bridge, and the tip is a manmade, standalone octagon, the remains of a fourteenth-century fort.

The island was inhabited as far back as the early fifth century by refugees from the mainland escaping the barbarian invasions that would eventually destabilize the Roman Empire. The people on Poveglia (back then called Popilia, possibly in reference to the island's poplar trees) prospered for centuries as a fishing village while also taking advantage of its location to welcome trading ships into the lagoon. They built homes and the San Vitale church and largely kept to themselves. In 1378, the Chioggia War erupted, pitting Genoa against Venice for control of maritime trade in the Adriatic Sea. The inhabitants of the island were relocated to the mainland to escape the attacks in this predominantly naval battle, and the Venetians constructed the octagonal fort at its southern tip.

After three years, the war ended in a truce, and the Genoans retreated from the Adriatic Sea. But Poveglia Island was never the same. No longer the home of a thriving community, it remained unpopulated and empty, without purpose. Some accounts say it was used for executions after the war. Criminals would be taken to the island, shackled to a rock, and drowned when high tide washed in. If so, that still wouldn't be the worst thing to have happened on Poveglia.

The island eventually became an important part of maritime trade as a port of call and a storage facility for merchant ships from around the world. These ships would arrive with their holds brimming with silks and spices and all manner of supplies . . . and eventually, with the Black Death.

More scientifically known as the bubonic plague, the disease originally arrived in Europe in 1347 by ship from Asia (via the fleas on the rats on the ships) and ravaged the continent for five years. The plague caused high fevers, pus-spewing lumps at the lymph nodes, and black patches on the skin. Organ failure and death followed those symptoms after less than a week, and few survived once they contracted it. According to the

National Institutes of Health, twenty-five million people died in Europe from the plague, about a third of its population at the time. Italy was ground zero for the pandemic (technically the plague was first reported in Sicily, but soon spread to the mainland), although other ships bearing the plague soon arrived in ports elsewhere in Europe. By 1352, the plague had finally run its course. But that course was a labyrinth of horrors that left many scars throughout Europe—and Venice particularly. It's estimated that more than fifty percent of the population of the city was killed.

In the eighteenth century, Venice created stations on some of the islands in the lagoon to detain ships for forty days, ensuring that they were free from contagion before allowing them to continue further. The practice was called quaranta giorni, which means "forty days" in Italian. From it, we get the word *quarantine*. They also built hospitals on those islands for the infectious, which were called lazarettos (or *lazzaretto* in Italian). In a 2020 interview with *Sapiens* magazine, native Venetian and lazaretto expert Professor Francesca Malagnini of University for Foreigners, Perugia, explained, "They saw that the only solution was to separate people, to take away the sick people, or suspected sick people. This was the only way to protect everyone's health and allow the economy to continue." In essence, Venice implemented a modern methodology for protecting against contagion, despite knowing nothing about germ theory, which wouldn't be discovered until about a century and a half later.

Poveglia Island was one such quarantine station and lazaretto. In fact, the Venetian government is supposed to have disposed of somewhere between 100,000 and 160,000 plague victims on that island, either having died there or after dying elsewhere in the city. Plague doctors in eerie beaked masks full of aromatic herbs to hide the stench of sickness and death ministered to the afflicted and disposed of the bodies in plague pits and built massive bonfires of human remains. Some claim that half of the island's soil is made up of ash from those cremations and that the ground is pocketed with mass graves.

Much of the haunted reputation of the island comes from this phase of its existence. Screams are supposedly heard in the night and shadow people thought to be the spirits of plague victims are seen from time to time. People across the lagoon claim to hear a bell tolling on the island, presumably from San Vitale church, which was destroyed by Napoleon in 1806. Only the church's bell tower was left intact, to be repurposed as a lighthouse. But the bell itself is long gone, the tower mute in its position as the most prominent structure on the island from afar.

The only specific ghost story from this period of Poveglia's history is the ghost of Little Maria. According to various accounts, including a 2014 article in the *Daily Mail*, the story goes that Little Maria was a plague victim separated from her parents because of her illness. Today, she can supposedly be seen on the beach weeping and staring across the water in the direction of her hometown of Malamocco on Lido.

Curiously enough, no archaeological efforts to uncover these plague pits have ever been undertaken on Poveglia, while extensive digs have occurred on its sister islands of Lazzaretto Nuovo and Lazzaretto Vecchio. On those islands, archeologists have found mass graves containing thousands of skeletons, one of which, a female skeleton unearthed on Lazzaretto Nuovo, had a brick shoved in its mouth, prompting archeologists to theorize that the victim might have been thought to be a vampire or a witch.

It's almost like Poveglia is too foreboding for such a project.

Or, despite the stories, perhaps the body count of the island isn't as high as that of those other lazarettos. Explorers of Poveglia have found a stone in the undergrowth dated to 1793 and engraved with the Latin inscription, "Do not dig. Those who suffered contagion in life lie here." However, Lorenzo Pesola, the spokesperson for Poveglia per Tutti (Poveglia for Everybody), a group that once tried to buy the island to turn it into a public park, told the *Telegraph* in 2015 that "A handful of plague victims lie here, not the 'hundreds of thousands' of popular myth." And while most of the ghosts come from the island's time as a lazaretto, not all of them do. But that tale is even more controversial.

The lazaretto was shuttered in the early nineteenth century, and in 1922 a mental institution was established on Poveglia Island—a mental institution apparently haunted by the ghosts of doomed plague patients past. According to WorldAtlas, "From the beginning days of the asylum, patients were heard to complain about ghastly sightings, wailing voices, and other unnatural happenings but these reports were ignored as the laments of the insane inmates of the mental hospital."

One of those unnatural happenings is the sadistic doctor who is supposed to have practiced at the facility. He would experiment on the patients and force crude lobotomies on them. Eventually, he fell to his death from the empty bell tower. Some accounts state that he was driven mad by the ghosts of plague patients and jumped of his own accord. Other accounts state that he was pushed by his patients to avenge their friends and protect themselves from his cruel surgeries. The strangest part of the story, though, is that the fall did not kill him. Instead, his broken body was enveloped by a sudden mysterious ground fog that suffocated him.

The hospital closed in 1968, and today the island is

completely abandoned. A firsthand account in a 2015 article in the *Telegraph* describes it this way: "A forlorn air hangs over the place. In the old hospital, boundaries between inside and out have been blurred. Floors are tiled with leaf litter, lianas twist through glassless fanlights and a roof has been replaced by vegetation. Beyond the buildings, the old vegetable plots and orchards are obliterated by brambles." A 2016 article in *L'Italo Americano* magazine places a finer point on it:

"While the rest of Venice is governed by Comune di Venezia, the island of Poveglia remains firmly in the jurisdiction of the Devil."

Visitors are technically barred from the island for safety reasons, although based on the number of social media influencers who have filmed videos there and paranormal shows that have camped out there, it's not too difficult to pay someone with a boat to take you to the island . . . and hopefully pick you up again afterward.

In 2014, the city of Venice tried to auction off a ninety-nine-year lease to the island, along with a few other historic properties, in an attempt to infuse some cash into its meagre budget. Only two bids were put in. A local businessman named Luigi Brugnaro offered €513,000 for it to either rehabilitate the island into a clinic for those with eating disorders or a luxury resort (apparently his purpose wasn't completely clear). The other bidder, Poveglia per Tutti, offered €420,000. As previously mentioned, they wanted to transform the island into a public park. The group's marketing materials feature a giraffe that once quarantined on the island, a gift from the Viceroy of

Egypt to the Austrian Emperor in 1828. According to the 2015 *Telegraph* story, one of the reasons the group bid on the island was that "It holds fond memories for many Venetians of young middle age . . . for when they were growing up it was a piece of campagna [countryside] in the lagoon." Pesola is quoted in the article as saying, "Young people came here to smoke their joints, have sex, have some shade from the adult world. It's tied to a lot of people's biographies."

The city rejected the winning bid as being far too low. Brugnaro at first tried to fight the decision, but then lost interest when he campaigned for and became mayor of Venice after his predecessor was caught taking bribes.

However, Poveglia per Tutti never gave up, and in 2025, more than a decade after their initial loss, they were finally successful in gaining control of the island. Or at least part of it. According to the terms of the agreement with the city, they obtained a six-year-lease for the base section of the tripart island. The group told *USA Today* after the deal was made, "Our main goal is to ensure that the island does not get sold to private owners, as has already happened to other islands in the lagoon that have become inaccessible to non-paying visitors. . . . We are now working to make it more accessible by building safer moorings. The island will always be open to everybody, not just local residents."

So maybe Poveglia Island will no longer be a blight on the Venetian Lagoon, although that won't necessarily stop the island from being a home for ghost stories and strange legends. Especially since it seems that the majority of Poveglia, including the section with the ruins, will remain inaccessible and populated only by lost souls for the time being. A 2024 piece in *Far Out* magazine eulogizes it this way: "Perhaps the most terrifying aspect of the island is its emptiness, a quiet entity occupied by nothing other than a once-filled location. The suffering sounds of those close to death are heard in the soft whispers of the wind, and the hushed tones of horrifying histories appear loud and clear only by virtue of once being true."

And then there's what the locals say about the island: "Quando muore un cattivo, si sveglia a Poveglia." Translated:

"When an evil man dies, he wakes up in Poveglia."

EILEAN MÒR

KEEPER OF LOST LIGHTHOUSE KEEPERS

LOCATION: Flannan Isles, Scotland	**NAME TRANSLATION:** Big Island
SIZE: 43 acres	**INFAMOUS FOR:** Disappearing lighthouse keepers

Three victims. Sometimes that's all it takes to warn the public that we need to avoid a place. Other locations can devour hundreds of lives before we start to catch on, but sometimes it only takes a memorable few—like the lost lighthouse keepers on the mysterious island of Eilean Mòr in Scotland.

Scrutinizing a map of the Hebrides archipelago—the hundreds of islands that line the west coast of Scotland—you can find multiple islands with the name Eilean Mòr. For instance, the Eilean Mòr of the Crowlin Islands, where evidence of human habitation during the Mesolithic period was found. Or the Eilean Mòr of the MacCormaig Islands, famed for being the seventh-century retreat for Saint Cormac. That's because Eilean Mòr is Gaelic for "big island." But in this case, we're talking about the Eilean Mòr of the Flannan Isles (also known as the Seven Hunters), a grouping of unpopulated islands in the Outer Hebrides, so far west and isolated from the mainland that it seems more a feature of the Atlantic Ocean than of Scotland.

Eilean Mòr is little more than a grass-topped rock, some

forty-three acres in size. It's visited by puffins, storm petrels, and other seabirds. Rabbits were introduced to it at some point, but they are its only inhabitants now. Three buildings cling desperately to the island, the only evidence of its peopled past. Two are ancient ruins: one a small hut and the other a tiny, rough chapel, little more than a pile of unmortared stones, dedicated to—and some say built by—seventh century Irish Saint Flannan, namesake of the islands. The third is a more modern edifice, set on the highest point of the island: a lighthouse. It's seventy-five feet tall, white with mustard highlights, and a black lantern is perched atop it. The towering building was completed in 1899 after four years of arduous and delayed work caused by the difficulty of the island's location and its exposure to the full force of the Atlantic and its storms. The lighthouse is automated these days. Nearby is a helipad where workers land to perform maintenance and upkeep and then get the heck off the rock. As noted in a 2003 article by the BBC, "Flannan Isle was not a place to stay for any length of time." But before 1971, it was permanently populated by a rotating crew of lighthouse keepers. One of those crews was not so permanent, though, and the mystery of their disappearance is the island's claim to fame.

In late December 1900, only a year after the paraffin-fueled lighthouse lantern first burnt its way through the night, a few ships passing by noticed that they couldn't see the signal. The lantern would normally be visible for twenty miles or so, although it was sometimes overpowered by the fog that seemed preternaturally pulled to the island. On December 26, the steamship *Hesperus*, the relief boat for the lighthouse keepers, arrived at the island, albeit delayed for a week by storms. Normally, it came by every two weeks to restock stores and relieve the lighthouse keepers, three of which maintained the tower on a rotating schedule of six weeks on, two weeks off. The last time the *Hesperus* had tied ashore was December 7.

The current crew on Eilean Mòr was James Ducat, who was the head lighthouse keeper, and two assistants, Thomas Marshall and Donald McArthur, the latter of whom was a substitute keeper filling in for another assistant William Ross, who had taken ill. All three men on that shift were hardened and experienced mariners, able to deal with both the physical challenges of the island and the metaphysical challenges of solitude.

As the *Hesperus* neared, they witnessed none of the usual welcome by the lighthouse crew. Usually, the keepers would fly a flag in greeting and hurry down to the landing out of excitement for the break in their dreary routine, but also to help moor the boat, which was a difficult task. The island is rimmed with sheer cliffs and battered by waves. The footpath from the landing to the interior of the island includes long, steep ramps and stairs set into the cliffs. But all the captain of the *Hesperus*, James Harvie, could see were empty rock and a dark lighthouse, even after blowing his horn and firing a flare.

Captain Harvie sent a group to shore, who somehow found a way to land unaided. Joseph Moore was the first to leave the boat and enter the lighthouse. He, after all, knew it best. Moore was part of the rotating crew of keepers on Eilean Mòr and was coming to relieve one of his colleagues. What he found in the lighthouse chilled him. In a letter Moore wrote two days later, he claimed that when he approached the lighthouse, the gate was shut, as was the main door. In the kitchen, the fireplace seemed to have been cold for days. The clocks had stopped. He went to the bedrooms and found all the beds empty. According to his letter, "I did not take time to search further, for I only too well knew something serious had occurred. I darted out and made for the landing."

That night, Captain Harvie sent a telegram to the mainland communicating the disappearance of all three men and detailing what little they knew about it: "A dreadful accident has happened at Flannans. The three Keepers, Ducat, Marshall, and the occasional have disappeared from the island. . . . Poor fellows they must been blown over the cliffs or drowned trying to secure a crane or something like that. Night coming on, we could not wait to make something as to their fate."

A subsequent and more thorough search revealed little amiss. The lighthouse was full of fuel and clean. The only noticeable clue to their activity was that two of the three coats were missing from their pegs (McArthur's was the only one still in the lighthouse). The eastern landing was tidy and ready for boats, too. But the western landing was in disarray. A crate where they kept ropes and tackle was missing, its contents strewn across the rocks. Some of the iron railings on the footpath to the water were broken or missing, as was a life buoy. A one-ton boulder had fallen on the path.

On December 29, the superintendent of the Northern Lighthouse Board, Robert Muirhead, who had handpicked the lightkeepers himself, arrived at the island to investigate the disappearance. He submitted his report a week later. His conclusion:

> *The most likely explanation of the disappearance of the men is that they had all gone down on the afternoon of Saturday, 15 December to the proximity of the West landing, to secure the box with the mooring ropes, etc and that an unexpectedly large roller had come up on the Island, and a large body of water going up higher than where they were and coming down upon them had swept them away with resistless force.*

Basically, a freak wave—the roller—had taken all three in one gulp.

Muirhead ended the report, "I visited Flannan Islands when the relief was made so lately as 7th December, and have the melancholy recollection that I was the last person to shake hands with them and bid them adieu."

This explanation seemed to fit most of the evidence, including the left-behind coat. It was theorized that Ducat and Marshall had gone down to secure the box (losing it would have been a major problem for the keepers, in addition to the fines they would face for any lost items) and that McArthur saw something amiss from inside and rushed out to help them, leaving his coat behind.

But this theory does little to satisfactorily explain the mystery. Why were all the doors and gates fastened tight if McArthur was in a hurry? Nor does Muirhead's account explain the most mysterious clues on the scene, clues that have caused some to doubt his theory of a freak wave. First, the kitchen apparently held more evidence than a cold fireplace and a stopped clock. A chair was supposedly upturned and a meal laid out on the table untouched, meaning that whatever happened wasn't some run-of-the-mill concern over the security of the box, but something sudden and surprising.

And then there were the final log entries ostensibly recorded by Marshall:

> *Dec. 12: Gale, north by north-west. Sea lashed to fury. Stormbound 9pm. Never seen such a storm. Everything shipshape. Ducat irritable. 12pm. Storm still raging. Wind steady. Stormbound. Cannot go out. Ship passed sounding foghorn. Could see lights of cabins. Ducat quiet. McArthur crying.*
>
> *Dec. 13: Storm continued through night. Wind shifted west by*

north. Ducat quiet. McArthur praying. 12 noon. Grey daylight. Me, Ducat, and McArthur prayed.
Dec. 15: 1pm. Storm ended. Sea calm. God is over all.

A few items from the log demand attention. First, no storm was recorded by any of the other outposts or ships in the area on those dates. In addition, how could a mere storm—which were frequent in the area—have terrified these seasoned old salts to the point of tears? Finally, the phantom storm was over by the fifteenth, and the keepers safe enough to record their survival in the log. What happened afterward that plucked these lighthouse keepers from the planet?

Over time, every theory possible has been advanced to explain the mysterious doom of these poor keepers. One is that they were captured by pirates or some foreign power. Another is that they hopped a boat on their own and didn't look back. Yet another is that one of the keepers went a little island-crazy and killed the other two before jumping into the water himself. From there, the theories gets weirder: that the keepers were abducted by aliens or a race of pygmies long rumored to inhabit the Hebrides. Or the culprit was a sea serpent, drawn from its dark depths by the bright lure of the lighthouse on high.

However, more than likely, the disappearance of these men was nailed right away by Muirhead. A deeper look into the more befuddling clues is pretty revealing. The first is that the detail of the overturned chair and the unconsumed meal were not in the original reports. In fact, Muirhead's report stated, "The pots and pans had been cleaned and the kitchen tidied up, which showed that the man who acted as cook had completed his work." The idea that the lighthouse keepers had been interrupted mid-repast didn't appear until 1912 when

Wilfrid Wilson Gibbons published what would become a popular poem that tells an embellished version of the discovery of the disappearance of the lighthouse keepers. The poem ends:

Like curs, a glance has brought to heel,
We listened, flinching there:
And looked, and looked, on the untouched meal,
And the overtoppled chair.
We seemed to stand for an endless while,
Though still no word was said,
Three men alive on Flannan Isle,
Who thought, on three men dead.

As to the log entries, it seems they are also completely fanciful. There was a logbook found at the scene that covered that timespan (the log in the book ended on December 13, but there were entries chalked on a slate through December 15 where logs were first recorded before being transferred to the book). However, those were mere factual recordings of weather and sea conditions. The log wasn't a diary of events and feelings. In fact, a 2018 piece by Skeptoid points out that the Northern Lighthouse Board's statement on the matter in 2014 was, "We do not hold the log book and no-one is aware of its whereabouts but lighthouse log books would not generally extend beyond recording tasks carried out at the lighthouse and the weather and sea conditions etc."

So where did these entries come from? Well, they're printed in a 1965 book called *Invisible Horizons: True Mysteries of the Sea* written by a paranormal author named William Gaddis. According to Skeptoid, Gaddis claimed to have transcribed the log text from a 1929 piece by Ernest Fallon in the magazine *True Strange Stories*. According to a 1998 *Fortean Times* investigation by Mike Dash, the Fallon article was a work of fiction under a pen name by an author named John L. Spivak.

Without that disordered kitchen and the strange log sequence, the story we are left with is that three men in a very dangerous location where it's easy to disappear . . . all disappeared.

But that doesn't completely mundane the mystery. We still don't know the details, or have any confirmation of Muirhead's freak wave, which is technically as much a theory as attack by sea monster, if more easy to believe. So what exactly happened to James Ducat, Thomas Marshall, and Donald McArthur on that fateful day? Maybe we don't want to know.

Today, Eilean Mòr, like the rest of the Flannan Isles, is owned by the National Trust of Scotland, and, other than the lighthouse being automated and a helipad having built for maintenance of the beacon, the island is pretty much just as those doomed keepers left it. But you can visit it. You just need a boat. And calm seas. And a bit of courage.

In December 2017, the village of Breasclete on the Isle of Lewis, where the wives and children of those three lighthouse keepers lived, erected a memorial to those lost souls, a small sculpture in the form of a bronze wave sweeping over a lighthouse on a boulder.

In that memorial are depicted the only firsthand witnesses to the tragedy: The ocean, omnipresent but obstinate; the rock of the island itself, solid but mute; and the lighthouse, bright but blind. Eilean Mòr remains keeper of lost lighthouse keepers, and of secrets.

GAIOLA ISLAND

RICH PEOPLE BEWARE

LOCATION: Naples, Italy	**MAIN FEATURE:** Abandoned villa
SIZE: 1 acre	**INFAMOUS FOR:** Deadly curse

Gaiola Island rises from the ocean a mere thirty yards off the coast of Naples, Italy. Swimming distance, really—not that I'd recommend it. However, it looks more rock formation than conventional island: two thick pillars of limestone connected by a walking bridge. The surface area of those two islets combined is about the size of a small estate, and that's exactly what it is. One of the islets has an old, crumbling villa atop it. The other is a terraced yard—or it would be if the whole rock hadn't been abandoned for half a century. And that's a good thing, because almost every owner of the island has suffered misfortune and death—including suicide, murder, drowning, heart attack, car accident, loss and maiming of loved ones, insanity, imprisonment, and bankruptcy. Some of those owners suspiciously don't seem to appear in the record other than in connection to Gaiola, while others are quite famous and their ownership of the island well-documented. It's hard to disentangle truth and fiction when it comes to this island. Regardless, locals believe the island to be cursed, and they call that curse the Gaiola Malediction.

The island's name is derived from the Latin word for small

cave—caveola—because the nearby shoreline of the mainland is perforated with them. That shoreline is part of Posillipo, a residential area of Naples populated by the affluent in luxurious villas. From the beach, the island looks like the exotic subject of a painting, rising out of twinkling sapphire sea, the kind of backdrop that belongs in an influencer's social media post. The island is the centerpiece of the one-hundred-acre Parco Sommerso di Gaiola, or Gaiola Underwater Park, a preserve dedicated to watery wildlife such as octopuses, moray eels, breams, and damselfish ... as well as submerged Roman ruins.

Back in the first century BC, the now-submerged park was dry land, but it and all of the surrounding shoreline were still the domain of the wealthy—in this case the Roman aristocracy—who built their sumptuous villas on the coast. The most notable house on the block was called Pausilypon ("place where sorrows end"). It was built by Publius Vedius Pollio, a high-ranking nobleman and friend of Emperor Octavian Augustus. Ruins of his villa still exist on the remaining coast, while much of his holdings have sunk into the gulf along with other structures due to movements of the earth's crust caused by volcanic activity. Today, if you know what you're looking for and have a diving mask on, you can see, beneath the surface, the waterlogged ruins of villas, quarries, nymphaeums, and fish corrals, the latter of which were a high-end feature of expensive Roman villas.

Meanwhile, Gaiola Island, once it became one, was originally known as Euplea because it was the site of a small temple devoted to Venus and dedicated to safe navigation of the seas. In other words, the opposite of a cursed island.

But that's all ancient history. The modern and much darker history of the island began in the nineteenth century, before the villa was constructed, when the only inhabitant was a hermit the locals called Il Mago, or the Wizard. Little was known about this solitary man on this small island, including how he got his enigmatic nickname. Fishers would give him some of their catch on their return from the sea, which helped him survive. And then one day, he disappeared. No note left behind, no body. Just gone. Swallowed by the sea like so many of the surrounding ruins.

The next inhabitant of the island was a businessman named Luigi de Negri. He owned a successful fishery and bought Gaiola in 1871. He was the person who built the villa that currently decays on one of the islets. Soon after building it, though, de Negri went bankrupt. So far in the history of Gaiola, not such a strange story—vagrants vacate and businessmen go bankrupt all the time.

In 1910, the Italian navy christened a new armored cruiser called *San Giorgo*, which left its berth to join the Italo-Turkish War. However, a month after they cracked the champagne bottle on its hull, it hit a reef near Gaiola and ran aground, flooded with over four thousand tons of seawater. The navy had to refloat the ship and repair it, sidelining its use in the war effort for about two years. Again, boats wreck all the time—the sea is a harsh mistress and all that. But there's more.

The next year, another boat, this one owned and piloted by a Captain Gaspare Albenga, also sank near the island. He had taken the boat out because he was interested in acquiring Gaiola and wanted to give it a closer look. However, he crashed into some rocks, capsized his boat, and drowned. According to the lore, neither his body nor the wreck of his ship were ever recovered.

In the 1920s, a Swiss businessman named Hans Braun bought Gaiola Island. And then he bought it. He was found murdered in his home, his body wrapped in a rug. The details are scant on this tragedy, including the motivation for the murder and if the murderer was ever caught. In addition, whether the morbid burrito of his corpse was found in the villa itself or in another of his homes is also unclear. What is clearly recorded, though, is that not too long after his murder, his widow went swimming out in the gulf and drowned.

It's getting difficult to scoff at the Gaiola Malediction—and it's about to get even more challenging. A German perfume dealer named Otto Grunback was the next victim to catch island fever, purchasing this seeming gem of a residence off the coast. However, while staying at the villa, he suffered a heart attack and died.

The next wealthy man to place the island in his portfolio was a pharmaceutical scion and author of supernatural fiction named Maurice-Yves Sandoz. He would end his days in a mental asylum in Switzerland, and then end his life there by suicide in 1958.

The subsequent owner of the villa, in a surprise twist, didn't die tragically. A wealthy German businessman in the steel industry named Baron Karl Paul Langheim bought the place, lavishly decorated it, and threw parties there with guest lists that included princes and princess, counts and countesses. A first-person account of one of his parties in the Society section of a 1956 issue of the *Philadelphia Inquirer* by Gloria Bragiotti Etting described him serving lunch with "Ischia wine chilled in tall silver pitchers" and melon sherbert served in melon shells, which the guests ate while gazing at Vesuvius. Afterwards, the baron toured them through the palazzo with its tiled floors and "Neapolitan rococo gilt furniture." The party ended for him—similar to de Negri—as he soon went broke—although, according to multiple sources, the reason he lost all of his money wasn't due to a failed business, but his "wild lifestyle."

After Langheim, the next owner was none other than the richest man in all of Italy: Gianni Agnelli, owner of Fiat, the internationally famous and successful Italian car brand. Agnelli's tragedies seemed to target his whole family, some of which predated his purchase of the island (for instance, his father died in a plane crash when Gianni was a teenager and his mother died in an automobile accident ten years later). But those familial misfortunes didn't stop after he took ownership of Gaiola. In 2000, Agnelli's forty-six-year-old son Edoardo was found dead at the bottom of a 250-foot-tall viaduct on the Turin-Savona autostrada. The cause was ruled as suicide. Giannia himself died in 2003, and his brother would die of lung cancer the following year, having become CEO after his brother's death. Admittedly, Edoardo, Gianni, and Umberto died decades after Gianni Angelli sold Gaiola, but sometimes that's how curses work—you can't always shake them by getting rid of the cursed thing.

The island then passed from the hands of the richest man in Italy to the man who would become the richest in the world: J. Paul Getty. The Getty family troubles are legendary. His twelve-year-old son Timmy died from a brain tumor in 1956. Talitha, his second wife (of five), from a heroin overdose in 1971. His sixteen-year-old grandson John Paul Getty III was kidnapped in Rome by the Italian mafia in 1973 and had his right ear severed to impel his grandfather to negotiate $2 million in ransom. The five-month ordeal in a cave in Calabria would haunt John Paul Getty III for the rest of his days, both mentally and physically. In 1981, he suffered a stroke brought on by drug and alcohol use, which left him paralyzed, partially blind, and unable to speak for the rest of his life. He died thirty years later in 2011.

But even a world-famous name like Getty wasn't enough to

satisfy the hungry island. Gaiola had one more private owner after Getty: Gianpasquale Grappone. He ran an insurance company but made his real money in white collar crime—fraud, embezzlement, and the like. He was eventually caught and jailed for those crimes. While in prison, his wife died in a car accident in 1978.

Now, not everybody who owned the island has been impacted by the curse. In fact, the island has quite the literary history. Besides author Maurice-Yves Sandoz, it was also owned by Nelson Foley, the brother-in-law of Sir Arthur Conan Doyle. After him, Norman Douglas, British author of the popular 1948 travelogue *Siren Land*, nabbed the keys to Gaiola (possibly, at least; some accounts are less specific, mentioning merely a villa in Posillipo). Oscar Wilde is even supposed to have spent time writing on the island during his exile, unscathed. Maybe the island considers being an artist as curse enough. Writers aside, Homer Byington Jr., an American diplomat, was born on the island in 1908 while his parents were renting the villa. Byington would go on to enjoy a distinguished career as an ambassador and consul in Malaysia and Naples before dying at the age of 79 while partying on a cruise ship—so he did okay, too.

And even though the island has been vacant since the late 1970s, the Gaiola Malediction still finds a way to strike. In 2009, in a villa on the mainland just across the water from Gaiola, wealthy husband and wife Franco Ambrosio and Giovanna Sacco were both bludgeoned to death in what appeared to be a robbery. A tangential episode, to be sure, but that didn't stop the media from drawing the connection between the crime and the curse.

With most of these deaths and misfortunes being well documented, one could posit that if Gaiola Island isn't really cursed, maybe nowhere is. However, if the Gaiola Malediction is real, where did the curse come from? Is it some malicious parting gift from the mysterious Il Mago before he disappeared from the island and from history? Or does it date back further, to the ancient Roman ruins now buried in the gulf and turned into a playground for octopuses?

Remember Publius Vedius Pollio from earlier? Turns out, some really bad stuff happened on the grounds of his villa Pausilypon. Pollio was apparently infamous for his cruelty, which was recorded by such ancient philosophers and historians as Seneca, Pliny, and Cassius Dio. Pollio was known for feeding his slaves to the moray eels he kept in his fish corrals (giving the translation of the name of his villa, "place where sorrows end," an ironic and tragic meaning). At one point, while hosting his friend the Emperor Augustus, a slave broke a cup made of fine-wrought murrhine glass. Pollio immediately ordered him fed to the carnivorous eels. Augustus, appalled, intervened and stopped the horrific execution. He then ordered Pollio to break his entire collection of glass right there in front of him and to fill in his fish corral, humiliating him. Perhaps it was Pollio's cruelty that seeded this land with the curse, manifested in the island that survived the submerging of his estate.

Whatever the case, there is good news when it comes to Gaiola Island: Unless you're own-an-island rich, you're probably safe from its malediction.

SEEKING THE LEAST SCARY PLACES

Forests are scary, the ocean is scary, the desert is scary, mountains are scary—almost everywhere on the planet is scary. Except maybe for one specific type of place.

Scientists divide the planet into multiple environments that they call biomes. According to the National Geographic Society, a biome is defined as "an area classified according to the species that live in that location." For instance, the ocean and forest represent two different biomes because of the types of adaptations local species have made to survive in those distinct environments.

Biomes can be summed up in five major types: aquatic, grassland, forest, desert, and tundra (the forest category represents all types of densely treed habitats, like jungles). This book is divided into six types of places you shouldn't go. And they almost exactly correspond to the five major biomes, except that we've added islands and ruins as categories, neither of which are biomes, and left one biome out entirely: grasslands.

Grasslands are wide areas of flat space and low-growing vegetation in warm, dry climates. Think of the American Great Plains or the African veld. Grasslands have a lot of other names and varieties, too, depending on where they appear, including steppes, shrublands, savannahs, rangelands, drylands, meadows, prairies, llano, and pampas. According to the 2023 Grasslands, Rangelands, Savannahs and Shrublands Alliance paper *Valuing Grasslands*, this biome covers 49 percent of land on Earth. *National Geographic* puts the number somewhere between 20 and 40 percent, "depending on how they're defined."

And however grasslands are defined, they are apparently incapable of being creepy. There's just nothing spooky about large, open fields. Probably because there are no places to hide. Nowhere for bigfoots to disappear into. No respectable site for a ghost to haunt.

But they do have skies. They have most of the skies, in fact. But even UFOs seem to visit grasslands merely to doodle in the crops. And that just makes tall grasses and crops scary (which they are . . . we definitely need to find a new way to grow corn).

But if you're looking for a bit of safety in this terrifying world with all its risks to both body and soul, check out the grassland. However, you still might have to dodge the errant lion or lightning storm. Because no place on the planet is *really* safe.

DEADLY DESERTS

The phrase sounds redundant: *deadly deserts*. After all, many of us think of deserts as intrinsically dangerous places—empty and lifeless and perilous to creatures such as ourselves who are composed of sixty percent water. But the truth is that deserts are thriving ecosystems, full of plants and animals adapted to the extremely low moisture. Hell, entire civilizations have thrived in the desert for millennia. But more sinister phenomena thrive in these desolate dunes, too—strange electromagnetic phenomena, hidden military bases, wailing ghosts, bizarre creatures not catalogued by science, UFO activity, and worse. If someone disappears in the desert, it's safe to assume they got got by dehydration or a venomous reptile—probably. But it could have been a fate much, much more bizarre.

SKINWALKER RANCH

HERDING HORRORS

LOCATION: Uintah Basin, Utah, USA **SIZE:** 512 acres **AS SEEN ON:** *The Secrets of Skinwalker Ranch*	**INFAMOUS FOR:** Strange creatures, UFOs, poltergeists, sky portals, cattle mutilations, real estate billionaires

Skinwalker Ranch is a 512-acre cattle ranch in the northeast corner of Utah where for decades people have witnessed UFOs, cattle mutilations, bigfoots, crop-circle-like designs in the landscape, blue orbs, portals in the sky, unusual illnesses, bullet-proof dire wolves, harmful magnetic fields, disembodied voices, and other bizarre phenomena. It's also quite possibly the most heavily monitored paranormal site on the planet, with the combined financial resources of the United States government and two different billionaires invested in attempting to document and explain the surreal goings on in that patch of desert.

The Uintah Basin covers 9,300 square miles and is populated by some 140,000 people across six counties. Its largest communities are Duchesne and Vernal, and it's also the location of the Uintah and Ouray Reservation, home to the Northern Ute Tribe, from whom the state of Utah gets its name. The basin contains craggy mountains, dusty mesas, plains of sagebrush, open skies, and everything else that goes with a soundtrack of whip cracks and wagon wheels. And apparently the whole area has been frequented by UFOs since the 1950s. In a 1978 article, the local paper *Deseret News* called the Uintah Basin "famous for numerous UFO sightings over the past ten years," including "the flight of an awesome dome-shaped unidentified flying object with intense lights" which was witnessed by multiple people at multiple locations. And right in the middle of all of that sits Skinwalker Ranch.

Its name—ominous even before you learn its history—comes from a Navajo legend about evil sorcerers called skinwalkers who can transform into animals. In 2016, Joseph Hicks, a local author who spent years of his life documenting the UFO sightings in the basin, told UB Media (owner of the *Vernal Express* and the *Uintah Basin Standard* newspapers) that the association of skinwalkers with that region came out of a territory dispute between the Ute and the Navajo before white settlers invaded. He said, "The Navajos lost and they, in turn, cursed the Utes with the skinwalker, saying a spiritual person that changes into a wolf will be here to harass you, and they accepted that . . . and so, the skinwalker animal seemed to be on that ridge that they now call the Skinwalker Ridge." A ridge that is now part of Skinwalker Ranch.

Once upon a time, though, it was the "ranch" part of Skinwalker Ranch that was considered more important (in fact, it doesn't seem to have been called Skinwalker Ranch until the 1990s). The ranch was purchased in 1934 by Kenneth and Edith Myers, and it stayed in the family for more than half a century. Apparently, those decades were a fallow time for weird occurrences on the ranch, as nothing enters the record from their time there. But then the Myers family sold it to Terry and Gwen Sherman in 1994. The Shermans would last a mere two years.

In 2002, George Knapp and Colm A. Kelleher released a book called *Hunt for the Skinwalker: Science Confronts the Unexplained at a Remote Ranch in Utah* that in part detailed what happened to the Shermans during their brief time as owners of the ranch. Knapp was a journalist who specialized in the paranormal and had written a few articles about the ranch in the past for the *Las Vegas Mercury*. Kelleher was a biochemist who spent time investigating the ranch after the Shermans sold it. According to the book, when the Shermans arrived, they were surprised at the level of security the previous owners seemed to have needed: "There were deadbolts on both sides of the doors. Even the kitchen cabinets had bolts on them. And at both ends of the house, iron stakes and heavy chains had been installed. [Sherman] guessed the previous tenants had positioned large guard dogs in the front and back of the home, but he had no idea why."

And then Terry and Gwen learned why. According to the Shermans, they almost immediately began experiencing a range of intense paranormal phenomena on the ranch. Glowing blue orbs the size of handballs darted around the property. They had hard, glass-like shells, were full of bubbling liquid, and would cause the Shermans intense emotional distress and—in one horrifying instance—incinerate three of their dogs to cinders. A wolf the height of a man's chest with "hypnotic blue eyes" attacked a calf right in front of them, impervious to the four .357 Magnum bullets and two thirty-aught-six blasts that they peppered it with. Strange orange "things" hovered in the sky, and objects would pass into and out of them as if they were portals to another location.

In addition, heavy equipment was found in trees, cattle were found dead and exsanguinated, disembodied voices would speak incomprehensibly to them, bigfoot-like creatures would run through their property, and fields would light up in the middle of the night. They even once awoke with their sheets covered in blood and small wounds in their thumbs. The Shermans quickly realized that they couldn't stay on this ranch, which, according to a 2006 article in the *Deseret News*, left them "financially ailing, mentally anguished, and in the end, horrified and afraid."

In 1996, newspapers in Utah and Nevada started reporting on the Shermans' stories, which brought the ranch to the attention of a billionaire named Robert Bigelow. He was from Las Vegas and had made his money by founding a successful chain of extended-stay motels called Budget Suites of America. He used his fortune to fund his offbeat interests, including projects to prove the existence of life after death and to create space hotels in orbit. He also founded Bigelow Aerospace, which developed an inflatable space habitat that is currently being used on the International Space Station. And, man, did he love his UFOs.

In 1995, a year prior to reading about the hub of strangeness that was Skinwalker Ranch, Bigelow had founded the National Institute for Discovery Science, or NIDS. According to its website, the organization was a "privately funded science institute engaged in research of aerial phenomena, animal mutilations, and other related anomalous phenomena." Skinwalker Ranch seemed the perfect place to sic NIDS on. It was remote and private, the phenomena seemed to cross all three categories, and Bigelow knew his way around a real estate deal. In 1996, he bought the ranch for $200,000 and assembled a NIDS team whose members specialized in the fields of physics, biochemistry, and veterinary science to stay at and study the ranch, included Kelleher. Terry Sherman, despite the terrifying experiences that forced him to sell the property, stayed on as caretaker.

For the next eight years, the team documented and investigated both the Shermans' and their own experiences until NIDS folded in 2004. According to a 2021 article in the *New Yorker*, NIDS was shut down due to a "purported decrease in domestic paranormal activity."

Bigelow didn't release any of the documentation or evidence gathered in that eight-year period at Skinwalker Ranch, but Kelleher did discuss some of the experiences of the group in his book *Hunt for Skinwalker*, including the occasional "strange sulfurous odor," mysterious cattle deaths, and UFOs, but he concluded that there was "difficulty obtaining evidence consistent with scientific publication." According to Kelleher's book, Terry Sherman believed it was so difficult for the outsider team to prove anything because the source of the bizarre disturbances "took extraordinary measures to become much more opaque and hidden almost immediately after NIDS assumed control."

If you feel that explanation is suspiciously convenient, you're not alone. In 2010, a biologist named Frank Salisbury released a revised and updated version of his 1974 book *The Utah UFO Display* about UFO activity in the Uintah Basin and elsewhere. In the new edition, he interviewed Garth Myers, the brother of Kenneth Myers, who owned the ranch before the Shermans. Garth explained that after his brother died in 1987, his sister-in-law Edith lived there by herself until 1992, at which point she moved to a nursing home where she died two years later. He told Salisbury, "I can tell you unequivocally that up to 1992 there had never been any signs of that [UFO and similar activity]." He went on to say that he received a call from Robert Bigelow himself about a month after he purchased the property, asking why the Myers had never reported any activity. Garth told Biglow that it was because the phenomena never happened. He also told Bigelow that, despite what the Shermans claimed about the giant dog chains and deadbolts on the property, his brother- and sister-in-law didn't keep any large guard dogs on the property, nor were there any other heavy security precautions. According to Garth, Bigelow's response was, "Oh, you're not telling me the truth." The conversation ended after that.

Even though NIDS was over, Bigelow wasn't done with Skinwalker Ranch yet. Kelleher and Knapp's book found its way into the hands of James Lacatski, an official with the US Defense Intelligence Agency. He contacted Bigelow, visited the ranch in 2007, and apparently experienced some kind of paranormal event. According to a 2021 *New Yorker* article, a figure appeared in the air that "went from pretzel-shaped to Möbius-strip-shaped." Bigelow then introduced Lacatski to his friend Senator Harry Reid of Nevada. Reid was interested in UFOs himself. Inspired by the meeting and the tales from the ranch, Reid then rallied Senator Daniel Inouye of Hawaii and Senator Ted Stevens of Alaska (the latter of whom had experienced a UFO event as a pilot in World War II), and the three conspired to insert a budget line of $22 million into the 2008 Department of Defense budget to investigate what the government would eventually call unidentified aerial phenomena (or UAPs) in an attempt to shed the baggage dangling from the UFO acronym. They called the initiative the Advanced Aerospace Weapon System Applications Program, and the recipient of that budget was a subsidiary of Bigelow Aerospace.

That meant Skinwalker Ranch stayed under the telescope, along with a few other paranormal hotspots. However, two years later, the program ended, having only yielded a few hundred pages of elementary documentation that did nothing to further the knowledge of UAPs, UFOs, or budgetary pork.

Bigelow's direct interest in Skinwalker Ranch also, eventually, ended. In 2016, he sold it to another billionaire for $4 million. The buyer at first stayed anonymous, but by 2020 had stepped out into the tractor beam light, revealing himself to be almost a carbon copy of Bigelow. His name was Brandon Fugal. Like Bigelow, Fugal made his fortune in commercial real estate, in his case transforming the skylines of his home state of Utah. Also, like Bigelow, Fugal liked to fund fringe science, including projects looking into the feasibility of antigravity power and the resurrection of the mammoth from extinction. Where Fugal differed was his love of toys, including movie props, exotic cars, and rare books, all of which he collected. Also, unlike the secretive Bigelow, Fugal seemed to love the spotlight and was adept at giving interviews.

After all, Fugal had a TV show about the ranch to promote. On March 31, 2020, the History Channel debuted *The Secret of Skinwalker Ranch*. In it, a team of specialists set up a command center and a network of sensors across the ranch in an attempt to finally solve the strange shenanigans supposedly afflicting the place. And all of it is led and funded by Fugal, who either video calls in for various episodes or dramatically arrives in his black helicopter on the helipad he had installed so that he could quickly make the commute from his office in Salt Lake City.

According to Fugal, though, he had hired a team, installed the cutting-edge monitoring equipment, and started formally investigating the ranch before the TV show was ever pitched. In interviews, Fugal always speaks in grand terms about his mission with the property. He told *Salt Lake* magazine in 2022,

"If we can approach the ranch as a sort of living laboratory for verifying that we are not alone in the universe, whether that means we are interacting with extraterrestrials, interdimensional phenomena or spiritual entities, it is all extremely compelling."

The catchphrase that appears the most often in his interviews about the ranch, though, is, "I believe it is the greatest science project of our time."

Fugal also claims not to favor any particular theory about the phenomena afflicting the ranch. He seems as though he'd be just as happy to prove the existence of extraterrestrials or angels (the latter perhaps due to his Mormon upbringing). He also claims to have never experienced any paranormal events until six months into his ownership of Skinwalker.

The History Channel show has so far aired seventy-two episodes across six seasons full of UAPs, strange illnesses, sensor anomalies, and cattle deaths. And while the show has raised the profile of the ranch and given unprecedented (if scripted) access to the property, Kelleher and Knapp's conclusion from twenty years earlier still holds true: There seems to be "difficulty obtaining evidence consistent with scientific publication."

Today, Skinwalker Ranch, far from being one of the most mysterious spots on the planet, is one of the most recorded, monitored, and analyzed paranormal sites ever. And still *The Secret of Skinwalker Ranch*, with all its funding and resources, yields only about as much evidence as the average ghost hunter show, which is to say, almost none. Nevertheless, the dogged determination, resources, and connections of people like Bigelow and Reid and Fugal have at least self-fulfilled a prophecy: There's never been a ranch like this one.

NEVADA TRIANGLE

FLY THE FIENDISH SKIES

LOCATION: Southern Nevada and Central California, USA	**TRIANGLE POINTS:** Fresno, Reno, Las Vegas
SIZE: 25,000 square miles	**INFAMOUS FOR:** Plane disappearances and crashes

Steve Fosset was one of the most accomplished sky jockeys in history. In 2002, he became the first person to circumnavigate the world by hot-air balloon. In 2005, he was the first to circumnavigate the world solo in an aircraft without stopping or refueling. In 2006, he took a glider to an altitude of 50,671 feet; another world record. According to the San Diego Air and Space Museum, Fosset set 116 records in his life, 91 of which were in aviation (he also set records in land and sea travel). The man could fly. But in September 2007, three months after being inducted into the National Aviation Hall of Fame, the sixty-three-year-old flew his single-engine Super Decathlon light aircraft into the Nevada Triangle—and never returned. He became one more victim of that mysterious stretch of mountains and desert that has claimed some 2,000 aircraft in the last half century.

The Nevada Triangle is mostly in California but includes a slice of the southwestern edge of Nevada as well. It extends from Fresno north to Reno and then east to Las Vegas, encompassing a whopping 25,000 square miles that includes parts of

Death Valley, the Sierra Nevada mountain range, and Yosemite, Kings Canyon, and Sequoia National Parks. It disappears three to four planes a month, if that 2,000 number is to be believed—and there certainly is some disagreement about that. The number is bandied about every time the Triangle is mentioned, but the source is unknown. Regardless of its accuracy, there have definitely been a lot of crashes and disappearances in the Nevada Triangle over the decades.

During the month-long, $700,000 search for Fosset in autumn of 2007, the rescue teams found the wreckage of eight other crashes which weren't previously known—and none of which were Fosset's. His fate wasn't discovered until more than a year after his disappearance when hikers stumbled across his ID cards. This led investigators to the wreck of his plane on the slopes of the Ritter Range in California's Sierra Nevada, as well as a few bones, which DNA tests determined were his. The National Transportation Safety Board found no mechanical issues with the aircraft which could have led to the crash.

Another infamous set of crashes in the region involved two B-24 bombers. In 1943, one took off from a military airstrip in Fresno with a crew of six for a night training mission. It never returned to base. The next day, the Air Force sent eight—or possibly nine—more bombers to search for the missing plane. They didn't find the AWOL bomber, but en route, one of the search and rescue planes disappeared as well. However, two of the crew of eight from that second missing bomber made it back to civilization safely.

According to the surviving crew, the plane had developed engine troubles, and the captain ordered everyone to abandon the craft. Only the two of them did, for whatever reason. But even with survivor testimony, nobody could find the second missing bomber, either. Finally, twelve years later, in 1955, the aircraft was discovered at the bottom of Lake Huntingdon when the lake was drained to repair a dam. The reason for the crash is still unknown. Some believe that the captain mistook the lake for a snow-covered clearing and tried to land on it, although the two survivors claimed that the lake wasn't frozen or snow covered when they passed over it.

As for the original missing bomber, it wouldn't be discovered for nearly two decades. The copilot of that bomber was Second Lieutenant Robert M. Hester, and his father Clinton Hester would spend the rest of his life looking for the wreckage of his son's plane—seventeen years, to be precise, until his death in 1959. A year later, two geologists discovered the wreck in another lake, this one isolated and unnamed. A retrieval effort was mounted, but only some of the crew's remains could be brought back. The difficulties of the environment halted any salvage or investigation of the aircraft. Today, that lake is named Hester Lake, and it still holds the bomber and all its secrets at its bottom.

The Nevada Triangle hadn't had its fill of young air force pilots yet. In 1957, US Air Force Lieutenant David Steeves took off in a Lockheed T-33A trainer jet from Hamilton Air Force Base outside of San Francisco. The twenty-three-year-old pilot's destination was Craig Air Force Base near Selma, Alabama. The jet never made it. And, of course, that fateful route took him through the Nevada Triangle.

But then, almost two months later and after being declared dead, Steeves strolled out of the Sierra Nevadas—well, not really strolled. He was bedraggled and thin and on the back of a horse led by a guide. According to Steeves, something blew up in the jet during his flight over Kings Canyon in the mountains, and, after a brief blackout, he ejected from the plane.

When he landed, he injured both ankles and then crawled for fifteen days over twenty miles of rugged, snow-covered terrain following the King's River, his only warmth the parachute that he had kept on him after his jump. He found a park ranger's cabin stocked with some canned food and fishing gear, and that—plus a deer that he shot with his service pistol—kept him alive until he was found by the guide.

Some people didn't believe the story. It was, after all, an extraordinary one. The nation was a decade into the Cold War, and some thought he might have sold the plane to the Russians, or that the whole story was an attention-seeking hoax. It didn't help that Steeves was unable to lead investigators and journalists to the site of any wreckage. He would die eight years later in yet another crash, this one in an experimental plane of his own design over Idaho.

In the late 1970s, a Boy Scout troop found an airplane canopy in Kings Canyon with a serial number that matched Steeves's jet. The rest of the jet was never found, but it was enough to substantiate Steeves's unbelievable tale of survival in the Nevada Triangle. But we still don't know why the plane crashed. Of course, there are a million reasons why a plane might crash, all of them involving gravity, but experts seem to have a good explanation of why it occurs so often in the Nevada Triangle. It's called the mountain wave.

The Sierra Nevada range is pretty tall, with peaks that range at the high end between eleven thousand and fifteen thousand feet. It's also parallel to a jet stream. That means air gets pushed by that strong wind over those towering peaks with a force that creates massive updrafts on one side and equally massive downdrafts on the other. These powerful drafts, or mountain waves, can tear planes from the sky and throw them to the ground as inevitably as a boat caught in a waterfall. Professor

Kelly Redmond, a climatologist with the Desert Research Institute in Reno, told KNPR's *State of Nevada* radio program in 2015, "It's quite easy for a small plane to get caught in the down draft on the downwind side and not have the power or just the capability to get out of the way of that."

For instance, if one of those jet stream–propelled drafts is rushing down a mountainside at 400 miles per hour, and a small plane's speed maxes out at 300 miles per hour, that plane is doomed if it is caught in the draft, no matter the skill of the pilot or the condition of the plane. This is exactly what is thought to have happened to Steve Fosset: He got caught in a mountain wave that no pilot, no matter how record-breaking, could have outmaneuvered.

As to the disappearances of the wrecks, the unending, rugged mountainous landscape can easily swallow a small plane whole. A 2008 article in *Smithsonian* magazine detailing the search for Steve Fosset and his tiny craft put it in this context:

"In this terrain, even a Boeing 747 could disappear."

However, all that said, it's not only small craft getting in trouble and disappearing. See those two aforementioned bombers, for example. And it's doesn't just happen to planes—it's also people on the ground who should beware the Nevada Triangle.

David Paulides, a former police officer and author of a series of books and documentaries called Missing 4-1-1, has dedicated his life to cataloguing unsolved missing persons reports. In his work, he has documented more than a thousand disappearances that stick out to him as strange or seemingly inexplicable and which are located in clusters throughout US national parks and forests. In 2019, he told 8 News Now in Las Vegas, "The largest cluster zone we've ever established is in that Nevada Triangle, and there are two other clusters that are also in that Triangle." However, like those 2,000 supposed plane crashes, some doubt his findings. Writer Kyle Polish analyzed Paulides's work for a 2017 article in the *Skeptical Inquirer* and concluded, "I've exhausted my exploration for anything genuinely unusual. After careful review, to me, not a single case stands out nor do the frequencies involved seem outside of expectations." As to any guesses about the fates of those missing people who vanished into the Nevada Triangle, Paulides himself says, "I don't think you could say it's just one thing."

Other people do say it's just one thing: Aliens. Located outside the eastern edge of the Nevada Triangle, and sharing some airspace with it, is the notoriously secretive Air Force base known as Area 51, a place whose borders are rife with ominous *Restricted Area* signs and whose skies are full of strange moving lights. Many are convinced that the government uses the facility to experiment with alien technology—more specifically, the alien technology recovered from a 1947 wreckage site in Roswell, New Mexico. This wreckage was officially declared the remains of a "weather ballon" by the US government, but the events of the crash sparked an alien fever which lasts to this day. Area 51 has become so synonymous with aliens from outer space that the nearby State Route 375 was officially named the Extraterrestrial Highway by legislators in 1996. (If you ever find yourself driving it, make sure you stop at the Little A'Le'Inn for a bite and a bed.)

These days, we know a lot more about Area 51 than we used to, but the US government only acknowledged its existence in 2013 in a document released by the CIA (if you can believe them). The official name of Area 51 is the Nevada Test and Training Range, and it's also referred to as Groom Lake—due to its location in a dry lake bed—and Paradise Ranch, which was a marketing tactic to convince people to work at a base in the middle of the desert.

The truth that's out there, though, is that, according to the CIA's website (again, if you can believe it), the base is used to test experimental *terrestrial* aircraft, including the U-2, A-12 Oxcart, Bird of Prey, F-117A Nighthawk, and Tacit Blue, all of which are stealth and reconnaissance craft. In fact, the website states that the U-2 and A-12 Oxcart craft "accounted for more than one-half of all UFO reports during the late 1950s and 1960s."

Still, the connection between disappearing planes in the Triangle and the rumors of alien technology at a base nearby is irresistible to make. But whether it's powerful mountain waves or extraterrestrial tractor beams, explanations are of little comfort in an area so strewn with human bones and plane wreckage.

MAPIMÍ ZONE OF SILENCE

COSMIC CHARYBDIS

LOCATION: Northern Mexico **SIZE:** Unknown **NOTEWORTHY MOMENT:** 1970 missile crash	**INFAMOUS FOR:** Device malfunctions, mutated wildlife, meteor strikes, blond aliens, underground civilizations

Something went wrong with the missile. It wasn't the launch, though. Athena missile 122 had taken off from the US military's Utah Launch Complex in Green River, Utah, as planned. All four stages fired in the correct sequence. But at some point, its course went awry. It wasn't on target, not at all headed for the White Sands Missile Range in New Mexico, where the military intended it to impact harmlessly as part of a test run. Instead, the fifty-foot-tall, sixteen-thousand-pound projectile overshot the intended destination by four hundred miles, crossing the border into Mexico and disappearing, pulled from the sky somewhere over the desert near the state of Durango, yet another victim of the infamous Zona del Silencio.

It's not entirely flippant to say that the most terrifying place on the planet a modern person can find themselves is a cell phone dead spot.

Cut off from everyone in the world. No internet full of vital and not-so-vital information at your fingertips. No GPS to navigate with. No games to alleviate boredom. No DoorDash (okay, that was flippant). But there is one spot in northwest Mexico that doesn't just drop your calls or interfere with your service—it drops missiles and meteorites out of the sky; interferes with radars and compasses; mutates the flora and fauna; and bears the uncomfortable attention of blond beings from beyond. In the Mapimí Zone of Silence, no one can hear you scream.

The Zone of Silence has no official dimensions or borders but lies somewhere in northern Mexico at the convergence of the states of Durango, Coahuila, and Chihuahua. It's part of the Mapimí Biosphere Reserve, thirteen hundred square miles of harsh but varied desert and unique wildlife distinct enough for it to be awarded a UNESCO designation. It's home to more than four hundred plant species and some two hundred and fifty animal species—two hundred of which are birds—including endangered species such as the puma, the Mexican fringe-toed lizard, and the Bolson tortoise, North America's largest land reptile. The reserve is also notable for its marine fossils and large salt deposits from its time millions of years ago at the bottom of the Sea of Thetys. And, if you believe the stories of the zoneros—people who say the area has strange properties—it is a magnet for all things cosmic.

According to Santiago Garcia, a local zonero who wrote two books on the Zone in the 1970s and 1980s, people have known that there was something different about the region since the mid-nineteenth century when "hot pebbles" would regularly rain from the sky. Certainly, the area in and around the Zone has seen its share of meteorite activity over the past century, including the famous Allende meteorite, often called the "most studied meteorite in history." Allende appeared in the atmosphere on February 8, 1969, as a massive ball of fire that was witnessed over Mexico, Texas, and New Mexico before the more than two tons of space rock crashed into the desert about a hundred miles from the general area of the Zone.

The first recorded instance of the Zone impeding communications seems to date to 1930, when a famous civilian pilot named Francisco Sarabia reported that his instruments ceased working and his radio died while flying above the area. It wouldn't get its ominous moniker for decades, though, not until 1966, when the national oil company Pemex was exploring the area for drilling opportunities. The leader of the effort, Augusto Harry de la Peña, is supposed to have christened it la Zona del Silencio after his radio kept failing. Hardly Bermuda Triangle levels of intrigue, to be sure, but sometimes a place needs time to warm up.

However, on July 11, 1970, when the errant Athena missile bit desert sand, the Zone of Silence rose to international prominence. The accident became global news and nearly escalated into an international incident between Mexico and the US (especially since three years earlier, another US missile had also overshot its target and hit Mexico). Athena was a scaled down version of a much larger and more dangerous intercontinental ballistic projectile, but it was still a giant bullet with radioactive material in its nose cone, which the Mexican government didn't take kindly to. It was carrying two cannisters of the radioactive isotope cobalt 57 to measure how protective the ablative material covering the nose cone was during reentry into the atmosphere.

It took almost two months to finally determine the crash site, and, fortunately, it was discovered in an uninhabited stretch of desert. The subsequent recovery and cleanup effort led by the US military was a sizeable affair and was dubbed Operation Sand Patch. A camp was set up, complete with an aircraft landing strip, and the teams lived in railroad cars in the nearby tiny village of Carrillo. To avoid any more unwanted attention, all US military insignia were removed from the rail cars and equipment. The soil contaminated by the pellets of cobalt 57 was dug up and either buried in trenches or shoveled into one of sixty drums slated for removal by train car. The project took about two weeks. After that, the military removed all traces of the camp as if no crash or cleanup had ever happened.

As to the cause of the missile's malfunction, it was never determined. The third and fourth stages of the rocket were never found, so important evidence couldn't be accessed. According to an official account on the website of the White Sands Missile Range, "instrumentation data of Mission 122 did not provide conclusive evidence of the failure mode."

Still, despite the semiclandestine nature and relative speed of the cleanup, that level of attention on an otherwise undifferentiated patch of sand (it wouldn't be named a UNESCO site until seven years later in 1977) was difficult for some of the locals in surrounding towns to ignore. Soon after, the more extraordinary claims about the region began to surface, including Garcia Santiago's first book, *The Enigmatic Zone of Silence,* which debuted in 1976. People started noticing balls of fire that fell and rose and rolled up the mountains. Wildlife seemed to sprout irregular features: Bolson tortoises appeared with triangular markings on their shells and green cactuses turned purple. Many of the animals and plants seemed larger than their counterparts outside the Zone.

Pseudoscientific theories were proffered, one of which was that all the strangeness in the Zone was caused by the meteorites, which seeded the land with magnetic rocks that blocked device signals and altered the DNA of animals. Another was that perhaps the meteorites were a symptom of the Zone and not a cause, sucked there as irrevocably as any wayward missile like the Zone was a Charybdis that pulled things from the sky instead of ships from the surface of the ocean. Rumors sprouted about the only building in the entire desert, a solitary and lonely research station known as Laboratorio del Desierto. It was said to be a secret government headquarters performing tests on the region and observing the sky, regardless of its publicly stated purpose to study the rich natural flora and fauna of the Mapimí Biosphere Reserve.

And then there were the blond extraterrestrials. Geraldo Rivera, a state bureaucrat and zonero who investigates UFO phenomena in the area, told Atlas Obscura in 2016, "There are lots of stories of aliens and unidentified flying objects in the Zone. People often get lost in the Zone. When this happens, sometimes tall blond beings appear out of nowhere."

Thought to be drawn by the same mysterious forces that draw the meteorites, these beings, sometimes called Nordics, stand out in a region where the populace is shorter and darker. But these Nordics aren't the terrifying midnight abductors of modern alien lore—they seem to be peaceful entities who speak perfect Spanish, are vague about where they hail from, and often just want some water. Some zoneros take these tales of fair foreigners even further. According to a group called El Centro de Investigacion de Antropologia Cosmica de la Escuela Filosofica Lu Men (the Research Center of Cosmic Anthropology from the Philosophical School of the Light), these stories support the existence of a race of tall, yellow Maya who live beneath the desert sands of the Zone of Silence, disguising their pyramids as naturally occurring hills. They call this civilization of underground Maya Magneto Tzen or Tierra del Magnetismo.

So the story of the Mapimí Zone of Silence spans from interrupted radio signals and small meteorites to extraterrestrial beings and ancient subterranean civilizations. At least, that's one interpretation. There is another, much less fun one, summed up succinctly by Andrea Kaus in her 1992 doctoral dissertation for the anthropology department of the University of California, Riverside. The title of her dissertation is *Common Ground: Ranchers and Researchers in the Mapimí Biosphere Reserve*, and in it, she says of this vast, mindboggling story of the Zone of Silence: "It was deliberately invented to generate tourism and sold to the world via the mass media."

Apparently, the 1970 crash of the Athena missile was the true inciting incident for the Zone's strange renown. According to Kaus and other sources, locals were hired to guard the missile impact site from nosy neighbors and vandals. One such guard, a man by the name of Jaime González, got the idea that if the US was so interested in this site that it would go to all this trouble of building infrastructure and digging up the soil, that interest could be leveraged into a lucrative tourist industry. He got together with a small group of other locals and basically invented the Zone of Silence. Excited zoneros took care of the rest, retroactively offering stories from the region's past as evidence and expanding on its present with new myths and legends.

Kraus's dissertation refutes all the claims of the paranormal uniqueness of the region. For instance, devices do, in fact, work in the Zone of Silence. Sure, sometimes there's spotty reception, but that's true everywhere in the world. Also, those strange tortoise shell markings and cacti colors? Naturally occurring desert phenomena, as are the bouncing balls of fire (ball lightning).

In Episode 682 of the Skeptoid podcast, Brian Dunning digs into the space debris angle. He checked the Meteorological Bulletin Database of the International Society for Meteoritics and Planetary Science and found that the region wasn't any more a bull's-eye for shooting stars than the average place. As for the hot pebbles, Kraus explains in her dissertation that many deserts have deposits of "pebbles with desert varnish, an iron manganese coating common in desert environments." Their strange appearance could explain the stories of heated pebbles falling from the sky.

But those wet blankets don't dissuade the zoneros, Today, you can book a tour of the Zone or stay at a UFO-themed ranch in the area. Zoneros hold overnight meetings in the desert to try to commune with extraterrestrials and gather some of the more interesting rocks and fossils. Visitors can even check out the small marble marker dedicated to Jaime González that overlooks the Zone. The place has turned into a crucial part of the local economy, one which annoys or amuses locals who sometimes keep a stash of sodas and candy on hand to sell to the zoneros. Kraus recounts the story of one rancher who, "upon being asked where la Zona could be found . . . told a carload of people that they needed to keep following the road until they saw Martians jump from one side of the road to another. The amazing part, he said later, was that they thanked him."

Still, even if there aren't anomalies interrupting communications and space debris falling from the sky and strange creatures and secretive underground civilizations and clandestine government activities and aliens from the stars, the Mapimí Zone of Silence is still a desert, with all the dangers that implies. Be careful out there.

LOP NUR

THE SEA OF DEATH

LOCATION: Xinjiang, China **SIZE:** 8,000 square miles **NOTABLE VISITOR:** Marco Polo	**INFAMOUS FOR:** Evil spirits, radioactive soil, disappearances, mummy graveyards, abandoned cities

The desert that is Lop Nur has vanished famous explorers, unleashed evil spirits on vulnerable travelers, rained radioactive soil onto local populations, swallowed entire cities, and buried cemeteries full of the mummified dead beneath its sands. No wonder it's called the Sea of Death. Although the real death is its own: The Lop Nur desert was once a lake—as recently as fifty years ago, in fact—if a strange one.

Lop Nur (sometimes spelled Lop Nor) is located on the eastern edge of the Tarim Basin in the Xinjiang Autonomous Region of northwestern China, the most barren part of the country. Basically, in the middle of nowheresville. Lop Nur is one of the most arid places on Earth, with a rainfall of less than 20 millimeters annually and an evaporation rate of more than 3,000 millimeters. If negative water were a thing, Lop Nur would have it.

However, once upon a time, Lop Nur was a large salt lake at the terminus of the Tarim River, China's longest inland river, which sluices through the parched sand of the infamous Gobi Desert. Thousands of years ago, the oasis surrounding Lop

Nur was the home of the ancient Kingdom of Loulan and other settlements on the fabled Silk Road, the network of cities throughout Asia, Europe, and North Africa that, from the second century BC to the fifteenth century AD, facilitated global trade from East Asia to Europe.

But even in its heyday, the desert surrounding Lop Nur had an eerie reputation. Venetian explorer Marco Polo stopped in the area before his famous trek across the Gobi Desert in the thirteenth century. In the book based on his explorations, *The Travels of Marco Polo*, he discussed the evil spirts that roamed the desert there:

> "It is asserted as a well-known fact that this desert is the abode of many evil spirits which amuse travelers to their destruction with most extraordinary illusions."

He explained that travelers who found themselves isolated from their caravan could hear their names being called by a familiar voice. When they followed the address, thinking it to be one of their traveling companions, they ended up lost in the desert, dying of thirst or hunger. Similarly, during the night travelers would sometimes hear a "large cavalcade" and, thinking it to be the sounds of their group, would follow the noise to certain death. The spirits could also take on the form of people they knew and lead them astray, or the form of a group of armed men, from which the lonely traveler would flee. Sometimes the spectral noises sounded like musical instruments or the clashing of swords. But the end result of all the ghostly phenomena was the same: Travelers found themselves lost deep in the deadly desert, awaiting a slow and painful death.

But then something perhaps even stranger happened to the Lop Nur lake . . . it moved. The Tarim River would change its course multiple times over the centuries, skittering across the desert like mercury on marble, changing the location of the lake that was Lop Nur. Once enough explorers couldn't find the lake after retracing their routes, they started comparing old maps of the region to see what was up. They discovered that Lop Nur wasn't always in the same place. As a result, it was awarded the nickname "Wandering Lake."

And the wanderings of that lake eventually became its death throes. By 1931, the lake covered only about 730 square miles, down from its estimated peak of up to 2,000 square miles back in 220 AD, when it was the largest lake in China. Finally, after some tens of millennia as a lake, Lop Nur dried up in 1972, thanks to declining environmental conditions and modern infrastructure diverting its water toward population centers. Lop Nur officially joined the surrounding desert, leaving behind almost 8,000 square miles of salt crust, with the accumulated desiccated salts as deep as three feet in some places.

Today, Lop Nur the desert supports no permanent human inhabitants, and the few native species that live there have had to get creative. It's the home of a unique species of Bactrian camel that can live off the seasonal pools of salt water that accumulate in the area—salt water that has a higher content of salt than even seawater. According to the Wild Camel Protection Foundation, there are over 600 members of this species in Lop Nur, making them rarer even than their fellow endangered country-beast, the giant panda.

While there are now far fewer travelers to Lop Nur for the evil spirits to lead astray, the place is still eerie—perhaps because below the surface of the sands dwells an entire population of mummies. In the early 2000s, archeologists dug into the ancient ruins of the Kingdom of Loulan to crack open some of the 330 tombs of the massive necropolis that would come to be known as Xiaohe Cemetery. There, they discovered hundreds of mummies, the largest collection of them in any place on Earth. These four-thousand-year-old corpses were laid in boat-shaped coffins and wrapped in airtight bags made of ox hide, perfectly preserved through artificial means, with a boost from the extremely dry climate. Sometimes called the Tarim Mummies (after the Tarim Basin), these preserved remains were dressed in tall felt hats and wool clothes, their faces covered in pale paste and their necks and chests adorned with what would turn out to be chunks of the oldest cheese ever discovered. These mummies are so well preserved that even their delicate hair and eyelashes remain on their heads. According to a 2006 article in the *China Daily*, when archeologist Idelisi Abuduresule, head of the Xinjiang Cultural Relics and Archaeology Institute, opened the ox bag of a young girl, she exclaimed, "She's so beautiful!" That girl mummy would be dubbed "Princess of Xiaohe" (or, Little River Princess). Are these mummies the sources of the evil spirits that would lure travelers into the desert in the time of the Silk Road? Some say yes.

Moving from ancient times to modern terrors, on October 16, 1964, Lop Nur earned the dubious distinction of being the site of China's first detonation of an atomic bomb. The Chinese military chose Lop Nur because of its remote location, providing some semblance of safety and privacy from the prying eyes of the world. The detonation made them the fifth country in the world with nuclear capabilities, after the United States, the Soviet Union, the United Kingdom, and France. Three years later, they would also detonate a hydrogen bomb on the site. The government would continue active nuclear testing there into at least the 1990s.

However, Lop Nur was apparently not remote enough. In 2009, a Japanese physicist named Jun Takada published the results of a computer simulation he ran based on China's nuclear testing over the decades. According to those results, as many as 190,000 people in China may have died directly due to radiation exposure from those tests. And he's not the only one concerned about the effects of China's nuclear program.

In 2009, *Scientific American* interviewed Enver Tohti, a surgeon who grew up in the city of Hami, a few hundred miles northeast of Lop Nur. He recounted a summer during his elementary school days in 2003 when it rained dirt. He said, "There were three days that earth fell from the sky, without wind or any sort of storm. The sky was deadly silent—no sun, no moon." He received no satisfactory explanation from the adults in his life. His teacher told him that it was just a storm from the planet Saturn, the name for which in Chinese means "soil planet" or "earth star." It wasn't until Tohti was an adult himself that he learned that "dirt" was in fact radioactive fallout from nuclear bomb detonations at Lop Nur. These days, Tohti is a medical doctor researching the effects of that radiation on the lives of his fellow Chinese citizens. He believes that cancer rates in communities closest to the bomb tests are 30 to 35 percent higher than the national average.

Meanwhile, as Marco Polo warned about seven hundred years ago, people keep disappearing in Lop Nur. Biochemist Peng Jiamu was one of China's most famous explorers and scientists. On July 17, 1980, at the age of fifty-five and a year after he was promoted to vice president of the Chinese Academy of Sciences, Jiamu disappeared in Lop Nur, never to be seen again—alive or dead. Although he had led multiple expeditions into the Xinjiang province over the past two decades, this one was particularly troublesome, with the caravan often getting stuck in dunes and sandstorms buffeting them daily. The heat was also intolerable, reaching as high as 150 degrees Fahrenheit. Two weeks into the expedition, the team was running out of water, so Jiamu struck out on his own in a desperate attempt to find a spring. He didn't, and when he didn't return, a massive search was launched by the Chinese government to find their hero. According to a 1981 UPI article, they eventually found his footprints, ration coupons, and markings in the sand that seemed to suggest he had sat down six miles northeast of where his camp had been. The government concluded that, "Peng lost his way, then sat puzzling on the ground and was eventually buried by strong winds blowing sand." After an unproven rumor that Jiamu's disappearance was a front for his defection to the United States, he was given up for dead, and a small, lonely stone marker was set into the sand of Lop Nur as a memorial.

In June 1996, another Chinese explorer, Yu Chunshun, died in Lop Nur at the age of forty-eight. He was an experienced survivalist, having tackled the Qinghai-Tibet Plateau, the Takalamakan Desert, and Xinjiang itself before. This time, he took off from his camp alone on June 11 with a two-day supply of food and water to explore the ruins of Loulan, despite gale force winds and 158-degree-Fahrenheit sand. He was reported missing by his colleagues when they lost contact with him on June 14, and a helicopter found him after a seventy-hour search, his dead body blackened and blistered.

Between 2005 and 2007, human remains were discovered on six different occasions in the sands and salt of Lop Nur, not all of whose identity could be conclusively determined. In 2016, a group of stone collectors found the skeleton of a man who had with him a flashlight, a newspaper clipping dated

September 13, 1960, and some letters. The authorities determined it to be the remains of a veteran and farmer named Li Zhonghua from Bazhong City, who disappeared in the 1960s. When they told his wife and two daughters, they were all surprised at the news. According to a 2016 article in the *Daily Mail*, one of his daughters explained, "We never thought that he were dead, we guess he was just not willing to come back." In 2023, four people driving through Lop Nur on holiday got lost and died. Three were found in the vehicle and a fourth in the sand not too far away about a day after they disappeared.

So many victims of the evil spirits of Lop Nur. And there seems to be no relief in sight for the desolate region. According to most scientists, the Lop Nur lake will never return. But the desert still makes the news every once in a while—because of the people who venture out and die there, but also because the government still uses parts of it for military purposes, such as the test missions for its reusable space plane in recent years. Meanwhile, Lop Nur remains, like so many of the bodies hidden in its salt-encrusted sands, a mummified version of its past: a land of evil spirts, of radioactive fallout, of extreme conditions, and death.

SUPERSTITION MOUNTAINS

LOST GOLD, LOST SOULS

LOCATION: Tonto National Forest, Arizona, USA **SIZE:** 250 square miles **HIGHEST POINT:** Mound Mountain (6,266 feet)	**INFAMOUS FOR:** Disappearances, deaths, cursed mine

In his 1973 book *Cactus Country*, author and outdoorsman Edward Abbey wrote, regarding the Superstition Mountains of Arizona: "Nobody gets in or out of the Superstition Mountains completely untouched. Even the most hexproof infidels cannot escape the power of such a magic name, the glamor of that sinister reputation, the occult touch of all those bored and restless haunts, the spirits of the place." And he's right. The name should be your first clue to be wary: Superstition Mountains. Super-suspicious.

The Superstitions rip a scar into the sky above the Sonoran Desert forty miles east of Phoenix. The range reaches heights of more than six thousand feet, including the five-thousand-foot summit that shares a name with the range: Superstition Mountain. The surrounding Superstition Wilderness area comprises about 160,000 acres inside of Tonto National Park. However, even though they're only a day's jaunt away from Phoenix, those desert mountains are exceedingly dangerous. In the summer, temperatures rise above 120 degrees

Fahrenheit, and in winter, they drop below freezing. There are sheer drops and rattlesnakes and it's easy to run out of water. You know, all the usual challenges of the desert. The old and oft-repeated saw about the Sonoran is that everything there either "sticks, stings, bites, or eats meat." According to John Annerino's 2018 book, *Exploring the Superstitions*, at least 654 people have lost their lives or disappeared in those mountains over the centuries.

The Superstitions have been inhabited by a few indigenous nations over the years. The earliest were probably the Hohokam, whose hieroglyphs and ruins still adorn the mountain flanks today. Their descendants, the Akimel O'odham (also called the Pima) called the peaks home, too, as did the Apache.

The Superstitions were so named by Western settlers in the nineteenth century, who were spooked by Apache stories about the mountains looming over their farmland. The Apache believed the mountains to be the home of thunder gods, due to the strange rumbling sounds that could be heard throughout the range—rumblings that can still be heard today (the result of seismic activity). The Apache also believed that the mountains guarded a hole to the underworld. The Akimel O'odham likewise told tales of strange sounds in the mountains, but also of mysterious deaths and disappearances. The settlers wrapped all those stories into the word *superstition* and jammed it onto those peaks forming the horizon.

Now, as with any exchange between cultures, you can never be sure if something was lost in translation—or if the white settlers were being messed with or even exaggerating the stories themselves. Regardless, all that aboriginal lore was soon overshadowed by a single story: the Lost Dutchman's Gold Mine. Of course, since it's an American legend, it's all about getting rich or dying trying.

The story of the Lost Dutchman's Mine has multiple variations but always starts at the end, in 1891, when a German man from Phoenix named Jacob Waltz gave a deathbed confession concerning the location of a massive mine full of gold. In the mid- to late nineteenth century, West Coast gold rush fever had gripped the nation, and many treasure-hunting hopefuls were scouring the Superstitions, looking to open its veins too. The recipient of that confession was a woman named Julia Thomas, who had befriended Waltz. At some point Waltz had given Julia gold to help fund their struggling bakery, and she had let him live on her property.

Waltz explained that he and his partner Jacob Weiser had found a mother lode in the Superstitions at some point in the 1870s, but that Weiser had died during an encounter with Apaches and Waltz was left alone as the sole owner of this mine full of gold. Another version states that the Apache story was a ruse, and that Waltz himself murdered Weiser to keep the location of the mine a secret.

After Waltz's death, Thomas convinced two local brothers, Rhinehart and Hermann Petrasch, to go on an expedition with her—possibly multiple—to hunt for the mine but they failed. Either Waltz's directions were too vague or it was inaccessible. And with that, Waltz's confession birthed the legend of the Lost Dutchman's Gold Mine (*lost*, *gold*, and *mine* are probably self-explanatory, but *Dutchman* comes from the term Deutsch, meaning German). But Thomas and Petrasch got off easy. Since that time, many have suffered a far worse fate than failure in trying to find the mine: death. They call it the Dutchman's Curse.

Byrd Granger's 1977 *A Motif Index for Lost Mines and Treasures Applied to Redaction of Arizona Legends, and to Lost Mine and Treasure Legends Exterior to Arizona* discusses the Lost Dutchman's

Gold Mine legend in detail. Granger learned from locals that at least one murder per year had occurred in the Superstitions during searches for the mine between 1930 and the publication of his work. He also claimed to personally know people who had been shot at near Weaver's Needle, a rock formation rumored to mark the vicinity of the mine.

The most famous victim of the curse—and the one that brought the mine story national attention—was Adolph Ruth, a veterinarian and treasure hunter from Washington, DC. From 1913 to 1914, his son, Erwin, served as a medical officer for General Venustiano Carranza, the leader of the Mexican Revolutionary army who would go on to become the president of Mexico. During that time, Erwin acquired a parcel of maps and old documents from a grateful officer whose life he saved. He gave them to his father a few years later. Adolph eventually got around to studying the documents and believed that one of them seemed to indicate the location of the Lost Dutchman's Gold Mine. That was enough to infect him with gold fever. In June 1931, at the age of sixty-six, he entered the Superstitions to locate the lost mine. He never returned, and a subsequent search for him came up empty. A few months later, however, his skull was found by a search party organized by Erwin. It bore two holes in it that examiners agreed were the entry and exit wounds of a bullet.

Another search was held, and, six months after his disappearance, they found the rest of Ruth's skeleton. The searchers also located some of his belongings, including a note with directions to a cave that ended with Julius Caesar's famous line, "veni, vidi, vici," (translated from the Latin: "I came, I saw, I conquered"). The theory that Ruth found the mine and was then murdered by a rival treasure hunter seemed to put itself together. Unfortunately, upon following the directions, the searchers found no treasure. Further complicating the story, a bottle was supposedly found in the Salt River with a note that claimed to be from Ruth. It read, "I'm sitting under a tree in a creek with leg broke. I've got to have help quick. Finder of this note please give to Howard Peterson. P.S. Have found the lost Dutchman." Whether the postscript was true or simply a tactic to get people to hurry to his rescue is unknown.

Regardless, whether Ruth found the mine or didn't—and whether he died from his injury and exposure or from murder—he was dead all the same, thus fulfilling the Dutchman's Curse.

And Ruth was just the beginning. An endless parade of treasure hunters who have entered the Superstitions to find the gold mine have been shot, fallen to their deaths, succumbed to the elements, or disappeared without a trace. Here are just a few examples.

In December 1936, Roman O'Hal, a stockbroker from New York, went to search for the lost mine. He died from a fall.

In November 1937, a prospector named Guy "Hematite" Frink was found dead in the mountains of a fatal gunshot wound to his stomach.

James A Cravey, a retired photographer and amateur gold hunter, entered the area in June 1947. His skeleton was found in February 1948—missing its skull. According to a 1948 article in the *Arizona Republic*, Cravey was the twentieth person to die searching for the mine.

In 1955, Charles Massey of Tucson, accompanied by a few friends, entered the mountains to treasure hunt. While in the

Superstitions, he became separated from the main party and was never seen alive again. On February 24, 1955, his skeleton was found. Massey had been shot directly between the eyes.

Jesse Capen, a thirty-five-year-old night-shift bellhop at a hotel in Denver, became so obsessed with the Lost Dutchman's Mine that in the winter of 2009 he traveled to the Superstitions to find it. He never returned. In November 2009, his skeleton was found at the bottom of a cliff on Tortilla Mountain. A can atop the peak hid a note that said, "Jesse Capen was here. Dec. 4, 2009."

The list goes on and on, stretching from past centuries to modern day. David Bremson, operations chief of the Central Arizona Mountain Rescue Association, summed up the situation to the *Arizona Republic* in 2013: "Most of the body recoveries we've done out of the Supes have been Dutch hunters."

And that doesn't even include the treasure hunters whose remains were never found, nor those who were successfully rescued. In 2013, a fifty-one-year-old woman was rescued twice by helicopter in one winter while searching for the mine. The second time she was found unconscious and suffering from hypothermia and dehydration. An author named Barry Stone (the pen name of John Griffith Climenson) claimed in his 1945 book *Thunder God's Gold* that during his search for the mine he escaped from a mysterious sniper who took shots at him.

In more than 130 years of searching, nothing has been found in the "Supes" but the bones of treasure hunters. Was there even a hidden gold mine to begin with? While Waltz is a historical character, some say he didn't find any mother lode—that he had stolen his gold from an already claimed lode called Vulcan Mine and invented an excuse to explain why he had it in his possession. Others say that he did find a gold mine, but shortly after his death, the mine was made public knowledge when a flash flood swept the area, opening up the extremely rich Black Queen and Mammoth mines, from which millions of dollars of gold were extracted in the 1890s.

Others say the Lost Dutchman's Gold Mine was merely the continuation of a previous bit of lore: the legend of the Peralta Mine. As the story goes, in 1848 a Spaniard named Miguel Peralta (whose family had come to the area a century before, when Ferdinand VI awarded them a land grant and tasked them with finding treasure for the crown) went to the mountains with an expedition of four hundred men and apparently found the mother lode to take back to Mexico. However, the expedition was waylaid and almost everyone massacred by the Apaches. The reasons for the attack vary depending on the story and include retribution for the intrusion of the treasure hunters onto sacred land and revenge for one of Miguel's sons attacking an Apache woman. Miguel escaped, and, in 1871, met Waltz and Weiser in Mexico. They apparently helped him out of a deadly situation involving a card game gone bad and, in gratitude, he took them to the mine, shared the gold with them, and then sold them his share to the mine. Another version states that he gave them directions to the mine but didn't accompany them.

Over time, those stories of a hidden treasure trove and all the misfortunates who died looking for it birthed stories of supernatural guardians of the cursed treasure. Evil spirits and cannibals are discussed in whispers over flickering campfires on the peaks. Reports of moving lights and marching shadow armies pop up here and there, as well. And hidden gold mines aren't even the only treasures rumored to be secreted in the Superstitions—there's also the so-called Jesuit Treasure. The Jesuits established some two dozen missions in the Sonoran

Desert between 1687 and 1704. According to the story, when they learned of their coming expulsion by the Spanish Empire, they gathered up all their gold and valuables from those missions and hid them in the Superstitions before fleeing.

Today, you can see evidence of many of these stories in the place names throughout the Superstition Wilderness: Peralta Canyon, Lost Dutchman State Park, Massacre Grounds Trail, Treasure Loop Trail. And then there's the Superstition Mountain Museum in nearby Apache Junction, which contains an exhibit on the Lost Dutchman's Gold Mine, including various maps to the treasure that have been drawn over the years. It's a good place to start for wannabe treasure hunters, and a good place to end if you don't want to end up a decapitated skeleton.

HITTING THE HOTTEST UFO HOTSPOTS

If high weirdness is happening on the ground, you can be reasonably certain it'll be mirrored in the skies. Most of the paranormal flaps (a term used for a series of strange occurrences in the same time and geographic region) recorded have accompanying sightings of UFOs. But where in the United States are the skies the most blinky with weird lights, objects, and strange aerial craft?

Well, that answer depends on the data you use. One major and longstanding source is the National UFO Reporting Center (NUFORC), which was founded in 1974 in the state of Washington by Robert J. Gribble, a Seattle firefighter who, according to the NUFORC website, started one of the first UFO organizations in the country, the Space Observers League. Eventually that became the nonprofit NUFORC, the purpose of which is to "receive, record, and to the greatest degree possible, corroborate and document reports from individuals who have been witness to unusual, possibly UFO-related events." To date, they've processed more than 180,000 reports in their five decades of existence. And that data is public.

In 2024, coauthors Alex Fitzpatrick and Erin Davis took data from both NUFORC and the US Census Bureau to create a UFO hotspot map for Axios.com. They wanted to determine the most visited counties in the US per capita. They found that between 2000 and 2023, the county with the most UFO reports was Lincoln County, New Mexico, at 820.9 per 100,000 residents. Punchline: That's the county Roswell is in. The second most visited county was Arthur County, Nebraska, with 618.6 reports per 100,000 residents.

Pulling back to the state level, the states with the most reported sightings according to NUFORC are:

- ▷ California: 16,801
- ▷ Florida: 8,656
- ▷ Washington: 7,452
- ▷ Texas: 6,511
- ▷ New York: 6,178

These numbers mostly correspond to the most populous states, with Washington being the aberration (it's the thirteenth most populous state). In addition, Texas is more populous than Florida, but the latter has more sightings. On the other end of the spectrum, the state with the fewest sightings is South Dakota, with a mere 403 sightings, followed by Delaware with 423, the fourth and sixth least populous states, respectively.

A 2024 analysis of the NUFORC data by *Newsweek* found that in proportion to their population, Washington and Vermont had the highest number of reports per capita (almost a thousand sightings per million people). The state with the fewest visitations when adjusted for population is Texas, with 215 per million people. The analysis also found that the states around Nevada and the New England states had a high volume of sightings relative to the size of their populations. And both the Axios and the *Newsweek* analyses found that sightings are reported more in the Western states than anywhere else in the country. On the whole, it seems like the most important element for a UFO sighting is, well, a sighter.

As to what those sightings actually are? Who knows. After all, there's a reason that the acronyms UFO and UAP have one particular word in common.

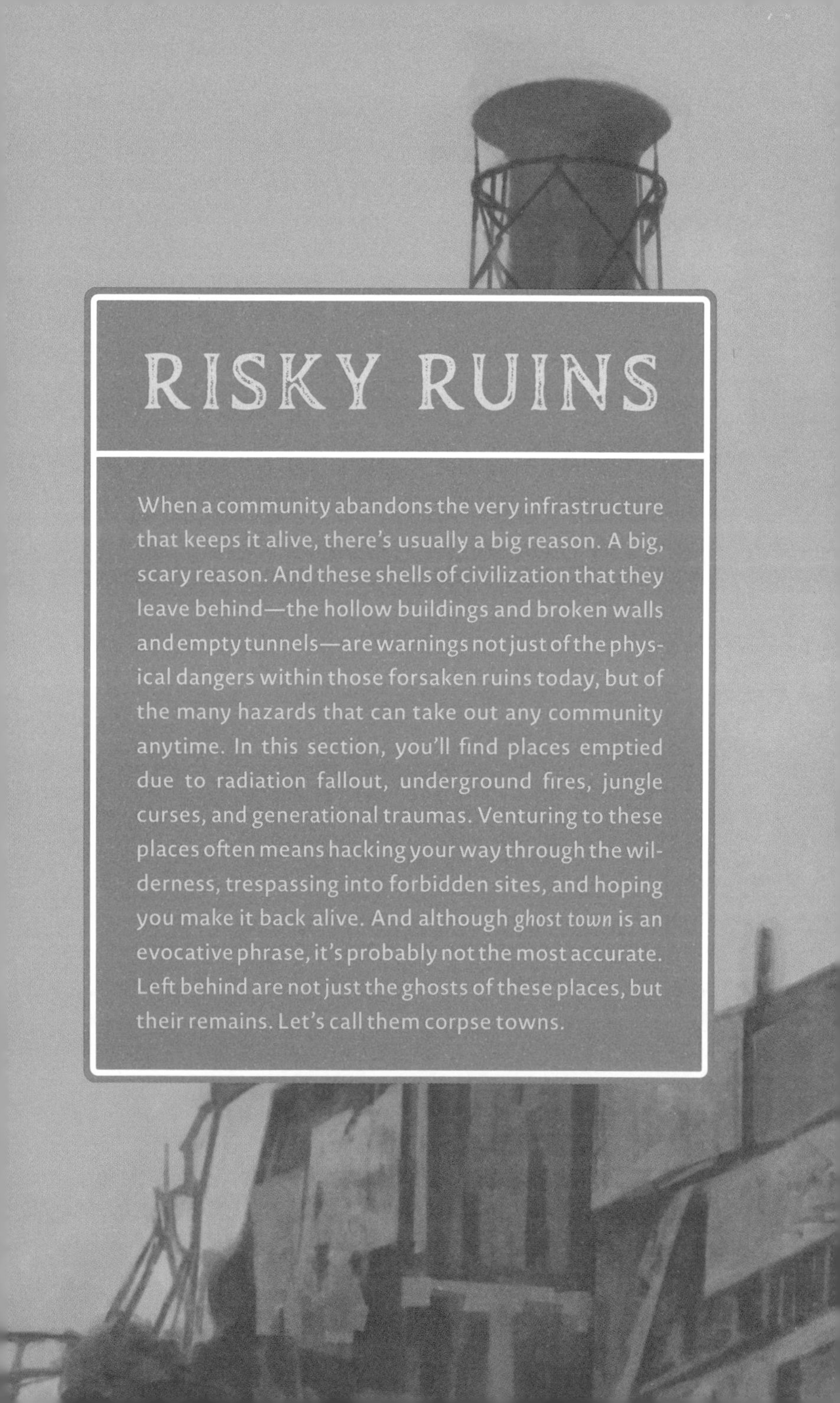

RISKY RUINS

When a community abandons the very infrastructure that keeps it alive, there's usually a big reason. A big, scary reason. And these shells of civilization that they leave behind—the hollow buildings and broken walls and empty tunnels—are warnings not just of the physical dangers within those forsaken ruins today, but of the many hazards that can take out any community anytime. In this section, you'll find places emptied due to radiation fallout, underground fires, jungle curses, and generational traumas. Venturing to these places often means hacking your way through the wilderness, trespassing into forbidden sites, and hoping you make it back alive. And although *ghost town* is an evocative phrase, it's probably not the most accurate. Left behind are not just the ghosts of these places, but their remains. Let's call them corpse towns.

CENTRALIA

A GHOST TOWN . . . ON FIRE

LOCATION: Columbia County, Pennsylvania, USA **YEAR ESTABLISHED:** 1866 **YEAR ENDED:** 2002	**INFAMOUS FOR:** Underground mine fire, sinkholes, toxic gases, eminent domain

When the British torched the White House and the US Capitol in 1814, we rebuilt those grandiose structures. When that clumsy cow burned one-third of Chicago to the ground in 1871, we rebuilt that city. But when the modest hamlet of Centralia, Pennsylvania, was set ablaze in 1962, there was nothing anybody could do to rebuild it—because the fire that ended that town was *underneath* it. You can't build much of anything on top of a fire. And you especially can't build anything on top of a fire that can't be extinguished and still burns to this day. That's right—Centralia is an ever-burning ghost town.

If you think of the shape of Pennsylvania—like I, and, I assume, the Pennsylvania-located company Hershey's do—as a giant chocolate bar with a bite taken out of its eastern border, then Centralia is located eighty miles west of that bite mark. Like many of the towns in that state, its history is black with coal mining—anthracite coal, specifically, as Pennsylvania is known for having the largest deposits of anthracite in the entire world. The state is practically hollow with mines.

Centralia itself got its start in 1832 when a man with the ironic name of Jonathan Faust opened the Bull's Head Tavern, which also became the town's first name, minus the tavern bit. In 1842, the Locust Mountain Cola and Iron Company bought up the land and commenced to mining the twenty-five million tons of coal in the region. Meanwhile, a mining engineer named Alexander Rae moved there and planned out a supporting village that he named Centreville. In 1866, when the town incorporated, the name Centreville was determined, not surprisingly, to be already taken, so they changed it to Centralia, which is a much better name for the ghost town it would eventually become.

For the next hundred years, the town prospered. At its peak in 1890, there were 2,761 residents, and its infrastructure included multiple churches, hotels, saloons, theaters, and general stores. It did have to deal with the Molly Maguires for a while, the Ireland-born secret society that used violence, arson, and murder to fight for mine workers' rights. Three members of the Maguires killed Alexander Rae, the town founder, in 1868. They were convicted and hanged for the crime ten years later.

Then, in 1962, something happened to Centralia that would simultaneously put it on the map and take it off the map: The massive seam of coal beneath the town caught fire.

How the fire began isn't exactly known, but there are a few plausible theories. One is that a previous fire from a mine explosion in 1935 never completely burned out and smoldered slowly through the mines until it reached a larger part of the seam beneath the town and expanded. Another theory is that someone dumped hot ash or coal into the open trash pit southeast of town (Centralia used an old strip mine as a landfill) and it caught the exposed seam on fire. The third major theory is that firefighters or sanitation workers lit the metaphorical fuse during their annual trash burn at that strip-mine-turned-landfill. The latter is the official explanation on the website of the Pennsylvania state government.

However it happened, fire touched coal and, as it does at every backyard barbeque, it conflagrated. Unfortunately, that bit of coal was the tip of the coalberg. The mass of anthracite beneath Centralia is known as the Buck Mountain Coal Bed, and the deposit is so big it's impossible to gauge its exact size with any degree of accuracy. However, the Pennsylvania Department of Environmental Protection estimated that the coal fire had the potential to spread across 3,700 acres. So, yeah, big.

But coal fires aren't rare, and attempts to control or extinguish the fire were quickly implemented. Water, clay, and ash were used to smother it. Trenches were dug and barriers put in place to halt its progress. Excavations of the burning coal were also attempted. But the failure of those methods and the true scale of the danger wasn't fully understood for almost two decades. The fire spread slowly and stealthily underground over the years, during a time when most of the mining activities in the area had already shut down due to the most lucrative coal seams having already been exploited. There were clues, though: Snow seemed to melt more quickly than usual on sidewalks and roadways. Vegetable gardens thrived in ways and seasons that they hadn't before. Houses seemed easier to keep warm, especially the basements. Hot water poured from cold water taps.

In 1979, almost two decades after the coal seam caught fire, a gas station owner named John Coddington (who was also mayor at the time) discovered that his gas tanks seemed strangely hot. He dropped a thermometer into them, and when he pulled it back up, the temperature of the gasoline registered an intense 172 degrees Fahrenheit. Coddington had to shut down his business, although he continued to live on the property. In 1981, the Centralia fire would come for his personal life, too—he passed out due to fumes from the inferno wafting up through his house. He told the United Press International news agency that year, "I was overcome by gas. I fell down on the floor. The family called the ambulance. I was taken to the hospital and given oxygen. The doctors said it was carbon monoxide that put me out."

That same year, twelve-year-old Todd Domboski was playing in his grandmother's backyard when a four-foot-wide sinkhole opened beneath him. He was able to cling to a tree root until he was rescued, but the fall would have deposited him 150 feet deep into a pocket of fire and carbon monoxide gas. He told the *New York Times* soon after the incident, "It was awful scary. I just grabbed some roots and hung there; the smoke was so thick I couldn't see anything."

Now everyone knew that something was wrong with this town—really wrong. Toxic gases from the fire continued to filter up through the ground and into people's homes. Sinkholes expanded. Trees died. Roads swelled and buckled, the asphalt twisted and humped like frozen rapids. Smoke blew across the landscape, and the air smelled of sulfur. One resident identified only as Jack told Cracked.com in 2017, "Every once in a while, you would come across a deer sticking out vertically with steam billowing out. They looked like they were crawling out. The poor deer had fallen into a sinkhole and had either starved to death or suffocated to death from the fumes. My friends would claim to see smoke coming out of its mouth." Meanwhile, the fire kept burning below.

By 1983, it was clear that the fire remediation efforts weren't going to work, despite various government agencies investing

$7 million into the project. It was time for a more drastic tactic. The US government had already helped some 34 families move away from the danger in the previous couple of years, but now Congress allocated $42 million to relocate everybody in Centralia. At this point in time, the town had about 1,100 residents. More than 1,000 people took the buyout and some 500 structures were demolished. By the end of the decade, the population was down to 63 people.

As for those who didn't take the buyout, some didn't want to leave their lifelong and sometimes generational homes. Others thought the amount the government was offering wasn't enough to start anew elsewhere. Some thought that the danger was overblown. After all, in more than twenty years nobody had died nor suffered any permanent ill effects because of the fire. Still others thought it was a conspiracy, that the government and its lobbyists wanted the mineral rights to the land to exploit all the anthracite still in the ground.

Ten years later, in 1992, the state government invoked eminent domain and condemned the entire town. A few years later, as the fire spread, the neighboring and aptly named town of Byrnesville was also evacuated (although another neighboring town with an even more apt name, Ashland, has so far been fine). In 2002, the US Post Office revoked Centralia's zip code. Centralia, Pennsylvania, no longer officially existed—except to the handful of holdouts who accepted the eminent domain as readily as they accepted the proposed buyout.

When I first visited the ghost town in 2007, only a dozen buildings remained in Centralia, including a couple freestanding row houses, buttressed by multiple brick chimneys to support them when the rest of the rows were razed. The town's four cemeteries were still maintained, including the Odd

Fellows Graveyard, near the origin of the blaze. This synchronicity led to a common local joke, according to a 2005 *Smithsonian* magazine article, that in Centralia "you can get buried and cremated at the same time, no extra charge."

Here and there, ghostlike wisps of smoke haunted the otherwise empty grid of streets, while in the distance, a solitary church on a hill overlooked the devastation with something like divine reproach. That's the Assumption of the Blessed Virgin Mary Ukrainian Catholic Church, a white facade against the trees with blue domes topped by three-barred golden crosses. It was built in 1911, and when the town was condemned, the leaders of the church commissioned a ground survey, which determined that underneath their church was bedrock, not coal, so it appears not to have been forsaken by God just yet.

On a grassy lawn of an American Legion building long since razed stood a bench—a veteran's memorial—and, for many decades, a time capsule, which was buried nearby and marked by a rectangle of stone on which was inscribed: "To be opened 2016." The capsule had been buried in 1966 at the hundred-year anniversary of the town—just four years after the blaze started. The time capsule didn't make it to 2016. That's because it was almost unearthed and stolen by one of Centralia's many dark tourists. As a result, in 2014, it was removed by officials and opened. Inside the box was about a foot of water, which had destroyed all the paper and photo contents, but a few items survived both the fire and the water: a miner's helmet and lamp and a pair of bloomers signed by the men living in the town at the time.

Also prominently placed at the time were various warning signs set up throughout the ghost town. One read:

Warning—danger
Underground mine fire
Walking or driving in this area could
result in serious injury or death.
Dangerous gases are present.
Ground is prone to sudden collapse

Another read: *These residents want absolutely nothing from our government. They want to live where they choose!* The latter sign exhorted people to call the governor and their senators and *demand they be allowed to remain in Centralia!!*

And then there was the mile-long stretch of Route 61 that was originally the main thoroughfare through town but was now abandoned. Google Maps calls it Pennsylvania 61 Destroyed—the name of an album Bob Dylan should have written. Everybody else called it the Graffiti Highway, based on the fact that it is covered in colorful spray paint from its many visitors. The asphalt undulated and buckled, making for an ideal obstacle course for the dirt bikes and four-wheelers that often tear down the road. A shallow, fifty-foot-long crack ran down the middle, sulfurous smoke wafting from it. The Graffiti Highway has its own Tripavisor entry (119 reviews; four out of five stars).

In 2013, officials reached an agreement with the seven remaining recalcitrant residents, who received a payout and were allowed to remain in their homes until their deaths, at which time their houses will fall under the eminent domain already in place.

In 2020, the owners of the land on which the Graffiti Highway ran, a mining company called Pagnotti Enterprises, decided to get rid of the broken roadway. Citing liability reasons, the company trucked in 400 loads of material to cover up the road, stating that the plan was to level it off and plant trees and grass on the surface.

My latest visit in 2024 revealed that the ghost town has gotten even ghostier. All the houses are gone, as is the veterans memorial. The church is still there, though, as is a municipal building. The cemeteries are still maintained. Wisps of smoke still haunt the landscape. Reports state that there are now even fewer residents than the seven holdouts in 2013, but the exact number isn't given. Otherwise, Centralia has been ground down to the street grid. The mining company never got around to beautifying the Graffiti Highway site, and it remains a series of large dirt piles that bury what was once the iconic strip of the ghost town and its tumultuous history.

But the story's not over yet. The fire below still burns and will, according to the experts, do so for another 250 years.

CIUDAD BLANCA

LOST CITY OF THE MONKEY GOD

LOCATION: Mosquitia, Honduras **ECOSYSTEM:** Coastal jungle **DESCRIPTION:** Large white buildings adorned with monkey statues	**INFAMOUS FOR:** Human-monkey hybrids, hidden treasure, tropical diseases, deadly wildlife, drug cartels

The story of Ciudad Blanca, the White City, is almost as impenetrable as the Honduran jungles that surround it. Some say this lost city from pre-Columbian times is a myth, that it never existed. Others say that it has already been found. Others yet say that it's real—but is not what we think it is. But the dreamers say it's still out there in all its legendary glory, hidden under thick rainforest vegetation and protected by the usual terrors of the jungle: a city of white buildings full of giant monkey statues, fabled for its riches and infamous for its curses, the home of gods and human-monkey hybrids. Grab your machetes. This one's going to be dense—and dangerous.

Mosquitia is 32,000 square miles of thick, hazardous jungle in northeast Honduras that also spills into Nicaragua next door. It is a place of unknowns, of unplumbed history, of undiscovered species. A place where you can't see more than a dozen feet in front of you due to the aggressive plant life. A place where, as a result, the primary mode of travel is bushwacking by machete. A 2015 *National Geographic* article said that the region features "some of the last scientifically unexplored places on earth." It is hard to get to, hard to traverse, and hard to survive. There are deadly vipers, large animals, venomous insects, and extreme heat and moisture. It's easy to lose your way or contract any of a range of tropical diseases that do everything from rot your face off to kill you painfully. And then there are the drug cartels that thrive in this lawless land. Some early maps refer to it as El Portal del Infierno—the Gates of Hell.

And yet, within that tangle of untouched rainforest supposedly hides the ruins of a vast city dating back a millennium or more, its advanced builders lost to time such that they don't even have a name today, despite the stone monuments and mounds they left behind scattered throughout the jungle. Local peoples such as the Pech and Miskito talk about Ciudad Blanca as a city that humans are forbidden to enter. It is a city where the local deities and mortals alike fled when the Spanish invaded, only to be cursed by those gods or the diseases that the Europeans brought with them.

Chris Begley, an archeologist who spent much of his career in Honduras, wrote a 2017 piece for *Sapiens* magazine in which he recounts that, while in Mosquitia, a Pech guide told him that Ciudad Blanca was nearby. When Begley asked to be taken there, the guide refused, explaining that "the site was sacred . . . and was the refuge of Indigenous gods who had fled when the Europeans had arrived nearly 500 years earlier. There were gods from all seven Indigenous groups, and if you went there and couldn't speak to each one, they wouldn't allow you to leave. You needed to know all seven Indigenous languages, and nobody knew them all—not even him." The Pech have their own name for the city: Kahã Kamasa, or White Town.

For invading Europeans, the legends started as soon as they neared the coast of Mosquitia. Many trace the first rumor of a wealthy city in that rainforest to Christopher Columbus. He apparently claimed that large gold nuggets could be found on the coast of Honduras and that there was an entire island of gold just off the mainland. Next came Spanish conquistador Hernán Cortés who, ever looking for El Dorado, wrote in a letter to Spanish emperor Charles V: "I hear of large and rich provinces and great lords who live in them in much state and magnificence; especially of one, called Hueitapalan. . . . Even if two-thirds of [the reports] should be untrue, it would nevertheless exceed Mexico in wealth and equal it in the grandeur of its towns."

It's even rumored that Charles Lindbergh, famed aviator, saw a gleaming white city in Mosquitia during a Central American flyover. He supposedly described the city as "an amazing ancient metropolis." Also in 1927, an ethnographer by the name of Eduard Conzemius mentioned Ciudad Blanca while reporting on the Pech to the Society of Americanists. He said he had learned that someone had stumbled across the ruins of a walled city in 1902 while looking for rubber trees. All the buildings and the wall around it were made of white stone.

And then a new name started appearing in the media to describe whatever lost city was hiding in the Honduran bush. In 1934, the *Calgary Daily Herald* quoted explorer Captain R. Stuart Murray, who was discussing an upcoming trip to Honduras. He said,

"There's supposedly a lost city I'm going to look for, which the Indians call the City of the Monkey God. They are afraid to go near it, for they believe that any one who approaches it will, within the month, be killed by the bite of a poisonous snake."

For the next decade, Ciudad Blanca continued to be searched for and reported on by explorers, discussed in the halls of academia and in the pages of newspapers, and its fame continued to grow among the people of Honduras as well. But the city was never found. In 1940, the legend achieved a new level of attention, thanks to an explorer named Theodore Morde.

Morde was an interesting guy. According to the 2013 book *Jungleland* by Christopher S. Stewart, when the twenty-nine-year-old Morde visited Honduras, he'd already encircled the world five times and had visited some one hundred nations. In addition, "He covered the Spanish Civil War with Ernest Hemingway and George Orwell, lectured on cruise ships, and later worked as a spy during World War II for the Office of Strategic Services, the US intelligence agency that preceded the CIA."

Morde traveled to Honduras with the backing of the Museum of the American Indian (now part of the Smithsonian Institution), and the tale of the hidden city he returned with was perhaps the most vivid so far. In a 1940 piece for the *American Weekly*, Morde wrote, "I am convinced that we have found the site of the legendary Lost City of the Monkey God." According to Morde, he was shown the remnants of buildings by the Pech and then regaled with the story of a large temple that was also part of Ciudad Blanca. In that temple, a set of stairs flanked by a statue of a crocodile and a statue of a frog led to a sacrificial place under the shadow of a giant monkey statue. He was also told about "hairy men who looked like Great Apes" who would steal woman and mate with them to create a hybrid primate race.

The rainy season put a stop to his explorations, but he was said to be planning a follow-up expedition. He never got around to it. In 1954, he died of suicide, hanging himself in the shower of his parents' home in Massachusetts, although other reports say that he was hit by an automobile. However it happened, Morde took the secret of the location of Ciudad Blanca with him and added to its aura of cursedness.

But the twenty-first century has so far been the greatest era for the legend of Ciudad Blanca. The newest installment in the story began with journalist Christopher S. Stewart, the aforementioned author of the book *Jungleland*, which was an account of his attempt to trace Morde's journey to Ciudad Blanca and the monkey temple. Stewart got his investigative journalist hands on Morde's journals, convinced archaeologist Chris Begley to be his guide, and in 2008, attempted to retrace Morde's steps.

Even though it was seventy years after Morde's expedition, Mosquitia hadn't gotten any easier to traverse. The pair navigated their way through a military coup, river pirates, bandit territory, deadly creatures, and viruses. They spent a month marching for hundreds of miles through solid green. Stewart told *Harper's* magazine in 2013, "At one of the lowest points in my journey, I wrote in my notebook, 'Go home.'" Which he did eventually, having found the adventure he was looking for—but not Ciudad Blanca.

Meanwhile, another American named Steve Elkins was also on the trail of Ciudad Blanca. He was a cinematographer and explorer who first attempted to find the lost city in 1994, but all he found were a few artifacts and an intricate carving of a man on a boulder. That carving was inspiration enough to convince Elkins that something was out there—that this land had not always been inhospitable jungle. But a fired imagination wasn't enough to fuel a second expedition until the invention of a new technology: light detection and ranging (lidar).

Although it wasn't a new technology (it had been invented in the 1960s for satellite tracking and military targeting) so much as a brand-new application for the technology. At some point, scientists realized that lidar could be used for high-res map making. When installed on a plane, it could shoot millions of laser pulses downward, creating a 3D map of the terrain. What Elkins wanted was to use lidar for discovery. In 2012, Elkins found the financial backing to put together a team to map a section of Mosquitia using lidar. For a week, they flew over thick jungle canopy in a Cessna with a hole cut in the bottom to accommodate the lidar system. Once they processed the data, they digitally stripped away the thick vegetation layer to see what was on the ground. And what was on the ground were the telltale straight lines that denote manmade structures.

What they saw were potential plazas, house mounds, canals, reservoirs, and earthworks that included a pyramid. It was a fantastic discovery. But they still had to "ground truth" it, to see it with their own eyes. In 2016, they returned with a team of experts and the backing of the president of Honduras and found the structures (the lidar map made it relatively easy, like following a GPS). They also found fifty-two stone sculptures sticking out of the dirt at the base of the pyramid, including stone ceremonial chairs called metates, carved vessels decorated with snakes, and figures that were half human and half animal, including one that was described by the party as a "were-jaguar." These findings prompted the government to rename the area Ciudad del Jaguar, or Jaguar City.

But despite their success, the team couldn't escape the curse. About two-thirds of them left the ruins with a bad case of leishmaniasis, a parasitic disease transmitted via sand fly bites. Douglas Preston, a journalist and novelist who accompanied the expedition, explained the disease to CBS News in 2017 this way: "The parasite migrates to the mucous membranes of your mouth and your nose, and basically eats them away. Your nose falls off, your lips fall off, and eventually your face becomes a gigantic, open sore." They received treatment, however, and were able to literally save face.

The team also returned to controversy. Some academics were peeved at the revival of interest in the sensationalized stories of Ciudad Blanca. In a book Preston wrote about the expedition called *The Lost City of the Monkey God*, he interviewed Rosemary Joyce, an expert on Honduran archaeology from UC Berkeley. She told him, "This is at least the fifth time someone's announced that they've found the White City. There is no White City. The White City is a myth, a modern myth, largely created by adventurers. I'm quite biased against this group of people because they are adventurers and not archeologists. They're after spectacle.... It's infuriating to see archaeology portrayed as a kind of treasure hunting."

Chris Begley also lent his voice to the choir of critics in his 2017 *Sapiens* article, writing: "La Ciudad Blanca keeps being discovered, over and over again; practically anytime anyone finds the remains of any settlement, they call it that.... In all cases, the 'discoverers' are outsiders, and their find is presented as a heroic accomplishment. They are seen as adventurers who have braved the impenetrable jungle and tropical diseases.... Nothing in their description is accurate. The cities aren't lost; the people living in these areas know all about them. And they aren't cities, by any reasonable definition."

Of course, academia being the way it is, some of the criticism smacked of professional jealousy—but they have a point that the Ciudad Blanca legends needs to be viewed with a more critical eye. For instance, the area is known for its white limestone cliffs, and those flashes of white through the dark green may have looked like the white walls of a city to weary jungle travelers. As for the Charles Lindbergh story, author Jason Colavito posted in 2013 on his website that "this legend saw print only in the 1950s, some three decades after the fact," casting doubt on its credence. Then there's Theodore Morde's shaky reputation—Stewart offers in *Jungleland* that pretty much everything Morde said about the Lost City of the Monkey God was fraudulent and a ruse to cover the fact that the entire expedition was a hunt for gold.

Despite the newspaper headlines, Elkins's team doesn't believe that they have found Ciudad Blanca. In fact, they think it might be the remains of two cities. Preston, in a 2015 *National Geographic* piece, remarked that "Archaeologists . . . no longer believe in the existence of a single 'lost city,' or Ciudad Blanca, as described in the legends. They believe Mosquitia harbors many such 'lost cities,' which taken together represent something far more important—a lost civilization."

In that dense jungle is a dense history ready to be unraveled, a history that could rewrite the story of the Americas and is more about the people of Honduras than the fame of its explorers. The discovery has become a source of pride for many Hondurans, whose country usually makes international news because of the corrupt government, the drug trade, and natural disasters. These ruins are not just of value to archeologists and anthropologists but are a connection to the mysterious forebears of the Hondurans and their accomplishments. It's probably why locals have kept the legend of Ciudad Blanca alive themselves.

In the end, the story of Ciudad Blanca seems to be a mix of

tales from natives and the Spanish augmented by twentieth-century explorers. But even if it never existed, Ciudad Blanca will always be a stratum of the story of this region, a symbol that some see as hopeful and others as fraudulent. But one thing is certain: Any who dare attempt to discover the truth of the lost city by entering the depths of its cursed jungle need to beware—and watch out for sand flies.

DUDLEYTOWN

VILLAGE OF THE DAMNED

LOCATION: Cornwall, Connecticut, USA **ESTABLISHED:** Late 1730s or early 1740s **OWNER:** Dark Forest Entry Association	**INFAMOUS FOR:** Cursed family, strange deaths, supernatural creatures, crotchety neighbors

The cover story of the August 1993 issue of *Playboy* magazine is an interview with actor Dan Aykroyd on the set of his sci-fi comedy film *Coneheads* (the cover photo is him in full Beldar costume with Pamela Anderson on his lap, suggestively fondling the pointy head of the character—this author does his research). The interviewer asks Aykroyd, star of the 1984 *Ghostbusters,* if he believes in the paranormal. Aykroyd's affirmative is immediate and impassioned. At one point he even says that ghosts are a "reality of life on this planet." He then offers, "The other day I read that Harold Ramis, my colleague in *Ghostbusters,* said he doesn't believe in ghosts! I'm going to bring him up to Dudleytown, Massachusetts, and scare the shit out of him sometime. I'll take him to the most haunted place on earth."

Dudleytown is not in Massachusetts, though. It's in northwestern Connecticut (close enough if you spend most of your time in Los Angeles). Or it *was* in northwestern

Connecticut—Dudleytown is a ghost town, although if we're getting technical, it's not really a town, either. Dudleytown is an unofficial settlement in the town of Cornwall, named after a group of residents who all had the surname Dudley . . . and who may also have brought a curse with them to the "most haunted place on earth," a place that many have been called the Village of the Damned.

The first settler of Dudleytown wasn't a Dudley. Sometime in the late 1730s or early 1740s, a farmer named Thomas Griffis dug a foundation in this forested Cornwall valley that is shaded by the Bald, Woodbury, and Coltsfoot mountains. The Dudleys came soon afterward. Five names always come up—Gideon, Barzillai, Abiel, Abijah, and Martin Dudley, who arrived separately over the next decade. Gideon, Barzillai, and Abiel may have been brothers, and Abiel and Abjiah might have been the same person, just conflated across stories. Regardless, a bunch of Dudleys gave the area its name. Previously, it was called Owlsbury, as it was apparently as infested with owls as it was with Dudleys.

The forested valley wasn't forested for long. Like much of New England during the colonial period, the trees were cleared for farmland, and the wood from those trees was used to fuel the smelting furnaces for Cornwall's iron industry. Over the course of the next hundred and fifty years, Dudleytown grew to some two dozen families.

And then began what Edward C. Starr would call in his 1926 book *A History of Cornwall* the "doom of Dudleytown." That doom took the form of madness and murder, freak acts of both nature and the supernatural, and demons, ghosts, and other monsters. And it all started because members of the Dudley family lost their heads in England.

In the early sixteenth century, an English nobleman named

Edmund Dudley was involved in some political shenanigans that, after the death of Henry VII in 1509, his rivals and victims were able to present as treasonous. He was beheaded at the Tower of London. A few decades later, his son John, Duke of Northumberland, continued the family tradition by vying for the crown himself. He married Lady Jane Grey, who had a claim to the throne, and she was installed as Queen of England after the death of Edward VI in 1553. She ruled for nine days, with the Duke as her consort, but Mary Tudor soon pulled the throne out from beneath her, and had Dudley and Grey beheaded. Maybe the Dudleys were just bad at the game of thrones. Or maybe the Dudleys were cursed.

Back in Connecticut, the exact nature of the "doom of Dudleytown" is difficult to parse, even with the British backstory. For every story of a tragedy that occurred in Dudleytown or to people who once lived in Dudleytown, there's a seemingly rational counter-story. For every anecdote, there's an antidote.

Strangely enough, in the stories, most of the Dudleys of Dudleytown seem to end up fine. It's their neighbors who need to watch out. Abiel is the exception: He fulfilled the curse of the Dudleys by losing his own head, albeit in a different way than the English Dudleys—he went insane as a result of the curse. At least that's one story. The other story is that he lived to the advanced age of ninety and, quite naturally, wound up infirm enough in body and mind that he became a ward of the town.

As for their unfortunate neighbors, there's no end to the tales of woe. In another Dudleytown story, William Tanner killed Gershon Hollister in Tanner's home in 1792. During the investigation into the murder, Tanner babbled about demons and ghosts and a strange creature that tore Hollister apart—another case of curse-induced madness. The curse-free version of the story tells that Gershon Hollister merely died from a fall off a barn he was helping Tanner build. Tanner would go on to live to 104, a ripe old age for a madman.

Then there was the wife of General Herman Swift, who was struck by lightning on her front porch and died. Her husband, of course, went mad in his resultant grief. The other side of this story is, well, the same—minus the madness. Swift's wife was killed by lightning on her front porch in 1804, but Swift didn't need a padded cell afterward. He would live to the age of eighty-one.

John Patrick Brophy and his family also suffered a tragic fate. His sons disappeared, his wife died of consumption, and his house burned down, all of which added up to Brophy losing his marbles. He found his way to Cornwall in a state that Jospeh Citro colorfully describes in his 2004 book *Cursed in New England*:

> "Haggard, tattered, wild-eyed, and wan, he raved about giant animals with cloven hooves and the ghastly green spirits that had chased and tried to capture him."

The prosaic side of that story is mostly the same, minus the monsters and the madness and with the addition of the fact that his sons didn't so much disappear as abscond with stolen merchandise.

The story of Dudleytown resident Nathaniel Carter doesn't have divergent variations, just divergent interpretations. He bought Abiel Dudley's house, but nothing bad seemed to happen to him or his family while living there. However, a few years later, when they moved to the wilderness outside of Binghamton, New York, their homestead was attacked by Native Americans. He, his wife, and his youngest child were killed, while his other three children were kidnapped. Was it the harsh reality of life as an invader in the New World, or the lingering effects of a curse from Dudleytown?

Finally, there's Horace Greeley, newspaper founder and presidential candidate. According to the story, his wife was from Dudleytown, and during Greenley's campaign to beat Ulysses S. Grant for the US presidency, she killed herself, either in Dudleytown or in New York City where they lived. The tragedy ended Greeley's campaign, implying that the Dudleytown curse altered the entire course of the nation. Greeley died a month later himself after checking into a sanitarium.

Turns out, that story is mostly fantasy. Unlike many enmeshed in the Dudleytown mythos, Greeley is a documented historical figure. His wife wasn't from Dudleytown, nor did she kill herself. She did get sick and die during Greeley's presidential campaign, though, and he did follow suit a month later in a sanitarium. But why Greeley was ever connected to Dudleytown in the lore is unknown.

Even our original curse story has a major caveat, and it comes from the research of an actual Dudley. According to Gary P. Dudley's 2009 book, *The Legend of Dudleytown [Connecticut]: Solving Legends Through Genealogical and Historical Research*, the Dudleys who made their way to Connecticut weren't even direct descendants of the treasonous Edmund Dudley, so we can't blame the curse on the crown.

Over time the town did leave itself to the ghosts, but not because of a curse that kept killing residents and driving the survivors mad. Instead, it was because the iron industry was waning, farms were failing due to the rocky soil in the valley, and the West was opening up with more appealing opportunities. By the late 1800s, Dudleytown had been abandoned; a bald spot in Cornwall, darkened by the shadows of the surrounding mountains.

What happened next reinvigorated both the land that was Dudleytown but also the curse. Dr. William Clarke, a surgeon in New York City, wanted some space away from the city, so in the early 1900s he bought three hundred acres of Dudleytown and built a house. He and his wife Harriet used it as a holiday home. From here, like those of most everybody connected to Dudleytown, his story splits in two.

In some accounts, Clarke left his wife in Dudleytown to attend to business back in New York. When he returned, he found that she had sunk into madness and killed herself (possibly as the result of seeing a ghost). The other story has her suffering in New York of a chronic illness and ending her life for that reason.

Had the former story been true, Dr. Clarke would probably not have done what he did next: doubled down on Dudleytown. In 1924, he organized a group of forty-one shareholders to buy eight hundred acres of it. According to the original prospectus, the purpose of the group was to "promote forestation, to run a wood mill, to promote conservation of bird, animal and wildflower life, and to afford a playground for you and your children and your children's children." The group began planting thousands of seedlings—red pine, Norway pines, Japanese chestnut trees, and poplars. Dudleytown hosted camping and riding and skiing activities.

The ghost town should have been drained of its dread at this point. But Clarke did something innocent that may have helped contribute to the legend of Dudleytown as much as anything else: He named the group the Dark Entry Forest Association. That's right—a group called the Dark Entry Forest

Association owns a cursed ghost town. About seventy-five years later, that ominously named association would take another action that would embed the lore even deeper into the ruins of the settlement.

But first, those ruins. Today, there's not much to Dudleytown. New England ghost towns are often anticlimactic; they're merely clusters of overgrown cellar holes, foundations, and stone fences hidden in woodland, and Dudleytown is no exception. And these days, around its few stones, the original tales of madness and death have been augmented with tales of ghostly forces that haunt its woods and attack visitors.

Now for another anticlimax: The origin of the legends of Dudleytown can be traced through literature. It all started in 1926, with the publication of the aforementioned book by Edward C. Starr, *A History of Cornwall*. Turns out, though, he made up all the stories of the original inhabitants. According to the Cornwall Historical Society website, "For reasons that have yet to be explained, Starr wove together a fanciful and inaccurate two-page account of Dudleytown residents over the centuries." Starr's stories weren't supernatural, however—those elements were added later. He focused on the misfortune and bad luck baked into the bones of the town by his own imagination. In 1938, *They Found a Way: Connecticut's Restless People* by Iveagh Hunt Sterry and Willim H. Garrigus, took Starr's stories a step further with supernatural embellishments and cemented the idea of a curse on Dudleytown.

And then Ed and Lorrain Warren came along to drag the tale of Dudleytown into the modern era. The Warrens were paranormal investigators from nearby Monroe, Connecticut, who never met a person, place, or thing that wasn't possessed ...and then milked and bilked those stories as part of their vast and spooky media empire. In the early 1970s, the husband and wife team filmed a Halloween special in Dudleytown, where they proclaimed it "demonically possessed." In their 1989 book *Ghost Hunters*, Ed says, "We can't vouch for the stories of curses visited on Dudleytown early in its history, but even if there weren't demonic forces at work then . . . there certainly are now." The Warrens were the first to bring national attention to the local campfire tale of Dudleytown.

In 1999, the movie *The Blair Witch Project* became a sleeper hit and made spooky forests cool again. Visitors flocked to Dudleytown, enough that the Dark Entry Forest Association, which is still extant and includes descendants of the original members, felt it needed to take drastic action. According to a press release put out by the group in 2001:

> *The owners of Dark Entry Forest, Inc. will seek the arrest and prosecution of all trespassers to the full extent of the law. . . .This year Law Enforcement Officers have been summoned 79 times to the Dark Entry Forest area, resulting in arrests for criminal trespass, disorderly conduct, illegal parking and littering. We will also assist the police by obtaining vehicle registration numbers and photographing them for evidence in citizen complaints.*

Journalist Robert Winkler visited Dudleytown for a 2002 *National Geographic* essay and described the early moments of his experience there: "We were met by a locked gate and signs announcing 'No Parking' and 'No Trespassing'. As we assessed the situation, an SUV came barreling down a nearby driveway. Out jumped a woman who warned that if we dared park there, someone would photograph my car and call the police. She raised the specter of towing, fines, and arrest before disappearing down the street."

A 2008 news item in the local *Register Citizen* newspaper

reports the arrest of a man who claimed to be hunting ghosts in Dudleytown. It quotes Connecticut Trooper Scott Aitken on the issue: "I would say we cite trespassers several times a month. Most of the trespassers we cite believe Dudleytown is haunted. A lot of them are looking for ghosts and stuff like that."

So not only do we have a cursed town owned by an ominously named association, but that association is unusually proactive about keeping visitors away. That has many people asking the question, "What are they trying to hide in Dudleytown?" and this author adding, "and is it worth invoking the Barbara Streisand Effect?"

In a 1989 *New York Times* article, Michael Gannett, then president of the Cornwall Historical Society, says, "Go to Dudleytown, they tell you. It's this real ghostly place. But the truth is, Dudleytown's a big fraud."

But is it? New England has so many ghost towns it's almost a lunar landscape of cellar holes, but it took a strange chain of events to give Dudleytown its reputation—British politics, a clumping of surnames, the deaths of settlers, a conservation-minded doctor, some books, a celebrity interview, a movie phenomenon, and an intense reaction to that movie phenomenon.

If that's not a damned ghost town, it's at least a damned interesting one.

PARIS CATACOMBS

EMPIRE OF DEATH

LOCATION: Paris, France **SIZE:** 200 miles **YEAR ESTABLISHED:** 1786	**INFAMOUS FOR:** Six million skeletons, partying trespassers

More than half a million people visit the famed Paris Catacombs every year. But those tourists don't die. They don't disappear. At worst, they exit those tunnels under the City of Light in the throes of an existential crisis, heavy with the dreaded truth conveyed by stacks upon stacks of ancient hollow-eyed skulls and piles upon piles of brittle bones: the truth that we will all die, become no more than those bones, our names forgotten. Death is the ultimate form of democracy in the city that invented it. And at best, the catacombs tourists exit with a T-shirt from the gift shop and another item checked off their bucket list. But that section of the Paris Catacombs—the heavily touristed section—is small. Just the fin of the shark; the foyer of Dracula's castle. Only about a mile of the Paris Catacombs are open to the public. The rest of the catacombs continue for some two hundred miles of dangerous skeleton-strewn darkness, flooded caverns, and tiny, airless passageways. People have gotten lost there. Died there. And… set up private banquets and cinemas there? Let's go down and see what that's about.

First, some historical context. The Paris Catacombs were

the solution to two big problems in eighteenth-century Paris: collapsing streets and overflowing cemeteries. Most of old Paris—from Notre Dame Cathedral to the Louvre—was built with Lutetian limestone, or Paris stone, a type of rock found in the basin where modern-day Paris exists (Lutetia was an older name for the city). Sometime in the fourteenth century, Parisians started mining it. They dug horizontal shafts down to the bedrock, and then mined sideways, pulling out the stone as they excavated. These mines were not an organized civic project, but rather an assortment of individual, unregulated projects, meaning that eventually, all these tunnels wound haphazardly underground as if dug by a colony of drunken ants. This wasn't really a problem until Paris started to expand over time, and its borders surpassed the tunnels below. Eventually, sinkholes started gaping out of the ground.

In 1774, a particularly bad sinkhole located on the Rue Denfert-Rochereau destroyed about a thousand feet of street. The next year, Louis XVI made it illegal to mine beneath public roads, and created the Department of General Quarry Inspection to make sure no more collapses occurred and to determine as best as they could the extent of those tunnels, which had never before been plotted or mapped.

Meanwhile, Paris had another problem from below. The ancient city was running out of space for the dead. Parisian cemeteries were so full that in some cases the ground rose six feet higher inside the cemeteries than outside, as the caretakers stacked the dead and dirt like a disgusting layer cake. French writer Rabelais wrote that Paris was "a good city to live in, but not to die in, since the beggars of Saint-Innocent [Cemetery] warmed their butts on the bones of the dead."

And Saint Innocent (more commonly known as Holy Innocents') was the biggest offender. It was the oldest and largest rotyard in the city, dating back to medieval times. According to a 2014 piece in *Smithsonian* magazine, Holy Innocents' Cemetery "exuded a strong smell of decomposing flesh—even perfume stores claimed they couldn't do business because of the off-putting smell." People around the cemetery complained about trouble breathing and about no trouble vomiting, as well as moments of delirium. Eighteenth-century French writer Louis-Sébastien Mercier wrote of the "cadaverous miasma" that he believed was the cause of these maladies and others.

And the dead kept rolling in—literally. In 1780, a restauranteur with the perfect name of Gravelot who ran an eatery on Rue de la Lingerie found said eatery overrun by corpses—corpses without reservations. Their weight had burst through the basement wall of his establishment, which was shared with the adjoining cemetery. Other buildings along the rue were similarly invaded. Dr. Philippe Charlier, a forensic pathologist who has studied the bones of the catacombs, told the *Paris Observer* in 2024, "People would be drinking, eating or dancing in a cellar tavern or cabaret when a wall would collapse and decomposing bodies fall in on them."

That's when Paris started closing the city cemeteries and trying to determine how to make everyone immortal so that graveyards would become obsolete. Actually, they had a much smarter and more feasible idea: Why not stick all those skeleton bones in the mines under the city? After all, that's what the Italians did over in Rome. And thus, in 1786, the Paris City Ossuary was established in the ready-made burial pits of the mines. Although everybody called it the Paris Catacombs (because, you know, do as the Romans do).

For the next three decades, with a brief pause for the French Revolution, authorities carted the bones of six million skeletons under cover of night—so as not to offend any citizens—and dumped them roughly down the mine shafts, sixty-five feet below ground level, where they shattered and were then scattered into amorphous piles.

In 1809, Napoleon Bonaparte himself opened the ossuary up to visitors, kickstarting the dark tourism juggernaut it is today. The opening of the catacombs to the public also inspired a quarry inspector named Héricart de Thury to rethink the presentation of the place for guests. Instead of sloppy piles of broken bones, he oversaw the transformation of those millions of human scaffolds into art and decor. He lined the walls with patterns of skulls and tibias and femurs. These walls dotted by skulls and dashed by bones are called hagues, and also include plaques inscribed with such meditations on death as, "Think in the morning that you may not make it to the evening and in the evening that you may not make it to the morning." It took four years to finish the installation, but the result was a macabre masterpiece that continues to draw tourists more than two centuries later.

The entrance to the public part of the catacombs is at the Place Denfert-Rochereau, from which visitors must descend 131 steps into its depths, some five stories below the street. A sign welcomes visitors with *Arrête! C'est ici l'empire de la Mort!* Translated to English:

"Stop! This is the Empire of Death."

The tour takes about forty-five minutes and covers less than a mile. It's safe, well-maintained, and a highlight of Paris. Go there, for sure. But it's the other two hundred miles of catacombs you have to watch out for.

Technically, only the mile of tourist-ready hagues are the catacombs. The rest of the massive network of tunnels below the city are mere abandoned quarries, although everyone still lumps them under the umbrella of the "Paris Catacombs." How could you not? But it's there where the bad stuff—and the fun stuff—happens.

The first (and so far only) official casualty of the Paris Catacombs was Philibert Aspairt, a doorkeeper at the Val-de-Grâce hospital. He descended into the crypts in 1793 . . . and disappeared. His remains weren't found until the next century, in 1804. It seems he had gotten lost and died in the suffocating darkness, apparently not too far from a stairway that would have led him to safety. His skeletal remains were identified by the hospital key ring and the buttons on his jacket. Why he went down there is uncertain, although one theory is that he was trying to break into the basement of a local brewery. They buried Aspairt in the same place he was found in the catacombs, one of the rare sets of remains identified by a tombstone.

But although Aspairt was the only one to die lost in the catacombs, he wasn't the only one to die down there. In 2016, a forty-five-year-old man died of a heart attack while in the catacombs during an illegal party. Others have gotten close to shedding their flesh and becoming dutiful citizens of that empire of death. In 2011, three people got lost for forty-eight hours in the tunnels before being found by the authorities thanks to notes they left in the tunnels that led to their discovery. In 2017, two teenage boys were found after being lost in the dark catacombs for three days. They were taken to the hospital and treated for hypothermia (the catacombs maintain a chilly 57 degrees Fahrenheit), but otherwise survived their ordeal unscathed. They were found by a search party with rescue dogs that sniffed out the boys.

The catacombs are a dangerous place, which is why, in 1955, the Paris government shut down the maze of tunnels and made it illegal to enter anywhere except for the tourist attraction itself. But that doesn't stop the cataphiles.

Cataphiles are people drawn to the secret and unmapped areas of the catacombs, despite the law of the land. They find old entrances in sewer drains and abandoned rail tunnels and the basements of buildings. Once down in the labyrinth, they explore, create art installations, perform theater, and even swim and scuba dive in the flooded sections of the caverns. And, man, do they party down there. In 2012, a Flickr user named Agence WATO published a photo series of an elaborate banquet set up in one set of tunnels. Dozens of masked celebrants sat at long linen-covered tables in a bunker-like corridor, its walls covered in graffiti and the tables covered with white linen cloths and candles and a feast. Patrick Alk, an ex-cataphile who did much of his spelunking in the 1980s, told the BBC in 2004, "We did everything—from dance festivals, theatre, artists' happenings, exhibitions. We had a free kingdom underneath Paris, and the places there are really closed places, secret places."

But cataphiles do have natural predators: the cataflics. These are the French police officers in charge of enforcing the no trespassing law in the tunnels (*flics* being the French word for "cops"). The cataphiles and cataflics play a daring game of catacomb and mouse, as the latter seal up entrances and caverns and the former break through and continue their subterranean soirees.

In 2004, the cataflics were conducting a training exercise in the catacombs when they stumbled across a peculiar cavern: It was an underground movie theater, and a sophisticated one at that, complete with power and phones lines and a bar. No one was present to check their tickets, but there was a security camera that, when the cataflics triggered it, started a recording of barking dogs, apparently in an attempt to scare any nosy wanderers away. When the authorities returned a few days later to catch the culprits in the act, everything had been removed—the only evidence of the room's previous use a note that read, "Do not try to find us."

Every once in a while, a journalist or blogger gets permission to join the cataphiles and write about the adventure—keeping all names and means of ingress and egress secret, of course. They wander miles in the dark, navigating by chalked arrows on the walls or names of the streets above that were installed long ago. They slither through pet-door-sized openings called cat holes, wade through murky water, and crawl delicately over carpets of bones, past graffiti-covered walls, and through tunnels furry with mole crickets.

One such writer, Matthew Alison, joined a group of cataphiles in 2024 for a night in the catacombs and wrote about it for the website Venture the Planet. His photos show him sitting on thrones made of skulls and bones and shuffling through corridors half his height, army-crawling through holes and wading through waist-deep water. He writes, "The Catacombs were as dark and disorienting as I'd imagined. Numerous side tunnels branched off in different directions—some leading up toward potential manhole exits, others dropping down into shadowy pits. Colorful graffiti lined the ancient limestone walls, giving the place an odd, almost medieval funhouse vibe. But as we descended deeper, the graffiti gradually disappeared, swallowed by darkness and silence."

And while most of the cataphiles are innocent adrenaline junkies, others are not so harmless. In 2009, the catacombs were shut down for months to repair damage to the hagues by vandals. In 2017, in a modern echo of the possible motive for Philibert Aspairt's descent to his death, thieves used the catacombs to successfully break into a cellar for a wine heist, making off with $250,000 in vintage vino.

The world below the streets of Paris is a strange and dangerous one, stuffed with the remains of six million dead and their ghosts that haunt the hollow underbelly of one of the most famous cities in the world. They are eager to add to their number.

CHERNOBYL EXCLUSION ZONE

RADIATION NATION

LOCATION: Northern Ukraine SIZE: 1,000 square miles DATE OF ACCIDENT: April 26, 1986	INFAMOUS FOR: Radioactivity, ghost cities, Black Bird of Chernobyl

It was only a test, a test that was supposed to make the nuclear facility safer. Instead, it triggered the largest nuclear accident in the history of humankind, one that killed dozens in the explosions and their immediate aftermath and maybe thousands or tens of thousands over time from the radioactive fallout across Europe. It caused the permanent evacuation of 350,000 people and rendered a one-thousand-square-mile area uninhabitable. It's a dark spot on the planet that needs no introduction (even if this chapter does): the Chernobyl Exclusion Zone.

In the early months of 1986, Halley's Comet was a blurry smear in the sky and the Cold War was about to enter middle age. The Soviet Union had just launched the Mir Station into orbit, and England and France had announced plans to build the Chunnel to link the countries under the English Channel. The space shuttle *Challenger* launched into the sky, only to explode seventy-three seconds later on live television. It was a

teetering time for human technological progress. Soon another explosion would reverberate across the planet, further highlighting the fragility of human advancement.

On April 26, 1986, technicians at the Vladimir Ilyich Lenin Nuclear Power Plant in northern Ukraine were conducting a test on reactor number four. The power station was large, with four working reactors and two more in the process of being built. The facility was intended to be a technological showpiece for the then Soviet Union. It was located about eighty miles north of the capital of Kyiv and twelve miles south of the Belarus border. The purpose of the test was to make sure the core could be protected in the event of a power blackout. However, unbeknownst to the technicians, the core had become unstable in the buildup to the test, so drastically reducing power triggered the exact scenario those technicians were trying to prevent: a nuclear disaster. The website of the World Nuclear Association is harsher in its assessment, stating the reason for the failure as "the result of a flawed reactor design that was operated with inadequately trained personnel."

The reactor built up immense quantities of steam and pressure that caused a pair of explosions that ripped the one-thousand-ton cover plate off the reactor and ejected radioactive materials high into the atmosphere in an amount that, according to the World Economic Forum, was four hundred times more radioactive than the atom bomb dropped on Hiroshima, Japan.

One person was instantly killed in the meltdown and another died shortly thereafter at the hospital. Of the hundreds of first responders that showed up to contain the disaster, 134 contracted acute radiation sickness and about thirty died over the next few weeks. Evacuation of local communities and their 350,000 residents began soon after. The evacuation included the ancient town of Chernobyl itself, the town of Pripyat—built to house workers at the station—and another 187 communities and settlements within a nineteen-mile circumference of the power station across Ukraine, Belarus, and Russia. That nineteen-mile circumference would come to be known as the Chernobyl Exclusion Zone, and it would eventually grow to one thousand square miles.

More than half a million workers, called liquidators, were bussed into the center of that zone for the massive clean-up effort, and a giant concrete and steel shell called the sarcophagus was erected around the reactor by radio-controlled cranes and other equipment to contain the fallout and protect the outside world from the two hundred tons of radioactive materials, as well as the contaminated debris and soil.

But the damage couldn't be ameliorated just through clean-up of the site and removal of nearby residents. A hundred types of radioactive elements were injected into the air during the explosions and ensuing fires, with the half-lives of those elements ranging from a few hours to thousands of years. The most deadly isotopes were iodine 131, caesium 137, and strontium 90, the latter two of which each have a half-life of about three decades. In the immediate aftermath people received enough exposure to affect them both in the near- and long-term.

A decade after the accident, Vladimir Afonichkin, one of those liquidators called in to clean up the toxic mess, explained to the *Los Angeles Times* that merely breathing in the days that followed was hard: "It was as if you had pepper on your tonsils." The newspaper also quoted a doctor, Viktor Klimenko, who traveled to Chernobyl from Kyiv to take part in the relief efforts, as saying, "Children had radiation in their hair, their skin. Everybody was dirty with radiation."

It has been estimated by various organizations that between five thousand and fifteen thousand cases of thyroid cancer were diagnosed in children over the next few decades as a result of the fallout. The Chernobyl Union, an organization of former liquidators, has claimed that hundreds of thousands of people in Ukraine alone have died or suffered permanent damage from diseases caused by the fallout. Others say those numbers are inflated for political reasons. The United Nations Scientific Committee on the Effects of Atomic Radiation issued a report in 2008 that states that aside from those thyroid cancers and the deaths and conditions of some of the plant workers and first responders, "To date, there has been no persuasive evidence of any other health effect in the general population that can be attributed to radiation exposure."

It's almost impossible to distinguish between the long-term health effects of Chernobyl and those conditions and diseases that would have impacted the population naturally over time anyway. After all, life always finds a way . . . to kill us. In addition, the Soviet Union collapsed about five years after the Chernobyl incident, which impacted both the health and the health records of its former citizens. Mikhail Gorbachev, who was president of the Soviet Union at the time, claimed that the rampant mistrust as a result of the Chernobyl accident was the single most important factor in the fall of the Soviet Union. Although, admittedly, he was smarting from accusations that his economic restructuring plan was the death blow of the USSR.

Today, the Chernobyl Exclusion Zone is infamous in the popular imagination as a glowing wasteland full of mutant creatures and powerful radiation that can melt your organs if you step anywhere near it. But what is it like really?

At Ground Zero, reactors number one through three were shut down over the years, culminating in the final reactor going dark in 2000 in preparation for the official decommissioning of the facility. The quickly erected and almost brutalist sarcophagus has itself been entombed in a large, gleaming hangar-type building awkwardly called the New Safe Containment. The massive concrete and metal sheath was put up in 2016 and is 360 feet high and 540 feet long. Its job is the same as the aging, crumbling sarcophagus, which itself is also being deconstructed by automated equipment after taking a beating from radioactive forces for thirty years.

Pripyat, Chernobyl, and most of the other settlements are still ghost towns. Pripyat, once the lively home of some fifty thousand people, has become an evocative icon of the disaster, with its empty streets, decaying apartment buildings, and rusting amusement park. Inside the houses are pet skeletons curled up on the floor, clothes laid over the back of chairs, and toys scattered haphazardly on the floor, as if the inhabitants had only just left. When they were evacuated, residents thought they were only leaving for three days instead of the rest of their lives.

There's still plenty of life in the city, though. "It's really scary at night," Nikolai Rey, a policeman who guarded a checkpoint outside the Exclusion Zone, told the *Los Angeles Times* in 1996. "The animals come, and any sound echoes all over the city."

The animals have certainly taken over. Wildlife experts have witnessed more than two hundred species of birds and an abundance of large mammals such as wolves, lynx, boar, moose, bison, and deer. Przewalski's horses, although not native, were introduced twelve years after the explosion, and their herds are growing. Brown bears have even been caught on trail cams there despite not having been seen in the area for more than a century. Ecologists are delighted by this glimpse into a thriving post-human landscape.

However, other researchers are skeptical about whether the wildlife is actually thriving. Judging the health of these animal populations takes more than trail cam footage and in-person anecdotes, including examinations into how damaged these animals are at the cellular level. The 2024 book *Atlas Obscura: Wild Life* states, "Scientists have found a significant number of asymmetrical insects, albino barn swallows and cataracted voles in the zone, traits they have connected to the accident." Creatures in the Zone might not be mutated to 1950s monster movie size, but their mutations might still spell their doom.

So is the Exclusion Zone a wild paradise or a holding cell for sickly and mutated animals? The truth is probably somewhere the middle. A professor named Mike Wood from Salford University in England, who studied the wildlife in the Exclusion Zone, told the *Telegraph* in 2016, "We're not saying that radiation is not as dangerous as we thought. Rather it is possible that in the absence of humans, the stress of radioactive contamination is a manageable one for wildlife populations." Basically, it seems like humans are more of a threat to wildlife than a reactor meltdown.

And speaking of humans, there are plenty of them in the Chernobyl Exclusion Zone these days, too. About five thousand people work in the Zone, managing the New Safe Containment structure and other Zone-related tasks, their radiation dosage carefully monitored and shifts timed for minimum exposure. Some two hundred people also call the place home permanently. These are the mostly elderly displaced people who returned to their homes soon after the evacuation because it was all that they knew, regardless of the risk. And then there are the dark tourists who want to watch their dosimeters go up. Tourism opened in the Zone in 2000 for various reasons that included the economic boost and keeping attention on the site for political and financial aid purposes. These tourists must go with a tour guide, stick to predesignated areas, and pass through multiple security and radiation checkpoints. Chernobyl isn't so bad if you're careful. Your insides won't melt—at least, if you follow the rules. In 2019, President Volodymyr Zelenskyy signed a decree making the Exclusion Zone an official tourism site. According to a 2019 CNN article, Zelenskyy said, "We must give this territory of Ukraine a new life. Until now, Chernobyl was a negative part of Ukraine's brand. It's time to change it."

And while that might indeed be true, Chernobyl still isn't Niagara Falls or Miami Beach. While the more intense contamination is contained to a scattering of hot spots, its effects overall are hard to predict because of changing conditions such as weather and forest fires. The contamination isn't as orderly as concentric circles around the power plant, either. Plus, the hotspots are *really* hot—including the junkyard of highly irradiated robots and vehicles used in the initial cleanup efforts. And the Red Forest, a large area of pine trees that caught the brunt of the fallout, their needles turned a reddish-orange. And the Claw, which news.com.au called "the most dangerous thing in the Exclusion Zone." It's a ten-foot-tall metal crane attachment that looks like a rusting octopus. It was used in the original 1986 clean-up, moving dangerous material that had been scattered by the explosion back to the core area. It is, as a result, extremely radioactive, and was dumped in a forest outside of Pripyat without so much as a warning sign or a barrier fence.

The lingering danger within the Zone was highlighted by the Battle of Chernobyl in February 2022. During the Russian invasion of Ukraine, the two militaries clashed in the Exclusion Zone, raising the radiation in the region by kicking up toxic dust with their platoons and vehicles. The Russians even captured the plant itself, holding the workers inside hostage. The Russians would withdraw about a month later amid rumors that their unprepared soldiers were catching radiation poisoning.

With all this mystery and sickness and death around the site, it's a wonder there isn't more paranormal lore attached to the Chernobyl catastrophe. Maybe the metaphorical haunting of the area is far more powerful than any literal one. Although there is one story: the Black Bird of Chernobyl.

According to the story, workers in the control room of the plant started seeing a large black humanoid creature with wings flying about in the days before the explosion. It had no head, but red eyes in its chest. Workers would also have encounters with it that yielded intense nightmares. Some received strange phone calls from unknown sources often described in accounts as "threatening."

Archaeologist Robert Maxwell, who worked at Chernobyl, told news.com.au regarding the Black Bird, "It's become one of those fables that's difficult to track because it relies on the accounts of people who died due to radioactive contamination." The journalist asked Maxwell if he had seen anything paranormal during his time in the Exclusion Zone. Maxwell replied, "No, absolutely not. It was entirely very much real terror when you're there. What's truly frightening is that you've got the all-encompassing overwhelming threat of radioactive contamination if you do the wrong thing or go in the wrong place or lean against the wrong object."

Maybe the reputation of the Chernobyl Exclusion Zone is worse than its reality, but that reality is still plenty scary. Venture there if you dare. Just don't forget your dosimeter.

SEARCHING FOR THE SPOOKIEST CITY

Most of the strangest and scariest places in the world aren't just God-forsaken, they're also people-forsaken. Which makes sense. If it's a place run amok with paranormal dangers, people wouldn't stay there long. But that doesn't mean our cities, where people do congregate, can't be spooky. Many are downright haunted. Now, I'm not sure how to measure such a thing, but good news, I don't have to. Major media outlets have tackled this topic already. So I decided to compare some of those lists to see what cities are the most haunted in the world.

The rules of this comparison were that I could only include mainstream outlets, and their respective lists had to include, for parity's sake, exactly ten cities on them. I came up with four sources: a 2021 Discovery.com article, a 2017 *Condé Nast Traveler* article, a 2016 article in the *Guardian*, and a 2014 *National Geographic* article. That's forty haunted cities. And, important to note, none of these lists ranked them on a scale.

When I compared the four lists, I found that no city appeared in all four sources—so, no clear winner in this exercise. However, seven cities appeared in half of the articles, and two appeared on three out of four. The former cities were:

- Canberra, Australia: A weak case is made for this city, with mentions merely of a haunted hotel and the city's Old Parliament House.
- San Antonio, Texas, USA: Similarly, its reasons for inclusion on two of the lists were just the Alamo and San Fernando Cathedral.

- Prague, Czech Republic: This city has a headless Knight Templar galloping through its streets and a castle where Nazis messed with the occult and opened a gate to hell.
- Changi Beach, Singapore: Changi Beach is haunted by the ghosts of massacred soldiers, a hospital full of torture victims, and an amusement park full of dead bodies that guards the gates of hell.
- New Orleans, Louisiana, USA: Often topping lists of the most haunted cities in the US, along with Savannah, Georgia, this city is known for its cemeteries full of pirates, killers, and plague victims; the LaLaurie Mansion—home of a particularly infamous serial killer; and, of course, lots of voodoo.
- Poveglia Island, Venice, Italy: Oh, you know this place. It's in this book! See page 122.
- Port Author, Tasmania: A former penal colony for the UK in the nineteenth century where prisoners were forced to live in silence and solitude with hoods over their heads.

The two cities that three of the media outlets agreed were among the top ten most haunted cities (and a tie for the most haunted city in this exercise) are:

- Baguio, the Philippines: Covered in ghosts from both a series of atrocities during World War II (that include beheaded clergy) and the 1990 Luzon earthquake.
- Sighisoara, Romania: Birth city of Vlad the Impaler, who inspired the Dracula story.

I guess the real conclusion here isn't us discovering the world's most haunted city, but instead learning that the world seems to be mostly populated by haunted cities.

SPOOKY SNOWSCAPES

Death always comes with an icy chill. Sure, we love the cold and snow at Christmastime or ski season, when thick flakes waft outside while we bask by the warmth of a fire. But the cold, like all the worst dangers, is only safe and poetic from a distance. If you're caught outside in it, the cold will freeze your meat to burning, desiccate the moisture from your flesh, blacken your skin into leather, and slow your blood to a sludge. But it gets worse when you add the paranormal to the physical dangers of the snowscape. After all, you can't feel a cold spot in the cold. Can't spot a ghost against the whiteness. And the dangerous predators that are at home in those brutal, icy wastelands stay camouflaged against the white until you're red between their teeth. It's easy to lose yourself in the snow.

DYATLOV PASS

MOUNTAIN OF THE DEAD

LOCATION: Ural Mountains, Russia	**DATE OF INCIDENT:** February 1–2, 1959
NAMESAKE: Igor Dyatlov	**INFAMOUS FOR:** Mysterious deaths of nine hikers

In 1959, nine cross-country skiers entered the harsh Ural Mountains of Russia and died of hypothermia. Admittedly, that doesn't sound like too bizarre a story. A tragic one, for sure, but not bizarre. However, it was the aftermath of their deaths, the scene that the search party found, that was so bizarre, so morbid, and so shocking that it has fascinated the world for sixty-five years, inspiring scores of theories and imbuing that frigid, snowy area of eastern Russia with an aura of mystery and terror that lingers today.

The group were mostly college students and recent graduates from the Ural Polytechnic Institute in Yekaterinburg, Russia. They were burgeoning engineers and economists, one of them studying nuclear physics. All shared a passion for the great white outdoors. They were members of the college ski club and advanced hikers, skiers, climbers, and survivalists. There were originally ten members of the fateful expedition—eight men and two women. The youngest was Lyudmila Dubinina. She was twenty. The oldest of the students was Alexander Kolevatov, at twenty-four. The oldest in the group, though, was thirty-eight-year-old Semyon Zolotaryov. He was a sports instructor and World War II veteran who was added to the trip by the ski club administration, probably to watch over the students. But the entire adventure was really led by Igor Dyatlov, twenty-three, who had no idea that he would one day add both his name and his last breath to the mountain range.

The excursion was carefully plotted by Dyatlov and his friends and approved by the ski club. It wended two hundred miles through an isolated section of the Ural Mountains at a point 350 miles northwest of Yekaterinburg. If you have a globe handy, the easiest way to see that part of the world is by looking straight down at it from the top. The Ural Mountains run north-south and separate the continents of Europe and Asia. The mountains on Dyatlov's route were relatively tame and rounded, with plenty of forest, so the group wouldn't have to traverse sheer cliffs and extreme altitudes. The dangers were the arctic cold, the strong winds, and the deep snow. Also, you know, whatever killed them.

These athletes set out on January 23, 1959. Five days later, after a preadventure that included multiple train rides, hitching a ride on a logging truck, being led by a horse-drawn sleigh, and sleeping in an abandoned logging camp, they arrived at the mountains. The plan was to penetrate as far north into the Urals as Mount Oroten before heading south and then swinging back out to the town of Vizhai on February 12, give or take a few days. According to multiple sources, the meaning of the word *oroten* in the language of the native Mansi people is "don't go there." (He said the name of the book!) However, according to a 2019 BBC piece, a Mansi forest warden named Valery Anyamov corrected the translation of Oroten to "mountain with swirling winds." Still a synonymous meaning for me.

Before the friends could take off into the mountains and

history, a member of the party, Yuri Yudin, twenty-one, experienced an intense sciatica flare-up and was forced to quit the expedition due to the pain. The condition would save his life. Unlike his friends, he would die unmysteriously in 2013 at the age of seventy-five.

And then there were nine. They entered the Urals on January 28. The next time anybody would hear from them would be . . . never. February 12 came and went with no telegram announcing their return. By February 20, the margin of tardiness couldn't be rationalized, and a search and rescue party went out to look for the young skiers. Their last camp was found on February 26 on a mountain called Kholat Syakhl, a Mansi name meaning "Dead Mountain." Their final states were discovered, but not their fates.

The tent was in place where it had been erected on a gentle slope, but collapsed and covered in snow, a ski pole used to prop it up still standing. Inside, clothes, shoes, and food were laid out neatly. Rips in the tent turned out to have been cut from the inside. Footprints in the snow revealed the group had walked toward the tree line below without adequate footwear—in stockings and even bare feet. One walker appeared to be wearing only a single ski boot. Half a mile away, beneath a cedar tree, the rescuers found the dead bodies of two of the hikers—both in their underwear—around the remnants of a fire. One of the bodies had a piece of flesh bitten from his right hand in his mouth. Three more bodies were found in a position that suggested they were attempting to return to the tent. One of them was Dyatlov. It was a strange scene, one that seemed to indicate that the hikers had simply cut their way out of the tent and walked barefoot to their deaths.

The first mystery was a mild one. Why camp on the slope instead of in the shelter of the trees? Nobody knows, but it could have been that Dyatlov didn't want to lose the distance the group had earned, or maybe it was a more interesting challenge for the team. The next mystery, how they died, wasn't apparent and would need autopsies to get to the bottom of. The final immediate mystery, the whereabout of the other four hikers, wouldn't be solved for another month, after the start of the spring thaw. The discovery only metastasized the overall mystery.

The four remaining bodies were eventually found buried under ten feet of snow, half drenched in a still-running stream. Two were missing their eyes, and one of those was also missing their tongue.

The autopsies didn't alleviate the confusion. Two bodies suffered chest trauma with broken ribs and two others had skull fractures, one of which was serious. Adding to the confusion, no external wounds were evident, and the other five bodies had no such internal injuries. Some of the bodies were discolored, with gray hair and reddish-orange skin, and their clothes emitted strong levels of radiation.

The hikers had meticulously documented their expedition. There were multiple journals and five cameras that yielded around 150 photos of the trip. The story they told was about as helpful as the autopsies. It revealed a group of young adventurers excited and reveling in the challenges of their expedition. But it also revealed that whatever had happened, the group had died a few days into their journey, sometime between February 1 and 2.

Two theories were ruled out. It couldn't have been an avalanche as the slope was too gentle, nor was anything other than the four bodies buried. Rocks were protruding through the snow and some of the tent was still exposed. Plus, the hikers' injuries were inconsistent with those usually incurred in an avalanche. The cause of death for avalanches is invariably asphyxiation, and any trauma to the skeleton is confined to the spine. Basically, when an avalanche happens, it's pretty obvious. In the words of Douglas Preston, writing about the mystery for a 2021 *New Yorker* piece, "Snow does not lie."

The other theory dispelled was an attack by the local Mansi, perhaps enraged at the presence of the intruders. But the Mansi actually helped with the search and recovery, and the injuries were too extreme for a hand-to-hand fight. The medical examiner likened the damage to that of a high-speed car accident. Nor did the slope show any signs of scuffle or combat. Again, snow doesn't lie, and it was saying that these experienced hikers cut themselves out of their tent and walked away with inadequate footwear and died. And nobody could figure out why.

On May 28, Soviet authorities closed the investigation and, in typical fashion, classified the evidence and made Dead Mountain off-limits for years. The explanation they released for the deaths was attributed to—depending on the journalistic account and translation—a "compelling natural force," a "compelling unknown force," an "overwhelming force, which they were not able to overcome," or an "insurmountable force of nature." It was clearly some force.

Decades later, the mystery went global. During the fall of the Soviet Union—the late 1980s and early 1990s—the records for the incident were declassified. In 1990, the lead investigator, Lev Ivanov, told the newspaper *Leninsky Put* that he had been ordered to close and classify the case because of multiple reports in the area of glowing spheres in the night sky. He said, "I suspected at the time and am almost sure now that these bright flying spheres had a direct connection to the group's death." A few years later, the internet awoke, breathing in every photo, interview, and document from the incident to fill its nascent servers.

Cue the theories. According to multiple sources, at least seventy-five different theories have been proposed for what happened on that mountain. Theories range from the plausible—such as hallucinogenic mushrooms and panic-inducing infrasound—to the outlandish, including UFOs and an orgy gone very, very wrong.

The most popular theory in Russia, including the one most often touted by the grieving families and friends of the hikers, was the bugaboo of the Soviet Union itself. Many believed that the students stumbled onto secret military tests in those mountains and were either killed by accident as a result of the tests or on purpose to keep them secret. This theory would explain the bright globes in the air (missile launches or parachute bombs) and the radioactive clothes. In addition, some documents seemed to indicate that the government knew about the deaths of the hikers weeks before their official discovery, although those were more likely clerical errors.

Another popular theory is that they were killed by a yeti, the-monster-under-the-bed of snowy mountains. Evidence for this theory is a photo taken from the camera of one of the victims of a vague figure in the forest. It looks like a bigfoot photo in the sense that it's blurry, like all bigfoot photos are blurry. In addition, the hikers, as was a custom of the time, would write mock newsletters. In the science section of one composed during their trek, they write, "In recent years, there has been a heated debate about the existence of Yeti. According to recent reports, Yeti lives in the Northern Urals, near Oroten mountain." Of course, the more plausible interpretation is that the photo is of a bundled-up hiker and the newsletter a bit of amusement to leaven the time between grueling hikes.

These theories have been promulgating on the internet, on television, and in numerous books and podcasts since that time, building up interest in and pressure on the case until, in 2019, it was finally reopened by the Russian government and freshly investigated. Led by a prosecutor named Andrey Kuryakov, the final resolution of the mystery was determined to be . . . an avalanche. Now you're thinking, wasn't that ruled out in the very first investigation? However, it wasn't an average avalanche—it was the rare type known as a slab avalanche (although not, for some reason, a slabalanche). For this type of avalanche, a small, thick slab of snow not much bigger than a car and weighing as much as one thousand pounds detaches itself from the rest of the snowbank and slides down the mountain. In this case, the hikers had cut into the snow to form a wind break for the tent, which could have functioned like removing a retaining wall. Any slight pressure would have loosed that slab over the cut to slam into their tent and then, due to the small size of the icy material, blend into the surrounding snow, concealing the evidence that it had ever happened. Some say that to trigger a slab avalanche, fresh snow would have been needed to push the slab over the tipping point. However, it didn't snow the night of the tragedy. Still, that could be explained by another natural phenomenon: a katabatic wind. That type of wind shoots straight down a mountain, aided by gravity, and can move snow cover—in this case, directly onto the weakened slab. The slab avalanche would have been significant enough to trap the hikers in their tent and scare them into thinking it was a bigger avalanche, or that another was coming, so naturally, they cut themselves out and headed for the shelter of the forest without delay.

In 2021, a paper published in the journal *Communications Earth and Environment* supported the theory. Written by Johan

Gaume of the Institute for Snow and Avalanche Research in Switzerland and Alexander M. Puzrin of the Institute for Geotechnical Engineering, also in Switzerland, the paper details how they used computer modeling based on (no lie) the snow animation technology developed for the Disney movie *Frozen*. They combined the snow animation with data from 1970s air bag tests on cadavers to determine that the combination of slab avalanche and katabatic wind fit the wounds on the bodies and therefore was a likely scenario. With that extremely rare combination of natural phenomena as the inciting incident, the rest of the pieces of this mystery fit together, if not perfectly, then at least more easily.

What happened after they escaped the tent seemed to be exactly what experienced hikers should do. They moved to a more sheltered area, tried to start a fire, and when the avalanche didn't come, they broke into two parties, one to find the covered tent—mostly buried in the darkness—and the other to dig a snow cave. Unfortunately, in the below-zero temperatures, the former party didn't make it. The latter party might have broken through a hollow while digging for the tent and fallen into the stream, thereby burying themselves. This fall could explain their internal injuries, as could the impact of the slab avalanche itself.

As to their off color, mummification always discolors bodies. The missing eyes and tongue became food for fauna aiming at the softest and most vulnerable body parts. The near nakedness might have been because of the rush from the tent combined with those who lived longer borrowing clothes from the dead. (There's also a phenomenon called paradoxical undressing in which hypothermia victims start feeling hot and remove clothes.) The radioactivity could be explained by the lamps they used, the wicks of which were treated with thorium. Snow might not lie, but it also doesn't always connect the footprints for us, either.

The theory offers a strong narrative. Douglas Preston wrote in his *New Yorker* piece, "The most appealing aspect of Kuryakov's scenario is that the Dyatlov party's actions no longer seem irrational . . . everything they did subsequently was textbook. . . . Had they been less experienced, they might have remained near the tent, dug it out, and survived. But avalanches are by far the biggest risk in the mountains in winter, and the more experience you have, the more you fear them. The skiers' expertise doomed them."

But not everybody agrees with these findings out of Russia and Switzerland. Some experienced mountaineers and scientists believe the prospect of those two natural events occurring simultaneously in that region and under those conditions too implausible, and others require a far more extravagant explanation for such an extravagant death scene. Even the authors of the paper admit that their findings don't fully clarify the mystery of what happened that night in February 1959.

Today, seven of the nine hikers are buried in a communal plot in Mikhailovskoe Cemetery in Yekaterinburg. An area not too far from their final camp has been dubbed Dyatlov Pass in their honor. A nearby column of rock bears a metal plaque that memorializes them.

And while the slabalanche answer might not be as exciting as abominable snowmen or Soviet secrecy, it is a more terrifying answer. It means that no matter how prepared we are for anything—how skilled, how careful, how experienced, how expert, how protected—we are still at the mercy of the simplest horrors. We are never safe from the basic workings of this planet. But that might be especially true if you are on an icy Russian mountain.

Yury Yudin, the sole surviving expedition member, probably summarized the mystery best when he told the *Moscow Times* in 2013:

> "If I had a chance to ask God just one question, it would be, 'What really happened to my friends that night?'"

MOUNT EVEREST

THE WORLD'S HIGHEST GRAVEYARD

LOCATION: The Himalayas, Nepal and China **HEIGHT:** 29,031.69 feet **FIRST SUMMIT:** May 29, 1953, by Edmund Hillary and Tenzing Norgay	**INFAMOUS FOR:** Deaths, ghosts, corpses, rich people, shit

It's the highest point on the planet, and possibly the most haunted. Yetis roam its flanks, hundreds of frozen corpses dot its snows and expel their ghosts, and it's covered in tons of shit and garbage—and that's on top of the extreme conditions and mortal danger inherent in a giant, icy mountain. But all this might not be the worst thing about Mount Everest. It might be the rich people crawling all over it. Let's talk about this majestic wonder of the world.

Things started auspiciously enough for this mountain. It formed, along with the rest of the scar tissue that is the Himalayan mountain range, during the Eocene Epoch, when two tectonic plates—the Indian and the Eurasian—smashed together and pushed the bedrock up out of the Tethys Sea and into the stratosphere.

Mount Everest wouldn't be recognized as the tallest point on the planet for another thirty to fifty million years, though: not until the British colonized India and decided to map their

latest acquisition. In 1802, the East India Company launched the Great Trigonometrical Survey, a mammoth project to measure the subcontinent down to the centimeter. People died performing it. Hell, people died just of old age while superintending it. It didn't wrap until 1871. In 1852, a young mathematician named Radhanath Sikdar, who worked for the survey, burst into the office of superintendent Andrew Waugh and shouted, "Sir, I have discovered the highest mountain in the world!"

Sikdar was correct, and math—not mountain-climbing—finally crowned a monumental champion. Sikdar clocked the peak at 29,000 feet above sea level (about 5.5 miles high), putting it a solid 800-plus feet taller than the highest known mountain at the time, Kangchenjungaat (which is actually the third highest, at 28,169 feet, behind K2, at 28,251). However, when the survey announced the new record-holder, they gave its height as 29,002 feet to avoid suspicions of inexactitude by the public. This decision spawned the wonderful joke that Waugh was the first person in the world to put two feet atop the mountain. Still, the survey pretty much nailed the height. Today, we measure it at 29,031.69 feet.

But now that mountain needed a name—or at least a name for English speakers to call it by. The mountain cut through both Nepal and Tibet. The Nepalese called it Sagarmatha, or "Goddess of the Sky," while the Tibetans called it Qomolangma, or "Goddess Mother of the World." It might have had other names as well, because, you know, it's a big mountain. Lots of people could see it. At the time, the survey merely called it Peak XV. Waugh decided to name the mountain after his predecessor at the survey, Sir George Everest.

Once Mount Everest became widely known to the Western world as the tallest mountain on the planet, people inevitably tried to summit it. In 1921, the British military launched a reconnaissance mission to find a suitable route up the mountain, and the next year they returned to charge up its flanks. After weeks of climbing and camping, the unit got as high as 27,300 feet. Their attempt ended when an avalanche killed seven of the Sherpas accompanying them.

Sherpas are an ethnic group in Nepal known for their climbing skills and altitude endurance. Climbers today still employ them as guides and porters. The record for the most Everest ascents is held by a Sherpa, Kami Rita. He has summited thirty times and is still active as of the writing of this book. He's probably up there right now as you read this.

But before somebody could complete thirty summits, somebody had to complete one. The second attempt to climb Everest was in 1924 and was mostly comprised of the same Brits who had struck disaster in 1922. They made camp at 26,900 feet. On June 8, George Mallory, who had been on both previous expeditions, and Andrew Irvine, participating in his first, took off for the summit in the hopes of being the first humans to reach the top of the world. They were seen from afar by their camp at about 800 vertical feet from the goal. It was the last time anybody in their expedition saw them. Whether the duo reached the top before disappearing is one of the most debated topics in mountaineering. In 1999, Mallory's body was finally found, about 2,500 feet below the summit. In 2024, one hundred years after the expedition, Irvine's body was found on a glacier below Everest's north face. The bodies didn't offer any substantiating evidence of their possible summit. The camera they may have taken with them is still missing.

The conditions on Everest are severe. Nights can get as cold as minus 76 degrees Fahrenheit, and since the mountain is so tall it touches a jet stream, wind speeds can hit one hundred miles an hour. Even flora and fauna avoids the place. Above 20,000 feet the only wildlife that can survive is some moss, a couple of hardy bird species that fly away when it gets too rough, and a jumping spider that lives off whatever hapless bugs get blown up the mountain.

Over the next three decades, another ten or so attempts would be made to summit Everest. None of them succeeded. A few of them ended in death. Everest loomed above the planet with its stony arms crossed.

Then, on May 29, 1953, a New Zealander named Edmund Hillary and his partner, a Sherpa named Tenzing Norgay, were the first to crunch snow with crampons on the highest peak of the planet. They were backed by a large British expedition, and Hillary's first words on return to camp were to fellow expedition member George Lowe: "Well, George, we knocked the bastard off!" Hillary and Norgay made a pact to tell nobody whose foot was the first on the summit, believing they deserved equal shares of the glory, but years later Norgay would reveal in his autobiography that it was Hillary's.

Today the ascent to that patch of snow atop the mountain is replicated ad nauseum. Some eight hundred people a year try to climb Everest—that "year" being a six-month window that gives a wide berth around monsoon season, which renders the climbing route impassable for most. According to the website of renowned climber Alan Arnette, who analyzes climber data, since Hillary's summit, 7,269 climbers have summited Everest for a total of 12,884 summits. Most of those summits occurred in the last twenty-five years. Only about a hundred people reached the top between the 1950s and the 1970s, growing to almost nine hundred in the 1980s, followed by a spider jump of some three thousand in the 1990s. According to the 2020 article "Mountaineers on Mount Everest" in the journal

PLOS ONE, between 2006 and 2019, almost two-thirds of Everest climbers reached the top, whereas in the previous fifteen years, it was about one-third (the paper excluded Sherpas).

Over the years, Everest has been summited by a blind person, a double-amputee, multiple thirteen-year-olds, septuagenarians, and octogenarians, and many have climbed it in the double digits of times. It's a fixed-line climb, meaning much of the route to the top is marked by rope handrails. Along those handrails is often a slowly shuffling line that would rival the wait time of any Disney World ride. On May 23, 2019, 396 people left base camp for the top—the greatest number on any single day. The congestion was fiercer than the mountain. These days, you don't even need any mountaineering skills to make it to the top. It just takes time and lots of money. Sir Edmund Hillary himself told the BBC in 2003, "Having people pay $65,000 and then be led up the mountain by a couple of experienced guides . . . isn't really mountaineering." If Alan Shepard were alive today, he'd probably say the same about Jeff Bezos's tourist space capsule.

And the price has gone up since Hillary's statement. According to a 2024 Kipling.com article, it can cost upward of $200,000 to climb Everest once you factor in climbing passes, guides, equipment, training, and travel costs.

All that to get to what's a pretty gross destination these days. The mountain is, after all, a graveyard. So far, some 340 people halved the distance to heaven by dying on Everest (or doubled it to hell). That's a death rate of about one in ten. It even killed an astronaut. In 1993, Karl Gordon Henize joined a team to ascend the mountain, eight years after his only space flight. The sixty-six-year-old had trouble breathing on the ascent, however, and had to return to base camp, where he died in his sleep. The cause of death was ruled a pulmonary edema caused by the high altitude. The place is still dangerous, although it does have a lower death rate than at least a dozen other mountains, including Annapurna in Nepal and the already mentioned K2 that straddles the border between Pakistan and China.

And those 340 deaths? Most of the bodies are still up there. It's often too difficult to bring that dead weight down under those dangerous conditions. Plus, the bodies become so cemented to the rocks by ice that they are basically part of the mountain. One area of Everest has earned the nickname Rainbow Valley because the dead bodies are all wearing brightly colored gear. Sometimes climbers have to step over those bodies, and other times they're used as landmarks—like Green Boots, an unfortunate climber with neon footwear, or Sleeping Beauty, a woman who died wearing a purple coat (both bodies have since been removed by special missions sent to do so). Most deaths come from avalanches, but falls are common, as is hypothermia. The majority of deaths occur on the descent after that high point of the climbers' lives.

The dead might leave behind their bodies, but the living leave behind their waste. According to a 2015 *Washington Post* article, some 26,500 pounds of human shit are left behind on the mountain each season. An *Outside* magazine article from the same year states, "Some expeditions have started bringing in rolls of carpet to throw down as a base layer for their tents because, at this point, the muddy slush on the ground is as much feces as it is dirt." Climbers also leave a massive amount of trash behind that includes oxygen bottles, abandoned tents, clothing, food wrappers, and whatever else people carry up but don't carry out. In 2024, the Nepalese army removed eleven tons of garbage from the mountain (along with four corpses and a skeleton). A 2024 BBC article estimates that the mountain is covered in about fifty tons of it.

In 2003, Jamling Tenzing, a son of Tenzing Norgay who himself ascended Mount Everest in 1996, spoke to the *Guardian* about all the wealthy bucket listers who had started regularly hitting and littering the summit. He said, "You still have to climb this mountain yourself with your feet. But the spirit of adventure is not there any more. It is lost. There are people going up there who have no idea how to put on crampons. They are climbing because they have paid someone.... It is very selfish. It endangers the lives of others."

And we haven't even gotten to the monsters yet. Because the mountain is legendary for two spooky entities: yetis and ghosts. (We already talked about the jumping spiders, right?)

Parallel to the attempted and eventual conquering of Everest was an interest by the Western world in the bigfoot of the East, the abominable snowman. Tales had circulated of the creature from the original British expedition way back in in 1921, which came across footprints in the snow and were told by their Sherpas it was from *metoh-kangmi*, a "man-bear snowman." The real mania was kickstarted after a 1951 reconnaissance mission to Mount Everest. The members of the team were there to scout possible climbing routes for the mountain when one of them, Eric Shipton, took photos of footprints in the snow at an elevation of 15,000 feet that he believed belonged to a yeti. They were large and humanoid, with a big toe so bent it almost looked like a thumb.

Hillary would go on to have his name almost as connected to yetis as it was to Mount Everest, despite once telling *Stars and Stripes* magazine, "I have never believed in the existence of the snowman." Nevertheless, in 1959, he was part of an expedition into the Himalayas with the explicit purpose of searching for the beast. His team was given a memo by the Nepalese government outlining some of the regulations around yetis that included needing a permit, not hurting the beasts, and surrendering any photographic evidence or live specimens caught to the government. The party came up empty-handed yeti-wise, but later Hillary would find himself taking a supposed yeti scalp from a monastery to Western scientists to test for its authenticity. It turned out to be the scalp of a goatlike creature called a serow. And while these days, Everest is too crowded for yetis, there's always plenty of room for ghosts.

The annals of Everest are full of stories of climbers feeling invisible presences or seeing shadow people while climbing the mountain. Perhaps the most terrifying is the tale told by a Sherpa named Pemba Dorje. In 2004, he was accosted by black humanoid shapes near the summit, who begged him for food. He told the press shortly after returning,

"I think those were the spirits of the many mountaineers killed during and after the ascent of Mount Everest."

Of course, he also claimed that the ascent was a world record for the fastest, at eight hours ten minutes, a claim that has been doubted as fiercely as his encounter with ghosts of the dead.

Frank Smythe, one of Britain's legendary climbers, saw his share of weirdness during his attempts to summit Everest in the 1930s. According to his grandson, Simon Smythe, who wrote a piece about his grandfather for the *Telegraph* in 2003, his grandfather was once so sure a climber was beside him that he offered him some of his mint cake, only to discover there was nobody there. He also once saw strange creatures hovering above him. Smythe wrote: "[One had] what looked like squat, underdeveloped wings, whilst the other had a beak-like protuberance like the spout of a teakettle. They distinctly pulsated . . . as though they possessed some horrible quality of life." They soon vanished into the mist.

Frank Smythe never did get to the top of the mountain, and he once wrote in regard to his failure that "those who have failed on Everest are unanimous in one thing: the relief of not having to go on. The last 1,000 feet of Everest are not for mere flesh and blood." Little did he know how things would change.

Even if Mount Everest isn't crawling with our bravest and most adventurous anymore, it's still the highest point on the planet and an icon in its own right, although it's also an icon of what has changed over the years. In 2023, Freddie Wilkinson, an expert alpinist and author, wrote a piece for *National Geographic* in which he said, "the mountain has become an icon for everything that is wrong with climbing."

Maybe it's an icon for everything that's wrong with us in general.

THOMAS BAY

DEVIL'S COUNTRY

LOCATION: Southeast Alaska, USA	**FOUND IN:** *The Strangest Story Ever Told*
PART OF: Tongass National Forest	**INFAMOUS FOR:** Madness, disappearances, lost time, Kushtaka, Charlie Sheen

Don't let its name fool you. Thomas Bay might sound like a small town in Connecticut where the local veterinarian also solves crimes on the side, but in actuality, Thomas Bay is in wild, rugged Alaska, and it's a place of monsters and madness. It has left hardened locals and tenacious prospectors barking on their hands and knees like dogs and fleeing the state, demanding to never hear the phrase "Thomas Bay" spoken to them again.

Thomas Bay is, well, Alaskan. That means a few things you can guess: Moose, bear, whales, seals. Gold in them thar hills. Glaciers. Snow, although below-average snowfalls for the state. That's because Thomas Bay is in southeast Alaska, that thin panhandle that parallels British Columbia and is the closest point in the state to the lower forty-eight. It's about one hundred miles southeast of Juneau, with the Bay itself being fed by both the Baird and Patterson Glaciers. Mountains rise in the distance, most prominently the nearby peak named Devil's Thumb. It's part of Tongass National Forest, the largest national forest in the United States, and the land around the bay is spiky with spruce, hemlock, and cedar, as well as being dotted and dashed by lakes and rivers.

But the stock-photo beauty of the place is only dirt-deep, and its ominous reputation is underscored by not just one, but two menacing nicknames: Bay of Death and Devil's Country. It earned the first moniker in 1750 after an event that's more recounted than documented. The Tlingit, an indigenous people whose territory extends through what is now southeast Alaska, had established a village on the shores of the bay, but a landslide decimated it, killing some five hundred people. After that, the Tlingit called the area the Bay of Death. It wouldn't be called Devil's Country until two centuries later.

In the early 1950s in Petersburg, across the sound from Thomas Bay, a woman named Virginia Colp claims to have found a bizarre manuscript amongst her recently deceased father's possessions. Her father was Harry D. Colp. Colp was a prospector and frontiersman. He lived within paddling distance of Thomas Bay most of his life and died in 1950 at age sixty-eight. The manuscript, which he had apparently written in the 1930s, was an unsettling firsthand account focused on a series of journeys into Thomas Bay by himself and various fellow prospectors. However, the stories it told were not unfamiliar to Virginia or anybody in the area. Stories of the horrors of Thomas Bay had circulated for decades, but not in such a document. She published her father's manuscript in 1953 under the title *The Strangest Story Ever Told*.

The account began in the spring of 1900, when an eighteen-year-old Colp and three other prospectors (whom he only named as John, Charlie, and Fred) found themselves in the town of Wrangell, fifty miles south of Thomas Bay by boat. Charlie was excitedly telling his friends that he had finally convinced a Native American man to tell him where he had found a chunk of gold-embedded quartz. The answer? Thomas Bay.

In May, the prospectors sent Charlie ahead in a canoe to check out the place, while the other three got jobs in the timber field to save up money for an expedition. Charlie had provisions for three months, but a few weeks later, he returned—silent, famished, and exhausted, but with a chunk of gold-flecked quartz in his hands. Despite returning early, his canoe was empty of provisions and equipment. Charlie eventually told them what happened, but only on the condition that they give him money to catch a boat to Seattle, because he never wanted to see Alaska again.

After days of exploration looking for the geographical features that his Native American source had described, Charlie ascended a ridge and saw one of them: a lake shaped like a half-moon. While there, he stumbled upon a ledge of gold-speckled quartz and was able to break off a chunk with his gun barrel, ruining the barrel in the process. Then his story got weird. He said:

> *Right there, fellows, I got the scare of my life. I hope to God I never see or go through the likes of it again. Swarming up the ridge toward me from the lake were the most hideous creatures. I couldn't call them anything but devils, as they were neither men nor monkeys—yet looked like both. They were entirely sexless, their bodies covered with long coarse hair, except where the scabs and running sores had replaced it. Each one seemed to be reaching out for me and striving to be the first to get me. The air was full of their cries and the stench from their sores and bodies made me faint.*
>
> *I forgot my broken gun and tried to use it on the first ones,*

and then I threw it at them and turned and ran. God, how I did run! I could feel their hot breath on my back. Their long claw-like fingers scraped my back. The smell from their steaming, stinking bodies was making me sick; while the noises they made, yelling, screaming and breathing, drove me mad.

Charlie awoke adrift in the canoe with his piece of quartz and made his way back to Wrangell. After telling his story, he left Alaska and never returned. The three remaining prospectors assumed he'd gone a little crazy all alone out there in the wild. Plus, they couldn't get over all the gold stuck in that quartz. Two months later, Fred and John went up to Thomas Bay. Colp stayed behind to continue earning money.

Fred and John returned three weeks later in a similar state to Charlie and with maybe an even stranger story. After days of traveling to Thomas Bay and searching around, they found Charlie's old camp. They then split up to find the quartz ledge faster. John found the ridge and the half-moon lake, but before he could dig up the ledge, he heard three shots. Hurrying to their source, he found Fred on all fours barking like a dog and trying to pull pine saplings from the ground with his teeth. The gun Fred had heard was buried barrel down in the dirt. It took time, but John finally knocked some human sense back into Fred and convinced him to return to camp. Fred told him, "I'll go, but if you are just trying to scare me and fool me like the other devils, you can go to hell."

They made it back at nightfall, but after supper, Fred jumped up and shouted, "John, the devils are coming!" Fred ran to the bay where the canoes were tied and paddled off into the night. John tried to catch up, but before he could, he heard a gunshot and a loud splash. Fearing for his friend, John finally pulled up alongside, only to see Fred laughing and exclaiming that a devil had been in the boat with him, cursing at him, but that he had shot it in the head.

Most of this story came from John. All Fred would say to Colp was that Charlie was right about the gold and the devils. He added: "My advice to you is the same as Charlie gave us all. Just forget it." Fred left Alaska, never to return.

But Colp didn't want to forget it. He was intrigued by both the devils and the gold, but practical frontiersman that he was, also wanted to recover all the kit that everyone had left out there. He convinced John to go with him, even though John was trepidatious. John couldn't figure out how two "strong-bodied and level-headed chaps" like Charlie and Fred could go strange like that. The two men decided on a quick trip to grab the gear or stow it somewhere sheltered, and they spent a single uneventful night in Thomas Bay doing that.

In the summer of 1903, Colp and John returned to procure the stowed gear and explore the area. After two days, these hardened outdoorsmen got anxious. According to Colp, "It seemed as if someone or something with a menacing disposition was right behind me all the time, and that there were hundreds of angry eyes watching me." He brought it up to John, who agreed, and added that he had seen bushes move a few times without a source. They left. It was Fred's last foray into Thomas Bay. But not Colp's.

According to the account, Colp wanted to go back but could never find a companion willing to accompany him and didn't want to go alone. His next opportunity didn't come for three years, when a man named Mr. Bush, who had recently arrived in Alaska and opened a saloon, recounted a dream he had to Colp—a dream in which he described a landscape. To Colp, it sounded like Thomas Bay. There was even a crescent lake. Colp convinced Mr. Bush to accompany him into the Alaskan bush to his dreamscape. In July 1906, they took off for Thomas Bay, which Mr. Bush quickly acknowledged was exactly what he had seen in his sleep. As they trudged through the miles, Mr. Bush fell. Colp went to him and found him on his back, eyes open, but only the whites showing. Eventually, Colp got him talking, and Mr. Bush demanded they flee. As Colp led him out, however, Mr. Bush got angry and paranoid. He started calling Colp names and claimed that he was taking him deeper into the forest to kill him. Colp tried to prove otherwise, indicating the stream they were following was flowing toward the Bay, but Mr. Bush insisted that the stream was flowing uphill. They escaped without any other incident.

In August 1908, Colp went again into the Devil's Country, this time by himself. According to the account,

"I had to see what was there: gold, devils, or insanity."

Upon his arrival he immediately found a one-person camp that had been abandoned quickly and was months old. He took it as an excuse to immediately return home to report the missing person, but the authorities had no record of anyone who had gone missing. Colp decided to take it as a warning to never venture there alone again.

His last trip was in 1911. He found a "big husky Norwegian" man to accompany him. However, only a single night in Thomas Bay convinced them both to exit quickly. Colp kept thinking about all the strange occurrences that had happened there over the past decade, and the Norwegian wasn't feeling well. Much later, Colp asked the man why they only stayed one night. The Norwegian's answer was that they had actually stayed for two weeks prospecting but had come up empty-handed. Colp closed this particular story with, "Maybe we did, but if so, I am the one who was out of my mind because I can't remember a thing about it."

Over the next five years, Colp would send other prospectors to Thomas Bay, and they always came back with stories of misfortune or ones that conflicted. But one of these stories stuck out. Colp was informed about an old trapper out setting trap lines in Thomas Bay in the winter of 1925. One night, his dog went wild, barking and howling. The next morning it had vanished. The trapper was able to track it in the six inches of snow on the ground. He soon found a second set of tracks that seemed to be stalking the dog. He described the hind tracks as looking like a combination between the tracks of a young bear and a small barefooted man, and the front tracks as similar to a large racoon's. Sometimes the creature walked on all fours, other times only on its hind legs. The dog's tracks ended abruptly, like it had been snapped up mid-step. He followed the other tracks until he realized he was going in circles and that whatever the beast was, it was tracking *him*. He beat it back to civilization to tell his story. The next time he went trapping in Thomas Bay, he disappeared forever.

So what is the story of Thomas Bay? It starts out like a bigfoot story, but those devil-monkey things that Charlie saw don't seem like bigfoots. They were smaller, attacked in a group, and then there was the strange but evocative detail of open sores and scabs, like some plague had infected these creatures. Then there were the other stories. The invisible forces and lost time. The temporary madness. The feelings of dread. It all smacks of cosmic horror, as if Thomas Bay is a weak spot between dimensions, mixing worlds that never should be mixed.

Basically, it sounds way scarier than a bunch of ape-people.

But what if they were . . . otter-people?

The Tlingit tell stories of beings called the Kushtaka (or Kóoshdaa Káa), which translates to "Land Otter Men." These furred humanoids can shapeshift—for instance, appearing like a loved one to their victims—or mimic the sounds of a baby crying, all to lure people deeper into the wild to either kill them or turn them into Kushtaka. Some even say the hundreds of Tlingit victims of the Thomas Bay landslide were all turned into Kushtaka.

Bjorn Dihle, an author who grew up in southeast Alaska, has written a lot about Kushtakas and even, in 2012, retraced Colp's trek into Thomas Bay to determine if he could experience any of the phenomena described by Colp. In his 2017 book, *Haunted Inside Passage: Ghosts, Legends, and Mysteries of Southeast Alaska*, he interviews a Tlingit elder named David Katzeek, who describes the Kushtaka as a spirit, saying: "It basically tries to steal your mind; tries to steal, in a way, your self-esteem. It takes away from you. It causes you to become a person you really were never intended to be."

In 2013, actor Charlie Sheen decided to catch himself a Kushtaka. He had recently returned from a failed mission to find the Loch Ness Monster, so he set a Land Otter Man firmly in his sights. He took his private jet and some friends to Alaska but returned with the same results as his Scotland trip. Sheen told the tabloid website TMZ, "It obviously knew our group was far too skilled to be snowed in this fashion so it stayed hidden like a sissy."

These days, Thomas Bay is very much a changed place. It's easier to access. More frequently traveled. It's heavily logged and cleared. Small cruise ships dock in its waters. Colp would probably not even recognize it anymore. Perhaps whatever cosmic confluence occurred in previous centuries has ended or mended, or was rescinded. Maybe today it's safe now. Maybe you can go there.

Or maybe that is exactly what the Kushtaka want you to think.

MOUNT SHASTA

PEAK PARANORMAL

LOCATION: Siskiyou County, California, USA **HEIGHT:** 14,163 feet **STATUS:** Active volcano	**INFAMOUS FOR:** UFOs, lost civilizations, strange creatures, hippies

John Muir, the explorer and naturalist known as the "Father of the National Parks," described Mount Shasta in an article for the 1877 issue of *Harper's New Monthly* magazine as having "a far more impressive and commanding individuality than any other mountain within the limits of California." And he described it that way without even knowing that its snowy flanks were covered in bigfoots, lizardmen, and batsquatches. Without even knowing that it was regularly visited by UFOs. Without even knowing that an entire cult would one day start within its icy crags. Without even knowing that it hid an entire city built by the advanced refugees of a sunken continent. And without even knowing that it would lend its name, in the future, to a popular soda. He just thought it was a cool mountain.

That cool mountain towers 14,163 feet above the surrounding area of northern California and is the second largest peak of the Cascades range (losing to Mount Ranier in Washington by a couple hundred feet). Mount Shasta is snowcapped year-round, sporting seven glaciers large enough to have names. In February 1959 it received, at 15.75 feet, the most snowfall during a single storm of any place in the contiguous United States. Oh, and it's an active volcano.

The snowy exterior of Mount Shasta has a fiery heart. According to the United States Geological Survey, it's one of the top five volcanos in the country considered a "very high threat." It goes through 3,000-year-long periods of dormancy, after which it has eruptions every half a millennium or so. And with the last eruption on Mount Shasta being 3,200 years ago, it's about due. For nonvulcanologists, signs that the mountain has heartburn are the hot springs and fumaroles (openings that expel sulfurous gases). In fact, John Muir survived a freezing night of snow on Mount Shasta by laying down on the warm rocks around the hot springs. He described the sensation in the same article referenced above as "the pains of a Scandinavian hell, at once frozen and burned."

All that snow makes it a popular spot for winter sports and outdoorspeople. But that's not what makes it famous. A mountain of weird lore makes the mountain famous, as if its giant white peak gathers strange stories (and stranger people) like an antenna gathers radio waves.

The Native Americans were the first to make the mountain a stage for the strange. It figures into the lore and practices of such local peoples as the Shasta, Modoc, Wintu, Klamath, Atsugewi, and Achumawi. The Wintu trace the origin of their people to a spring on Mount Shasta. The Modoc believe the creator G'mokumk resides there. The Klamath tell the story of a massive battle that occurred when the sky spirit, Chief Skell, threw fire and rocks from the top of Mount Shasta at the underworld god Llao over on Mount Mazama. Some have interpreted this latter legend as evidence that the Klamath people witnessed volcanic eruptions at Mount Shasta in days gone by and preserved the tales in their oral history.

But gods and monsters aren't the only things topping the mountain. Mount Shasta is known for giant lenticular clouds that form at its peak. These clouds look unnatural and, frankly, flying saucer-shaped. Under the right lighting conditions, the clouds can look like the burnished metal of UFOs themselves. Others says that these lens-shaped clouds hide UFOs that are docking at the top of the mountain. Of course, you have to ask, why are UFOs docking at the top of Mount Shasta? To access the crystal city hidden inside that was built by the refugees of a drowned continent after a nuclear war with Atlantis, of course. There really *are* dumb questions.

This story starts with lemur fossils. Somehow.

In 1864, a British zoologist named Philip Sclater was pondering an oddity of the fossil record. Lemur fossils had been found in India and Madagascar, but not on any of the landmasses connecting the two countries—not in the Middle East and not in Africa. He theorized that a land bridge must have once connected the subcontinent and the island, a land bridge that—at the size it needed to be to cross the oceans in between—was basically a continent. He called that continent Lemuria. Land bridges were being postulated almost everywhere by scientists at the time, but the idea was rejected after the discovery of plate tectonics and the resulting continental drift theory. However, the idea of the Lemurian land bridge was rescued from scientific obsolescence by occultists and theosophists. They really dug the idea of Lemuria, treating it almost like a hip version of Atlantis that only the cool kids knew about.

These spiritualist writers postulated many things—that humanity had started on Lemuria, that the civilization on Lemuria was advanced beyond current knowledge, and that it was the realm of giants. Basically, a lot of Atlantis-adjacent stories. In fact, one of the theories as to why Lemuria eventually submerged was that it and Atlantis took each other out in a nuclear war.

At this point in the story, we've traveled almost as far away from northern California as is possible. But we go back there now thanks to a teenage boy named Frederick Spencer Oliver.

In 1883, the seventeen-year-old Oliver started writing a book called *A Dweller on Two Planets*. Oliver claims to have channeled a spiritual being named Phylos the Thibetan while he wrote the book. Phylos's stories were mostly about Atlantis, but Lemuria figured in, as well. As did Shasta, near which Oliver lived. According to the text, inside of Shasta lives a "mystic brotherhood" in a city called Sach, with walls "polished as by jewelers, though excavated as by giants" and shot through with veins of gold, silver, and green copper and inset with precious stones. The floors are covered in soft gray minerals that look like fur carpeting. The book wouldn't be published until 1905, six years after Oliver's death at the age of thirty-three.

Over the ensuing decades, various writers eagerly grabbed at the idea of a hidden civilization of refugee Lemurians in Mount Shasta and elaborated upon it. Astronomer Edgar Lucian Larkin wrote an article about it in the *San Francisco Examiner* in 1913. A writer known only as Selvius wrote about it in 1925 in the magazine the *Rosicrucians Mystic Triangle*. Edward Lancer wrote a piece about it in 1932 in the *Los Angeles Times*. That same year, Harvey Spencer Lewis, writing as Wishar S. Cerve, published his book *Lemuria: The Lost Continent of the Pacific*.

This game of literary telephone firmly wedged the Lemurians inside of Shasta. Over the course of these writings and others, the subterranean city became known as Telos, the City of Light, and featured levitating walkways and crystalline walls.

The inhabitants were seven feet tall and clad in long white robes. They would venture sometimes to the towns around Shasta, talking to people, making purchases with large gold nuggets, and flying the UFOs docked in the lenticular clouds at the top of the mountain (or trading with and refueling the extraterrestrials who flew them).

In 1934, a man named J. C. Brown claimed to have found a way into Telos. He was a seventy-nine-year-old geologist who had been employed by a London mining company to prospect for gold on Mount Shasta. Brown lectured about his adventures there in the town of Stockton, two hundred miles south of Shasta. He described finding a tunnel into the mountains and traversing it for some eleven miles until he found chambers full of gold, copper, and radium, plus twenty-seven skeletons that ranged in length from 6'6" to 10' tall. According to the *Stockton Record*, on June 9 of that year, eighty people who had attended those lectures showed up at the local docks to join an expedition into the mountain with Brown. But Brown never showed up.

Stories of tall, berobed people are still swapped in the towns surrounding Shasta. But the question really is, are these white-clad figures refugees from a drowned continent or are they the reincarnated forms of George Washington and Jesus Christ?

In the early 1930s, Guy Ballard hiked Mount Shasta to find immortal beings called Ascended Masters who he believed oversaw the spiritual evolution of humanity. Its membership included Jesus Christ, George Washington, Buddha, Krishna, and others from humanity's greatest hits. These figures had skipped death and entered a higher level of existence. While at Mount Shasta, Ballard managed to meet one, a chap named Saint Germain, who was dressed in a white robe and surrounded by a bright aura.

According to Ballard's account in his 1934 book, *Unveiled Mysteries*, Germain preached to Ballard for days about love and light while flying him through time and space to witness his past lives, as well as mines full of treasures. Germain also led Guy deep inside Mount Shasta to see the fabled Lemurian wonders and even introduced him to a Venusian or two. According to Germain, Ballard and his family were all Ascended Masters, too. Or were destined to be, at least, when it was their time to ascend.

With his anointment by Germain, Guy was ready to kickstart a religion, and he and his family moved to one of the best places on the planet to do so: Los Angeles. There, they started I AM. The name of the cult was a reference to Exodus 3:14, in which God calls himself "I AM THAT I AM." Ballard's doctrine of personal betterment, miraculous healing, and prosperity were well received by many. Some accounts number his followers as high as one million by 1938. Others placed it at 700,000 or 400,000. A 2003 article for the International Cultic Studies Association estimated it more conservatively, between 10,000 and 50,000.

In 1939, Ballard made the awkwardly timed decision to ascend. He died at sixty-one. Besides the practical effects of losing a leader, the movement found itself in an awkward spot—because Ballard wasn't supposed to die. He was supposed to ascend, like Jesus's resurrection into the clouds. However, his wife and son tweaked their theology and announced that physical death could be part of the ascension process.

Edna, Ballard's wife, would ascend in 1971. An article from the McClatchy Newspapers and AP services from June of that year wrote of her passing, "The event went unpublicized because the movement does not believe in death." As for I AM itself, the movement is still around and claims a network of hundreds of temples and sanctuaries all over the world. The most interesting place to see them, however, is at Mount Shasta, where they perform pageants every year.

But aliens, ancient civilizations, and immortal prophets aren't the only beings populating the icy sides of Mount Shasta. Many cryptids call this place home, too. Like the matah kagmi, a bigfoot-like creature from Modoc lore who guards the forests, and sightings continue to this day of the tall, dark, and hairy. There's also the tall, dark, and scaly. Rumors that the Lemurians are actually lizard people abound, as well, although lore locates lizard people all over California. Then there are the winged bigfoots—batsquatches, which entered the record in 1994 with a sighting near Mount Ranier in Washington. Mount Shasta's first batsquatch sighting on record was in 2009. It was relayed by a paranormal investigator named Paul Dale Roberts, who got a call from a man claiming to have seen one. According to the story, the man and his friends were hiking Mt. Shasta when they saw a creature the size of a man with the face of a bat, leathery wings fifty feet long, and "stocky as Hulk Hogan."

Today, in addition to being a lightning rod for lore, Mount Shasta is a New Age mecca. It's considered one of the root chakras of the planet, and the towns in its shadow are lined with shops that sell crystals and tarot decks. According to a 2015 Slate article, some 25 percent of Mount Shasta's visitors are "spiritual tourists." But it's not all vision quests and psychic channeling on Mount Shasta. People die regularly on its snowy slopes. Even more must be rescued from its dangerous flanks. According to a 2024 piece in the *San Francisco Chronicle*, the mountain averages one death and twelve rescues a year for hikers and climbers who get lost on the mountain or caught in its avalanches and snowslides.

Mount Shasta is a game of chance, one where you could go and get your energies cleaned, meet Jesus Christ, and be welcomed into a secret city full of treasure. Or you could get mauled by a batsquatch, abducted by aliens, and freeze to death at the bottom of its cliffs. In the end, though, the house always wins, and Shasta will one day cover the land with fire.

DIVING INTO THE HOLLOW EARTH

This book focuses on the terrifying surface of this terrifying planet, but what about below the surface? Is it terrifying down there, too? Well, that depends on whether you subscribe to the hollow earth theory.

The theory that the earth is a hollow sphere has been a common idea throughout history. Early proponents were religious groups. The center of the earth is where many belief systems placed their underworlds—Hades, Hell, Patala. Some went even weirder, like Cyrus Teed, who in the mid-nineteenth century started a religion around the idea that not only was the earth hollow, but we were already living inside it, with it being a sphere eight thousand miles in diameter that circumscribed all of Creation.

Early scientists played around with the idea as well, including the seventeenth-century English astronomer and physicist Edmond Halley (the namesake of Halley's Comet). He thought that a hollow earth with a series of concentric spheres rotating around a core might explain the magnetic anomalies he was detecting in his research (they were accounted for half a century later without needing the earth to be hollow).

One of the biggest proponents of a hollow earth was John Symmes Jr. Symmes was a veteran of the War of 1812 and a businessman. In 1818, he started writing and lecturing about the habitable concentric spheres he believed made up the interior of the planet, as well as the 1,400-mile-wide opening to them at each pole—Symmes Holes. He even got the federal government to consider funding an expedition to prove the existence of those holes, but it just never happened.

Modern scientists believe that the center of the earth is layered, with a solid iron and nickel sphere at the core almost the size of the moon that's surrounded by a semisolid mantle made of rock and minerals. It's all delicately topped by the flaky crust that we walk on, which ranges in thickness from a mere four miles to a mere fifty. In other words, there's just no vacancy in the basement.

Still, we've had some good times down there. Edgar Allan Poe perforated the planet with references to pole holes in his short stories "Ms. Found in a Bottle" and "The Unparalleled Adventure of One Hans Pfaall," as well as in his only novel, *The Narrative of Arthur Gordon Pym* from 1838. Jules Verne took us downstairs with his 1864 novel *Journey to the Center of the Earth*. And Edgar Rice Burroughs dubbed the interior of the earth Pellucidar and explored it in a series of novels between 1914 and 1963. We've also kept the idea going on the big screen, with movies such as *The Mole People* (1956), *At the Earth's Core* (1976), and *Godzilla vs. Kong* (2021).

As for Symmes, he's six feet closer to the truth, in Hamilton, Ohio, where the town throws a Hollow Earth Festival every year. His son Americus even erected a hollow earth sculpture—complete with Symmes Holes—for his gravestone.

EPILOGUE

SO WILL YOU GO THERE?

The title of this book is an imperative statement. However, I do have a question. And that question isn't whether you will heed my warning or not (despite the title of this epilogue). After all, I didn't. I found myself face-to-face with the *No Trespassing* signs of Dudleytown. I had to be pulled out of two feet of thick toxic muck and fish skeletons on the shores of the Salton Sea (RIP, Timberlands). I've breathed in the hellish vapors and crossed the fragile topsoil of Centralia. Driven the dangerous curves of Haynesville Forest. I've flown blithely through the Bermuda Triangle and come out the other side unvanished. I explored the varied strangeness of the Bridgewater Triangle, wandered the ruins of the Pine Barrens, and saw the skies of the Nevada Triangle (although not from a plane—never from a plane). I even risked getting marooned on Thrice Cursed Island.

No, my question isn't whether you'll take the title of this book as a warning, as a challenge, or facetiously. You do you as only you can do. My question—the question this entire book poses—is: Why are these places, among all the many places on this suspended blue ball, infamous for being strange and dangerous?

What I mean is, the planet's surface area is seventy-one percent water. So among all that wet acreage, why is the relative kiddie pool that is the Bermuda Triangle the spooky spot? North America hosts millions of lakes in which thousands of people drown and disappear every year. So how did Lake

Lanier become the serial killer lake? People kill themselves everywhere in the world; life is hard. But for whatever reason, Aokigahara is the spot that gets the word *suicide* in its nickname. There are thousands of coal fires smoldering beneath the basements of the world—but only one Centralia.

These parts of the planet somehow, through an odd aggregation of mysteries and legends, histories and fictions, truth and errors, have earned extremely spooky and deadly reputations. The chain of events that got them those statuses are sometimes followable, sometimes not, but in every case are fascinating.

But don't get me wrong. Every locale in this book is dangerous. And, yes, technically you can die or disappear anywhere in the world. Human beings are really good at the former and pretty good at the latter. But many of these places, even ruling out the paranormal, have a suspicious and unnervingly high body count that includes death and harm and disappearances. And the thing about a body count is . . . it can always be added to.

And whatever you believe about UFOs or monsters, dimensional portals or curses, ghosts, or merely your ability to navigate and survive harsh conditions, in the end you can't say that I didn't warn you.

I end this book with a clear conscience.

FURTHER READING

Annerino, John. *Exploring the Superstitions: Trails and Tales of the Southwest's Mystery Mountains.* Skyhorse Publishing, 2018.

Cervé, Wishar S. [Harvey Spencer Lewis]. *Lemuria: The Lost Continent of the Pacific.* Supreme Lodge of AMORC, 1931.

Coleman, Loren. *Monsters of Massachusetts: Mysterious Creatures in the Bay State.* Stackpole Books, 2013.

Colp, Harry D. *The Strangest Story Ever Told.* Exposition Press, 1953.

DeKok, David. *Fire Underground: The Ongoing Tragedy of the Centralia Mine Fire.* Globe Pequot, 2009.

Dooling, Michael C. *An Historical Account of Charles Island: Milford, Connecticut.* Self-published, 2006.

Eichar, Donnie. *Dead Mountain: The Untold True Story of the Dyatlov Pass Incident.* Chronicle Books, 2013.

Hartling, Neil. *Nahanni: River of Gold, River of Dreams.* Canadian Recreational Canoeing Association, 1993.

Higginbotham, Adam. *Midnight in Chernobyl: The Untold Story of the World's Greatest Nuclear Disaster.* Simon & Schuster, 2019.

Kaus, Andrea. "Common Ground: Ranchers and Researchers in

the Mapimí Biosphere Reserve." Doctoral dissertation, University of California, 1992.

Kelleher, Colm A., and George Knapp. *Hunt for the Skinwalker: Science Confronts the Unexplained at a Remote Ranch in Utah.* Paraview Pocket Books, 2005.

Kusche, Larry. *The Bermuda Triangle Mystery—Solved.* Harper & Row, 1975.

McCloskey, Keith. *The Lighthouse: The Mystery of the Eilean Mor Lighthouse Keepers.* History Press, 2014.

McPhee, John. *The Pine Barrens.* Farrar, Straus and Giroux, 1968.

Pătruţ, Adrian. *Fenomenele de la Pădurea Hoia-Baciu.* Divia, 1995.

Preston, Douglas. *The Lost City of the Monkey God.* Grand Central Publishing, 2017.

Sims, Julia. *Manchac Swamp: Louisiana's Undiscovered Wilderness.* Pelican, 2008.

Starr, Edward Comfort. *A History of Cornwall, Connecticut, a Typical New England Town.* Tuttle, Morehouse & Taylor, 1926.

Stringfellow, Kim. *Greetings from the Salton Sea: Folly and Intervention in the Southern California Landscape, 1905–2005.* Center for American Places, 2005.

Unsworth, Walt. *Everest: The Mountaineering History.* Mountaineers, 2000.

ACKNOWLEDGMENTS

First and foremost and forever, I need to thank Rebecca Gyllenhaal, not just for being the originator and editor of this particular book, but for shepherding me through my previous three books with Quirk, which have been some of the most satisfying and successful of my book life. She is, in fact, one of the three most important people to my career, the other two being my agent Alex Slater (that counts as your acknowledgment for this book, Alex) and the first publisher who took a chance on me fifteen years ago.

I'd also like to specially call out my three daughters—Esme, Hazel, and Olive—not merely for being my daughters (although that is a burden to be acknowledged all to itself), but for being my enthusiastic travel companions to so many of the sites in this book, despite me explaining the concept to them. The four of us driving off to strange places squashed into my tiny Civic will be some of the most prized memories of my life. I'd also like to thank my friend Jacob Strunk, for showing me the Salton Sea and then saving me from it, as well as my friend Miklos Csere, for helping me understand certain nuances of the Romanian language while researching Hoia-Baciu, and Loren Coleman, who personally provided me original documents on the Bridgewater Triangle and who somehow always finds a way into my books.

Finally but not finitely, I would like to thank those who are directly responsible for this artifact you hold in your hands. Jane Morley, for grabbing the baton on this book. Kassie Andreadis, for making sure my prose was as clear and my facts as accurate as possible, as well as for wrestling with the perennial problem in my books of figuring out how to grammarize *bigfoot*. Elissa Flanigan for the book design, Mandy Sampson and Chadd Keim for the production management, and Adam Parata, whose atmospheric illustrations really make this book about place feel like a destination of its own.